T0265921

Shattered Innocence

A Shared Global Shame

Christine Dolan

Shattered Innocence

A Shared Global Shame

Foreword by Homayra Sellier

VINDICTA

Vindicta Publishing

Las Vegas ♦ Chicago ♦ Palm Beach

Published in the United States of America by Histria Books
7181 N. Hualapai Way, Ste. 130-86
Las Vegas, NV 89166 U.S.A.
HistriaBooks.com

Vindicta Publishing is an imprint of Histria Books and a joint venture of Histria Books and Creative Destruction Media. Titles published under the imprints of Histria Books are distributed worldwide.

Library of Congress Control Number: 2023919783

ISBN 978-1-59211-395-8 (hardcover)
ISBN 978-1-59211-417-7 (eBook)

Contents

This book is dedicated to CHILDREN GLOBALLY, those who are protected that their parents continue to protect them, for the victims whom we want to save and restore, and for those courageous survivors who have put their lives back together and those still struggling after so many years.

I also dedicate this book to special people in my life who fought for the protection of children along my side. To the Memory of My Mother and Father, Anne and Tom, who were extraordinarily protective parents and believed in the protection of all children, to Jan Coe and her husband, the late Doug Coe, who stood shoulder to shoulder with me in this fight from the day we met until God called Doug home, to Carolyn Ewing, and her beloved late husband, Tony, whose wit, support and insight kept me going, to Reverend Paul and Rivers Teske, whose prayers have lifted me up in trying times, to Charlie Black and Ann Holladay, who heard the call and answered, to JoAnn Muller, who prayed for me to stay grounded, to Homayra Sellier and her late husband, Patrick, who believed not just in Homayra's and my friendship, but "our global crusade commitment" in 2000 to protect children, when many thought we had lost our minds, and to Mark, who heard the truth in Dubai! What a ride it has been!

"Finally, be strong in the Lord and in the strength of His Might. Put on the armor of God, that you may be able to stand against the schemes of the devil."

— Ephesians 6:10-11

Foreword

We are transformed by what we accept.

> — Dr. James Mercy, a researcher with the Center for Disease Control
> and Prevention on child sexual abuse in America.

"Imagine a childhood disease that strikes one in four girls and one in six boys before they reach the age of 18 — a disease that can cause severe conduct disorders, a disease that breeds distrust of adults and undermines the possibility of experiencing normal men/women relationships; a disease that can have profound implications for an individual's future health by increasing the risk of deadly diseases such as cancer, multiple types of sclerosis and AIDS; problems such as substance abuse, and suicide, a disease that replicates itself by exposing future generations to its debilitating effects, a disease that causes brain damage and modifies its DNA in three generations,

What we, as a society, would do if such a disease existed?

We would spare no expense.

We would invest heavily in basic and applied research.

We would devise systems to identify those affected and provide treatment services.

We would develop and broadly implement prevention campaigns to protect our children.

Wouldn't we?

Such a disease does exist — it is called child sexual abuse. Our response, however, has been far from our response to traditional diseases or health concerns of equal or even lesser magnitude. Perhaps the perception of sexual abuse as a law enforcement problem or our discomfort in confronting sexual issues contributes to our complacency and inaction.

Whatever the reason, we have severely underestimated the effects of this problem on our children's health, future, and quality of life."

I am Homayra Sellier, Founder of Innocence en Danger/Innocence in Danger, an international organization of child protection against all forms of abuse, especially sexual and trafficking — on the street and over the Internet.

I learned about the tragedy of sexual violence and the exploitation of minors in 1999 when the United Nations Educational, Scientific and Cultural Organization (UNESCO) nominated me to carry out the action plan for a worldwide movement following the dismantling of what was then considered the most extensive cyber pedo-criminal network by a police operation called "Operation Cathedral."

I met Christine Dolan in 2000; she was then conducting the ongoing investigation of "Shattered Innocence." We met in Europe. At my invitation, she spoke at the U.N. in Geneva, Switzerland.

About two years later, we held several conferences in Washington, DC, and exposed the U.N.'s complicities and coverup when U.N. contracted employees were accused of sex trafficking in the Balkans, which led to a coverup and gaslighting of whistleblowers by eminent U.N. leaders. We stood side-by-side with the whistleblowers. Our efforts to exposure these crimes and support the whistleblowers led to three U.S. Congressional investigations and a change in policy at the U.S. Department of Defense and affected the company that hired the predators — DynCorp.

DynCorp operatives tried to get Christine to back off. One man, whom Christine knew from covering politics years earlier, and had not been in contact with her for years, reached out to her. He was working for DynCorp. Another man called her — "Do you know who DynCorp is" as if she would think twice and back down. DynCorp's origins had begun longer than she had been alive.

She not only was determined to expose all the players, but she also told them to their faces, "Game on! Take a seat and watch the exposure." They underestimated her.

The World Affairs Council in Washington, D.C. jumped in and hosted a panel where we both presented at the National Press Club. A World Affairs Council board member picked up the phone and made certain Capitol Hill was paying attention, which led to the three congressional investigations.

Back in 2000, no one was addressing this pledge strategically. It seemed too daunting. In all honesty, it was. We were among the few who broke the silence around this scourge and its various fertile grounds. We chose not to ignore this pledge — *Face it, fight it with courage and love for the sake of our children, our grandchildren, and a future that we all share with over a hundred million survivors of sexual abuse.*

Christine came to Paris to work with me on a criminal case of a collection of 8,000 photos of children being raped and tortured when discovered in Zandvoort (Netherlands) in 2001. Its owner was murdered in Italy. We were contacted by parents who believed their children were among those victimized in the case. We interviewed children with their protective parents in Europe.

Operation Cathedral was a police operation that broke up a major international child pornography ring called The Wonderland Club operating over the Internet. The British National Crime Squad led it in cooperation with 1,500 officers from 13 other police forces around the world, who simultaneously arrested 104 suspects in 13 countries (including Australia, Belgium, Finland, France, Germany, Italy, Sweden, the UK, and the US) on 2 September 1998. The case revealed widespread international attention to the highly organized nature of the ring, leading to public concerns about online child sexual abuse.

The case was poorly managed in France and Belgium. We were given permission to present evidence to the French National Assembly by the late President Jacques Chirac behind closed doors. Not an easy mountain to climb because of the resistance to shove its exposure under the rug.

Christine and I and three other journalists made a commitment in the early days that we were going to put "human trafficking" into the global vernacular. We did within five years, but we never thought we would create a cottage industry of non-government organizations (NGOs) that would receive grants and only focus on their financial survival and lie about their impact to gain more money.

"The measure of our success is putting NGOs in this arena out of business," Christine has stated for years.

I admire the tenacity, fearlessness, and moral strength of Christine Dolan to resist opposition and hardship for nearly 25 years. She pushes the truth wherever the facts and evidence lead her, and has forever said, "We must go upstream and take on the fertile grounds of human trafficking or this anti-human trafficking arena will be forever taking care of victims instead of getting to the root of this evil. This is all about the commodification of human beings in a transnational and trans criminal world. The lifetime misery is too harsh. We will either spend money upstream to curb this or downstream to care for broken human beings. We need to stop this at the beginning of this swamp."

From the start, Christine was in lockstep with me on tackling the Internet. She foresaw from her initial investigation what the tools of the trade were by dining and talking with traffickers, perverts, and victims. Early on, she was wise in her assessment that adult transvestites in European red-light districts were victims of child sex abuse and stood with them dressed as a hooker to assess the johns, but her eyes were focused on the impact of the Internet because of what she was witnessing. That part of this journey is truly ironic because anyone who knows Christine knows she is not a techie but was trained as a conceptual criminal investigator decades ago.

And, to date, she has always focused on social media like Myspace, and eventually, Facebook and Twitter, and games that entice children. Now, TikTok and the endless apps where predators prey upon children.

By 2009, she knew Facebook's leadership was not interested in protecting children no matter what they said publicly. No matter how many times they testified before governments, she never believed them. She knew Facebook turned down the opportunity to link every Facebook page with a symbol linked to the first international law enforcement taskforce on the Internet to protect children. It was created in 2003 without an Act of Congress or an Act of Parliament. It was created by five cybercrime law enforcement leaders in the U.S., U.K., New Zealand, Canada, and Australia. Christine knew Facebook turned down the Virtual Global Task Force's offer.

"Sorry, this is expensive real estate," Facebook told the Virtual Global Task Force officials.

Several years after we met, she discovered that Verizon in the U.S. was offering child porn-themed videos to its customers. Technically, it was deemed legal because the actors were legally of age, but the thought that this was being normalized by a major U.S. corporation was disturbing. Christine called me when I was extremely sick and told me, "You cannot die. We have a war on our hands," and told me about Verizon. Christine started mentioning Verizon in every public forum.

Audience members would whip out their cell phones to see if it were true. She got Verizon's attention. She named their board of directors.

As serious, dark, and head snapping as this topic is, there is a lesson to be learned from taking this war against evil on, faith carries every one of us into the trenches. Our faith has grown. As Christine has said many times — "If you flip EVIL backwards, it spells LIVE."

We give voice to those victims whose traffickers, pimps, and paedophiles have silenced, and focus on helping the victim heal and pick up the shattered pieces of their lives to move on. We at Innocence in Danger created healing camps as far back as 2002. Later, Christine organized the pilot program in America. It involved horseback riding and the arts and games.

Earlier, Sister Rosemary, who lived in Uganda, was introduced to Christine, who shared that she and her nuns took care of Kony's rescued female victims in Africa and gave them love, but they could not erase their horrible memories.

"Build new memories. Do not focus on the abuse. Create memories of laughter and learning and use the arts and music and the experience of bonding with animals and nature. Take them on an Africa safari where they will meet the Face of God," Christine told Sister Rosemary.

Christine earned the respect of law enforcement internationally from the get-go, which was quite unusual for an investigative journalist, especially someone like Christine who does not mince words. European law enforcement usually does not trust journalists. They put her through tests she was unaware of, and she laughed it off later. She had passed their test unknowingly. The Hague Porn Unit brought her inside the next day as did other law enforcement agencies across the world for nearly a quarter of a century. They brought her on their rounds. They opened the doors. She was going where other law enforcement could not go without an invitation from foreign governments as a journalist. Christine was able to connect the dots across the globe as a journalist and did so over 6 continents in 140 countries for nearly 25 years.

Scotland Yard brought her inside after she was told a lot of women were the predators on an Internet criminal case. Christine was curious about what these women looked like, about their ethnicities and ages. At the time, many world leaders and activists believed that men were the predators. The Internet changed that.

"Well, what do you know — another light bulb moment — these women are across the board in terms of looks and ages — they are young, old, pretty, ugly, and from all walks of life," she told me.

When Christine took on her own Catholic heritage and was committed to exposing the Catholic Church's sex scandals, she was truly shell-shocked by the volume going back decades. She attended a Sacred Heart school and later graduated from Georgetown University, a Jesuit university. She did not believe the Church leadership and diocesan lawyers in 2001 when they stated they did not know. Her instincts were prophetic.

She was hellbent on impeaching them with their own words with documents. She discovered 3rd and 6th-century documents. She collected sign-in books at rehab centers and cross-referenced them with cases exposing the perverted religious across the world. She interviewed a Jesuit leader who gaslighted two older disabled men who had been raped on a Jesuit provincial campus for decades and challenged the Jesuit provincial head on the spot. She had been to their bedrooms in the boiler house on the property and saw the room across the hall from their bedrooms where they were raped for years by well-known perverted priests. She made a phone call to the victims' attorneys after her interview with the Jesuit Provincial head she was so morally outraged by his dismissive attitude. The case was settled for $7.5 million shortly thereafter.

"We will impeach them with their own documents," and she did it. There is no other team you would want to be on but Christine's and ours because she thinks strategically and is humble enough when the going gets tough to admit that we need those more experienced than we are and brings them to the table and educates law enforcement, prosecutors, and judges.

In 2000, Christine had contacted Charlie Black, an old friend and Republican consultant in Washington, D.C. and told him, "You won't believe what I have been investigating." She told him about her first investigation and how they needed to get those from their socio-economic background involved. Charlie Black and his colleagues jumped in.

By 2005, she asked her friend, Charlie Black, to find her a Bible study because she could not figure out why people were ignoring that slavery was alive and well in the 21st century. Charlie was someone she had known for decades, and he had to pause and think who the person was to introduce Christine. She was on a mission.

She had never studied the Bible. She was disillusioned by 2005 by the cottage industry of NGOs — many of whom were Christian groups collecting monies from churches in America and telling Christians that law enforcement was not doing their jobs. She knew otherwise.

She was horrified that our efforts were resulting in endless NGOs which were only worried about their financial survivability, instead of taking on the heads of the snakes. Her faith was also shaken by the Catholic Church's leadership and persistent coverup.

By 2019, she and a colleague of hers in the mental health arena signed up to attend a "minor attracted persons" (MAPS) conference in Baltimore to see what "Maps" all were about. She had first heard about MAPS circa 2010, but their conferences were never opened to the press. In 2019, it was opened to therapists. The MAPs leadership was trying to enlist therapists to advocate for them to normalize MAPs as an accepted sexual orientation with the end goal of decriminalizing pedophilia.

To Christine's horror, more women than men were in attendance. They claimed that straight people were stigmatizing MAPS for being sexually attracted to young children. They claimed that they would not act out and needed therapists to advocate for them in the U.S. and change the law to a German model where German therapists were not mandated to report them to law enforcement as they were in the U.S. When one MAP at the conference stated publicly that he spent 10 years in jail for befriending a "friend," she asked him, "How old was your friend?"

"Eight years of age," he replied.

Unbeknownst to him, Christine and her colleague were advised before the conference by Bob Hamer, a renowned retired undercover FBI agent, who infiltrated

NAMBLA over a decade earlier and whose investigation led to the convictions of several men on sex tourism charges.

Christine then reported back to Bob.

"You hit the Motherload," Bob said.

Bob was also amazed that more women than men were in the room. Our mission is clear — wake up the ignorant, educate the public, expose the evil commodification of human beings, heal the victims, and never be intimidated by the scoundrels who cover up or participate, or want to normalize that which is unacceptable and intolerable. They are cowards only afraid of being exposed.

Today, Christine is taking on medical trafficking just like she took on sex, labor, the Internet, sex tourism, child soldiers, organ trafficking, skin trafficking, ritual abuse torture, and all the other faces of human trafficking. She has connected the dots across the spectrum.

Shattered Innocence — A Shared Global Shame is a book you need to read. Once upon a time, like many, Christine had a challenging time believing this type of evil existed even after having spent 20 years earlier covering politics, international issues and three wars. She thought she had seen it all and admitted to law enforcement in 2000 — if this is true — you need to educate me.

This book will demonstrate how she came to believe and hopefully, walk readers to that revelation too.

In 2000, while interviewing victims in Albania, she promised them that if they told her their stories, she would take it to the world. That is what she has done for over two decades.

Christine and I have shared the same motto from the start of this journey: One life is worth saving.

One day a man was walking along the beach when he noticed a boy picking something up and gently throwing it into the sea.

Approaching the boy, he asked, "What are you doing?"

The boy replied, "Throwing starfish back into the ocean. If I do not throw them back, they will die."

"Son," the man said, "Don't you realize there are miles and miles of beach and hundreds of starfish? The few you manage to save, out of so many, cannot possibly make a difference!"

After listening politely, the boy bent down, picked up another starfish, and threw it back into the sea. Then, smiling at the man, he said: "It will make a difference to that one; to that one, it is his LIFE."

Homayra Sellier, 2024

Introduction

How does human trafficking otherwise known, as modern slavery in the 21st century, exist?

Just ask the question, *why do we globally continue to commodify our fellow human beings?*

Anyone humane knows in civilized society we no longer must prove slavery is immoral and should be outlawed and wiped off the face of the earth, but now — even after 24 years of investigating this story and all its fertile grounds and faces as my colleagues and I have done, we still must prove that slavery has grown because of the continuation of commodifying human beings on all levels. We are sadly morphing human beings into statistics, data points, and collateral damage so quickly because of the digital age we find ourselves.

I have spent nearly a quarter of a century investigating and fighting to wake up people to this insidious horror. Today, society is reverting to the Middle Ages, not only normalizing taboos but embracing them. Our investigations have led us to a new Age of Digital Nihilism.

We live in a world where childhood innocence is being shattered, where some are pushing for the decriminalization of pedophilia, where tech companies are not on the side of protecting children, where parental rights are being removed legally, and even criminalizing parenthood, where educating children about oral, anal and vaginal sex in cartoons in childhood books is acceptable before the children can even put sex into context, where corporations sell child-themed porn to their customers, where breast binders and crouch puffers are sold in stores that sell cheap school supplies, where men with fetishes for breasts are deemed normal to dance before young children, where minor-attracted persons want to be accepted as a normal sexual orientation, where gender is now deemed to be different than sex, and the legalization of mutilating children without their parent's consent is acceptable human behavior. The list is endless.

Some who witness this cultural phenomenon are paralyzed by the willful ignorance, indifference, and self-justification. Others are gripped by emotions of hopelessness, anger, and helplessness. Others are traumatized and shamed because they succumbed to the trends and were sucked into a vortex that forever changed their lives and their bodies.

We are enslaved by this slippery slope, and it has manifested itself into A Shared Global Shame. We have shattered innocence and normalized evil.

And, despite history repeating itself, we have an inordinate number of citizens who want retribution and justice because other citizens' ancestors enslaved their ancestors. They call for reparations while they are consciously and without any consciences systematically refusing to look at reality in the 21st century and intentionally ignore the enslaved world that flourishes around us. They too have contributed to the 21st century slavery by their silent complicity, distortion of facts and reality, and by their consumerism.

The lack of introspection and reflection and knowledge about history and situational awareness today is staggering.

Slavery exists in the 21st century because of an inordinate amount of lack of empathy. Many individuals lack the moral compass to see the face of humanity in others and are truly ignorant of history, and how easy it is to repeat some of mankind's past evils.

Humanity is on very dark slippery slope and if the *elders in the room* do not respond to a Churchillian Call to Action, we will continue to raise generations of perverts, commodifies, and paedophiles, who are so narcissistic and self-serving, we will live in a world with no boundaries and no moral absolutes.

In 1990, I was privileged and honored to be the Spokesperson for the 1990 USA Nelson Mandela Tour shortly after Mandela was released from Robbins Island. I was brought in at the last minute about nine days before Mandela arrived in the U.S. His tour was hosted by cities from east coast to west coast — from NYC to Boston to Washington, D.C. to Atlanta to the Midwest to Los Angeles and then ended in Oakland, California. As a result of that, I later came to know the late Archbishop Desmond Tutu.

After Mandela was elected President of South Africa in 1994, he appointed Archbishop Tutu to chair the Truth & Reconciliation Commission (TRC) on apartheid. The TRC heard testimonies from victims and from those who engaged in horrendous acts during this era in South Africa.

The testimonies by those who suffered and were vilified, and from the families of those murdered by their countrymen were heart-wrenching.

Their testimonies left indelible impressions that would later serve me well to understand what happens to people when they commodify others and enslave them.

Concisely, their lights flip off. They do not see the face of humanity in another human being.

In 2000, the International Centre for Missing & Exploited Children's (IC-MEC) commissioned me to investigate the exploitation of children emanating from the Balkan Crises I have covered in the 1990s.

With that offer on the table, I called three friends and colleagues: Ed Turner, one of my former bosses at CNN, who was a consummate and gifted news executive; Dr. Noel Brown, then the head of the UN Environmental Program, and Zyg Nagorski, who sat on ICMEC's board.

Zyg and I had earlier worked together and implemented the ethics program for the World Bank at the request of then Chairman Jim Wolfensohn. Zyg was a Holocaust survivor, who was one of the most inspiring human beings I have ever met. Needless to state, I was honored to have worked alongside him.

"This is up your alley, Christine," Noel said.

"You need to have control. This must be done ethically. Do not give ICMEC what they want. Give them the truth, and shake them up," stated Zyg.

"ICMEC must have no say how you do the investigation nor have any control editorially. Just the facts," Ed deliberated.

My deal with ICMEC was that the organization had no say in how the investigation was conducted and no say editorially. I had been trained as a criminal investigator while in law school, had worked for four television networks and covered three wars. ICMEC agreed.

While conducting this initial human trafficking investigation, one of the earlier Truth and Reconciliation Commission panels flooded my memory like a tsunami.

White South African law enforcement officials testified before the TRC. Their *daily tasks* involved torturing, murdering, and even burning their countrymen's bodies while attending a barbecue. Literally flipping the bodies over coals for 7 or 8 hours to eliminate the evidence.

Desmond Tutu asked some of them if they even remembered the names and faces of all those they tortured. They claimed they did not remember.

Then Bishop Tutu did what only a man of God could think to do. He invited the men at the table to turn around so he could introduce them to those who had survived their tortures. Those men never forgot the torturers' names and faces.

That is the most poignant example I can offer the readers to educate you how evil predators view their prey.

It is a substantive example of what evil does to those who commodify and torture and those who suffer at their hands and actions.

That is how commodification exemplifies itself.

Victims become invisible. That is at the core of understanding human trafficking and slavery.

By 2002, two nurses from Nova Scotia said something to me that still resonates with me to this day.

"We live among individuals who inflict pain for their own pleasure."

If nothing else from the COVID-19's grip on humanity in the last several years, I have thought often of that testimony in South Africa and what my friends in Nova Scotia told me in 2002.

During COVID, many objected to and challenged the self-serving scientific operatives, government bureaucrats, PHARMA PR hacks, and politicians. And, then they were censored, and gaslighted ruthlessly and still are today.

The saddest part of that era was how the covid vaccine-injured were repeatedly gaslighted. The FDA, CDC, NIH, NIAID and even the Biden White House refused to acknowledge the neurological and vascular injuries as they acknowledged the cardio injuries in spring 2021. The fact that the neurological and vascular injuries are still not "officially" recognized by the FDA as this book goes to publication is morally unacceptable.

Those acts of omission were taken to prevent vaccination hesitancy.

What I do know as an investigative journalist is that the truth eventually surfaces.

Today, human beings are reduced to statistics and data points and profit as we wipe out the faces and emotions of others.

We are led to believe that if we object to hurting others and not protecting, especially the children from evil doers, we are liars, and provide disinformation and misinformation.

I not only highly disagree with this conclusion, but I also find it intellectually offensive and willing to challenge anyone — regardless of their position of power or fame.

There are moral absolutes such as protecting children and marginalized adults that stand the test of time.

Normalizing abuse, trafficking, and slavery in the 21st century is morally repugnant. Any domestic or foreign policy decisions by world leaders, politicians, and policy leaders that lead to the abuse of another human being is below the dignity of humanity, whether it is done by an act of commission or omission.

The US policy on its southern border is a prime example. Migrations and refugee camps are fertile grounds for smuggling that can easily morph into any face of human trafficking — sex, labor, organ, and medical trafficking - because predators prey upon those most vulnerable.

It happened during the Balkan Crises in the 1990s, as well as in Afghanistan, Iraq, across West Africa, Northern Africa, and the Middle East during the Arab Rising, and across the U.S. southern border during the Obama administration. Today, the U.S. southern border crisis is not an immigration problem. It is a trafficking operation with exploding numbers leaving unaccompanied minors in the hands of traffickers inside the U.S. during the Biden administration.

What does that say about us when we go backwards morally in the age of so-called universally recognized human rights? What does it say about us when we recognize perverted behavior as acceptable human behavior?

Experts have known since the creation of the Internet that isolated perverts found a new playground where they discovered like-minded perverts who validated and justified their own perversions and then they formed chatrooms and clubs and joined the Dark Web.

When I began this journey, the National Center for Missing & Exploited Children was receiving about some say 500 tips weekly. Others claimed 37,000 tips annually. Today, the center receives over 23,000,000 tips annually.

What follows is where I began my introduction to learning that slavery is alive and flourishing in the 21st century.

Admittedly, I was struck by how unconscious I was and leaned on law enforcement officials to educate me because I was truly ignorant of this dark side of humanity.

What I did possess was an abundance of curiosity and determination to not only get this story right, but to offer facts where they could pivot the minds of those who believe in righting wrongs and not afraid to stand up to evil. For nearly a quarter of a century, I have witnessed those in the gallows of this fight claiming a desire to right this wrong. Nevertheless, the depths of hell keep dropping lower to where we are today — a movement to decriminalize pedophilia and the normalization of childhood mutilations without parental consent, and a legislative movement to give probation to rapists of toddlers.

Over 20 years ago, Scotland Yard told me that they had an image of a newborn infant tied to an umbilical cord being abused.

Let that sink in.

That is evil.

Decades ago, there was a movement to end the female genital mutilation in foreign countries. Conservative and liberal activists joined hands to expose it and criminalize it. Yet, today, it has risen its ugly head in the West and in some places, there is a movement to decriminalize it once again overseas.

Hopefully, this book will educate the readers as I walk you through the tipping-point steps of epiphanies I reached in 2000, and beyond on why I have concluded that slavery in the 21st century is *A Shared Global Shame* and a wrong that needs to end and no one should be afraid to stand up to powers that be who lie, deceive, and distort reality for their lust for greed and power.

History has proven the power of one repeatedly when God calls forth moral courage. The contagion of courage shatters the bricks of evil.

It is fathomable to me to believe that we can turn the tide of history once again just like the abolitionists Thomas Clarkson and William Wilberforce and their colleagues did starting in the late 18th century in England, or former slave and international abolitionist Frederick Douglass, an orator of his day like William Wilberforce, who caught the attention of the world in their generations.

In summer 1885, British journalist W.T. Stead wrote an expose that shocked the public. "The Maiden Tribute of Modern Babylon" appeared in London's Pall Mall Gazette.

Stead warned his readership in the paper the ghastly four-part series was coming.

"… we have no desire to inflict upon unwilling eyes the ghastly story of the criminal developments of modern vice. Therefore, we say quite frankly to-day that all those who are squeamish, and all those who are prudish, and all those who prefer to live in a fool's paradise of imaginary innocence and purity, selfishly oblivious to the horrible realities which torment those whose lives are passed in London Inferno, will do well not to read the Pall Mall Gazette of Monday and the three following days. The story of an actual pilgrimage into a real hell is not pleasant reading, and it is not meant to be. It is, however, an authentic record of unimpeachable facts, "abominable, unutterable, and worse than fables yet have reigned or fear conceived." But it is true, and its publication is necessary," wrote Stead.

The newspaper published with graphic detail how wealthy Victorian men procured young girls for sex. Most of the girls were between 13 and 15 years of age. The johns of their day included a prominent member of Parliament, a doctor, a cabinet minister, a clergyman, and others.

Initially, the London solicitor ordered police to seize copies instead of investigating the scandal. *The New York Times* covered the story. The Salvation Army volunteers distributed copies. Found copies were sold above the cover price.

The story went far beyond the clients. Stead reported how women recruited the young girls and how law enforcement who knew looked the other way.

Who were potential victims and how were they targeted?

They were poor. Promises of jobs and money and even meals were made to entice them. The recruiters looked for orphans, girls who worked in shops, servants, cooks, and especially, nursemaids. Employment agencies served fronts for child prostitution rings.

No one was prosecuted in the end, but Stead. He served three months in prison after being charged with abduction after one of the recruiters delivered a 13-year-old named Eliza Armstrong to him to prove his story.

In the end, Stead won his campaign in the name of the public's right to know. The UK Parliament raised the age of consent for girls from 13 to 16.

Over a hundred years ago, King Leopold II of Belgium, cousin, and confidant to Queen Victoria of England, exhibited greed that cost the lives of 10 million in Africa devising a system of terror where Congolese villagers were forced to harvest rubber and ship ivory back to his homeland, or face death by Belgians who were to produce monthly quotas. That greed resulted in the Congolese population halved between 1880 — 1920.

It took a curious and morally outraged man, like Thomas Clarkson in his day 100 years earlier to stand up to the horror of Belgian's King Leopold's enslavement in the Congo at the turn of the 20th century. His name was Edmund Morel.

Morel worked on the docks in Antwerp and noticed the ships carrying rubber arriving, but only soldiers and ammunition and firearms returning on ships to Africa. He concluded the rubber industry was based on slave labor and not trade.

He became an investigative journalist and led a worldwide media campaign with Mark Twain, Booker T. Washington, W.E.B. Du Boise, the Archbishop of Canterbury, and others to educate those in his era on the genocide orchestrated at the orders of King Leopold II. Morel hammered away at the U.S. propping up the King's right to occupy the Congo that later became Zaire, which today is known as the Democratic Republic of the Congo.

In the end, Morel earned an audience with President Theordore Roosevelt in 1904. His ask was to end the Congo State that King Leopold II controlled based upon his evidence that genocide and slave labor were occurring in the territory.

Two years later, President Roosevelt and the U.S. Congress finally took a stand against the King and demanded an end to the Congo Free State.

So, I ask you, the readers, and journalists today, to educate yourselves historically, be not afraid, stand on the shoulders who have stood up to evil before, make the pledge to get off the bench, get in the fight and protect your loved ones, your communities, and your fellow human beings, especially, the children and those marginalized, and turn the tide of history once again.

Believe this is a winnable war and buckle up for some hard truths about evil.

Shattered Innocence
A Shared Global Shame — Summer 2000

In a nine-week period in 2000, I crisscrossed Western and Eastern European countries and went into Albania, traveling to 21 villages and cities, making 26 stops in all. I conducted over 500 interviews — children, pimps, transvestites, restaurant owners, concierges, bartenders, hotel maids, local and national police, Interpol agents, immigration experts, U.S. Custom Service agents, a paedophile expert, trafficking experts, traffickers, non-governmental organization (NGO) representatives, pornography experts, U.S. State Department employees, mafia dons, parents, prostitutes, a Ph.D. candidate specializing in sex tourism, members of the European Parliament, and heads of charities.

I went into the Red-Light districts in both Amsterdam and Brussels, and other cities, and drove around the boulevards of Milan, Rome, and Naples. I went into prostitution walkups in London's Soho district, hung out with pimps and traffickers in Vienna and Brussels, interviewed a Madam in Paris, and went to after-hours clubs in London, Vienna, Brussels, Amsterdam, Paris, Milan, and Rome, as well as in Bari, Italy. From sources in safe houses and traffickers on the streets, I collected names, numbers, and addresses of pimps and traffickers. In addition, I was able to parlay my experiences in other war-torn areas on the globe, and my travels in Africa, the Middle East, and other parts of the world.

As the story unraveled, I found myself tested not only professionally, but personally as well. It was a horrific and ugly story with grave ramifications. It is complex, multi-layered, and multi-dimensional. This investigation may have started with the Balkans, but it soon culminated into a global story extending beyond the Balkans, crossing Europe, and catapulting to Asia, Africa, Latin and Central America, and even into Australia.

There were days — and nights — when I saw or heard too much. There were a few times when I just had to change my schedule, find a cathedral — say a prayer, and hope that I could complete the investigation. What kept me going was thinking about the fact that these children and vulnerable adults had been kidnapped, coerced, threatened, raped, drugged, tortured, had their organs removed, and in some cases, murdered, and unknown to most of civilized society, especially in terms of ages, volume, and violence at this time.

All done before the dawn of the Internet onslaught as we know it today. And, because of how the Internet has evolved, this arena has only become more depraved.

The children and marginalized adults were in the hands of very evil human beings. A lot of what occurred was "behind closed doors," and "off the street."

Early on during this investigation, Dr. Louise Shelley, a Professor at American University in Washington, DC and a noted transcriminal expert, referred to this situation as the "Holocaust." It surely was. It was the Holocaust of the Millennium, but 24 years later, it has morphed into *A Shared Global Shame*. Too many people know about it and the truth is that nothing has really put a dent in the fight to stop it. In fact, the numbers are only increasing as people are becoming numb to evil.

Although this story may seem explosive, daunting, disturbing, unnerving, and even gross at times, these are evidence-based facts.

The underlying motives for exploiting human beings are money and power. The exploitation saga is about treating human beings as commodities, and flipping them into monetary gain, sexual pleasure, or exerting power over them. Predators are cold, deliberate, calculating, narcissistic, pathological, demeaning, demented, and sinister. The exploitation of anyone serves two groups: those who partake and those who profit. The third group is the victims — human beings — adults and children.

For the purposes of this first investigation, the focus was on children — those under 18 years of age. Note that the people who traffick and exploit adults also traffick and exploit children.

Trafficking is not an isolated industry. It overlaps with other criminal enterprises. This story is the result of individuals — from law enforcement officials to traffickers to victims and others — who wished to tell their stories. This is a collaborative effort connecting the dots about slavery in the 21st century.

Contemporary outcries about past slavery and reparations are loud and clear, but one must wonder, "How can contemporary man focus so much on the past when the present slavery is before our eyes?"

It would be far more virtuous and substantive for critics of the past if they were to open their eyes and look at the present global phenomenon of slavery in the 21st century. The slavery of children worldwide is not something in the future or a possibility if things go wrong. It is a current crisis. It is a crime against humanity now with catastrophic effects for future generations.

Repeatedly, individuals ask me "Why doesn't the world know about the extent of the exploitation of children, especially when we live in such a human rights age?" Quite frankly, the answer is amazingly simple. It is an unseemly topic, and if it does not directly affect someone, a lack of awareness becomes the protective bubble. If it does not touch one's life, if one does not encounter it, one doesn't see the full scope of the issue.

If there were sufficient co-ordination to battle this global phenomenon, one expert somewhere would have mentioned that there is a decline in the exploitation of children. The research finds just the opposite consistently. Coordinated efforts of organized crime are winning this war, and it is ugly. What is involved in this scenario? Kidnapping, coercion, torture, sexual and labor exploitation, geographical, physical, emotional, and psychological isolation, loneliness, and in the worst-case scenario, child soldiers killing other children, and in many cases, rapes, and gang-rapes, and disease if the victims survive. Sexually exploited children are at risk of contradicting AIDS.

AIDS numbers were staggering in 2000 when I did this first investigation. The United Nation's (UN) worldwide figure for AIDS cases then claimed 36 million people. At that time, 11 million children were orphaned due to AIDS. In 2001, 10 million orphaned children lived in Africa. According to the World Health Organization (WHO), AIDS was on the rise in the Soviet Union by 60 percent in 2000. In 2000, there were 250,000 new cases of AIDS in Eastern Europe and Central Asia. The AIDs epidemic hit this region after the fall of communism. One of the primary reasons Eastern European children were initially trafficked into Western Europe was because AIDs had not yet hit Eastern European cultures when this trafficking floodgate burst.[1]

Of the 5.3 million new cases of HIV infections in 2000, 600,000 were cases of children under the age of 15. In Africa, almost 25.5 million people were infected with AIDS. Of those infected, 55 percent AIDS cases were of women. According to a business report in *The Star*, a South African newspaper, AIDS then could reduce economic growth by 25 percent over 20 years, in addition to the fact that Africa was a continent then, as it is today, where poverty is a way of life for millions.

A WHO report years ago stated, "While the prevalence [of AIDS] in the adult population continues to be relatively low in many Asian countries, available behavioral data suggests an increased vulnerability," and the report went on to cite, as reasons — sex trade, illicit drugs, and migrations.

By the end of 2000, WHO expected 45,000 new cases of AIDS in North America and 30,000 new cases in Western Europe. In addition, the WHO found that there was an increase in the deaths of women with AIDS.

African children were particularly at risk because of the overwhelming numbers. If orphaned and taken in by their extended families, in many African countries, the government required that the families pay school tuition. If the extended families could not afford to educate the children, the orphaned were lost to street life where they could become easy prey for the predators.

So, we asked back in 2000 how do world leaders eradicate this horrific problem? Many thought more publicity was the answer. Activists declared that there should be an earnest and sincere war declared on pimps and traffickers. Many believed stiffer penalties should be handed down by the judges to human traffickers than drug traffickers. Another idea was for one international standard should be used. Multi-national institutions needed to eliminate the layering of bureaucracy and push through simplistic measures for definitions and everyone needed to comply. New laws were needed on all state levels, and they should have followed the international standard so that everyone agreed.

Two decades ago, there was too much legal chaos. In some countries, law enforcement could not do the needed investigations because privacy laws protected the predators. In other countries, there were no laws against the exploitation of children. In some countries, there were no simultaneous financial and criminal investigations. In others, the financial investigations ceased when there was a conviction. And, in other countries, laws conflicted. In many countries, there were no laws against what was known as child pornography.

There were calls for as little ambiguity as possible in the laws and in the definitions in the laws. Local law enforcement needed to be technically and logistically upgraded. There was a need to train law enforcement for cross-cultural, transnational, and international crime syndicate busting. There were shifts to train local law enforcement officials to be able to conduct simultaneous financial and criminal investigations and to continue these financial investigations beyond a conviction.

In the area of child exploitation, countries that did not have conspiracy laws were encouraged to pass them. Law enforcement wanted the ability to seize the traffickers' and syndicates' monies. After convictions, these seized monies were to be used for funding the local law enforcement and local NGOs' social services for the victims for rape counseling and reintegration.

I commended Europol and Interpol back in 2000. They were some of the agencies who brought me in on the inside, but what I learned then was that it was essential that local law enforcement be able to track these international organized crime predators and syndicates across country borders.

Throughout my initial investigation and later, I encountered true heroes in law enforcement — those who live on the front lines waging war against the exploitation of children. As in any industry — and law enforcement is no different — there is competition, but what has been striking to me is that when it comes to children and their safety, there seems to be little to no competition between law enforcement agencies. Repeatedly, law enforcement officials told me that the children's safety comes first. These law enforcement officials not only believed that, but they also practiced it as well.

So, what went wrong over the last 24 years after laws had been changed and billions had been spent where today, this criminal entity, when cross-referenced transcriminally and transnationally, is easily above $150 billion annually?

Society is numb to evil and commodifying human beings.

We in the civilized world claim we care but the truth is we have world leaders who do not, and we have citizens who are either unconscious or do not believe this could happen to their families, or powerful people partake and profit off these criminal acts.

Over the course of COVID-19, we were all targeted by PHARMA. That is medical trafficking. We were all guinea pigs.

The mere definition of trafficking is simple.

If human beings are lied to, forced, defrauded, or coerced for "X" for commercial profit — that is trafficking in its simplest terms.

It does not matter if the "X" stands for organs, medical experiments by PHARMA, labor and all its subcategories, sex on the street or over the Internet, institutionally or overseas for sex tourism involving BIG TECH or some pimp on the street, or within organized street gangs at cheap motels, or forced child soldiers, or for ritual abuse torture. It is still human trafficking.

There are a lot more Jeffrey Epsteins and Ghislaine Maxwells out there than the average person realizes.

Myths

MYTH: legislative and legal mandates to date are enough to combat the exploitation of those enslaved.

MYTH: the definitions of the exploitation of children and human trafficking are agreed upon by all.

MYTH: every country has laws prohibiting the sexual exploitation of children.

MYTH: trafficking of children does not have societal, economic, and health ramifications.

MYTH: all governments, non-government organizations, bureaucratic institutions, and law enforcement agencies agree upon the number of children who are trafficked and exploited.

MYTH: the exploitation of children is not a global phenomenon.

MYTH: child pornography is on the decline.

MYTH: child sex tourism is on the decline.

MYTH: adoptions for sexual exploitation do not exist.

MYTH: infants and toddlers are not sexually exploited.

MYTH: there is little demand for younger and younger children in the sex trade.

MYTH: law enforcement is staffed, educated, trained, and supported to eradicate the exploitation of children.

MYTH: children who are asylum seekers are not trafficked and sexually exploited.

MYTH: there is no correlation between rape and the increase in aids.

MYTH: wars do not exploit children.

MYTH: refugee camps are safe havens for children.

MYTH: rape is a new war weapon.

MYTH: international peacekeepers are trained to deal with the exploitation of children emanating from war.

MYTH: international peacekeeping are not exploiters and murderers of children.

MYTH: the exploitation of children in war zones is different from what is happening in other parts of the world.

MYTH: the media and the public have a global understanding of the magnitude and volume of the exploitation of children.

MYTH: groups are not committed to decriminalizing paedophilia and have it officially recognized as a "normal sexual orientation.

MYTH: pushing transgender medical procedures is not medical trafficking.

MYTH: medical industry is not involved in organ trafficking.

MYTH: institutional and corporate trafficking does not exist.

MYTH: the pharmaceutical industry is not involved in medical trafficking.

The Scope of
Human Trafficking

At the turn of the 21st century, tens of millions of human beings are being commodified, bartered, and sold throughout the world on the street and over the internet, and it has only grown since 2000 — 24 years ago — when I conducted this first human trafficking investigation.

This growing phenomenon is due to several factors albeit no one simple reason. They include, but are not limited to: the globalization of international economies searching for cheap labor, an increase of international organized crime syndicates ultimately connected to transnational and transcriminal black markets, rising unemployment in underdeveloped countries in marginalized sectors, an increased demand for services in developed countries, the every expanding onslaught of the internet, its social media and apps, discrimination, poverty, wars, migrations, and a basic need to survive by naive human beings who are taken advantage of by ruthless traffickers.

None of this is by accident. This is all intentional through the prism of commodifying human beings by individuals who consciously and without a conscience engage in this despicable behavior.

Human trafficking is a minimal risk business, but if successful, garners high payoffs. Some experts in 2000 claimed that the human trafficking trade generated $7 billion. In February 2001, Interpol announced that human trafficking generated $19 billion.[3]

Whatever the exact figure is, it is fair to state that the trafficking of human beings and the exploitation of them — adults and children — is a growth industry. In 1998, a United Nations Children's Fund (UNICEF) sponsored seminar found that economic globalization not only failed to reduce social ills plaguing children but exacerbated them.

Almost two decades later, modern day slavery is estimated to generate over $150 billion annually, but the figure is growing even more because of covid, the war between NATO/Ukraine and Russia and the impact upon European countries, and now in the Middle East.

Over two decades ago, UNICEF estimated that there were 10 *million child prostitutes* worldwide.[4] Some European experts estimated that there were 2 *million children* involved.

The May 2, 2000 REPORT on the Communication from the Commission to the Council and the European Parliament stated, "According to the UN and IOM [International Organization for Migration] estimates, *four million people* are trafficked worldwide and 500,000 victims of trafficking enter Western Europe *annually*; whereas according to all indicators the number of victims is on the increase and the flows from Central and Eastern European countries have dramatically increased, in addition to the already existing flow from Africa, Latin-America, the Caribbean, and Asia." [5]

Interpol officials, who wished to remain anonymous in 2000, claimed, *"No one really knows the numbers* — not the United Nations or Organization for Security and Cooperation in Europe. You must be careful with the numbers with everyone, *but there is a definite increase in prostitution, as well as child pornography, and child prostitution."* [6]

As staggering as these figures were then, some experts claimed that there were *"100 million children worldwide who are homeless: 40 million of them in Latin America alone. Many of them are engaged in begging, stealing, or even self-prostitution to survive... UNICEF estimates that 70-90 percent of child prostitutes come from abusive homes."*[7]

To understand the scope of the exploitation of children, one must examine the whole depth and breadth of human trafficking — both adults and children. Most of the published government and non-governmental reports had linked children directly with adults.

My initial investigation focused on *those less than 18 years of age, although it cannot be overemphasized that there is a definitive link between those who traffick children, and adults, and other contraband. Victims slightly older than 18 were interviewed during my first investigation because the same individuals and syndicates who were involved in the multi-billion-dollar world of transcriminal and transcontinental crime do not discriminate between ages. They have also witnessed young children in brothels, in the fields and manufacturing plants as well as on the street and over the internet. If someone can be sold, the traffickers will buy and resell the victims.*

Human trafficking is qualitatively different from other forms of illegal businesses. When traffickers smuggle tobacco from one country to another to avoid taxation, eventually, the tobacco goes up in smoke. When traffickers sell drugs the drugs are consumed. When toxic waste is shipped, eventually, it is dumped. When smuggled weapons and arms are traded, eventually, they find themselves in the hands of users.

Human beings, on the other hand, are trafficked, smuggled, moved, used, and reused for a variety of varied reasons — migrant workers, domestic slaves, sex slaves, indentured servants, prostitution, sweatshop workers, garment dungeon workers, begging slaves, and even mail-order brides, who are sometimes exploited by their own husbands. Human beings can be used and abused at every step of the trafficking game — sold and resold. There is cash staying power if humans are kept alive and trafficked. As heartless as it is, today's human beings are looked upon as just another commodity for trade by predators and traffickers, and every one of us who chooses to remain unconscious is complicit with our financial portfolios and the institutions we support.

Understanding war, poverty, discrimination, economic survival, greed and profit, and the unseemly definition of commodification are tantamount to understanding the exploitation of human beings. If wars exist, they go hand in hand with poverty and economic survival. Children are the least heard, protected, and guarded.

Graca Machel, the widow of Nelson Mandela, a world renown humanitarian, and author of the United Nations' 1995 Report, *Impact of Armed Conflict on Children,* wrote,

"In the past decade, *2 million children* have been killed in armed conflict. Three times as many have been seriously injured or permanently disabled. Millions of others have been forced to witness or even take part in horrifying acts of violence. It is impossible to give accurate statistics on this carnage. The conservative estimates available hide the numbers of children whose murders remain unrecorded, who are erased from the memory of humankind when whole families and communities are wiped out. Yet increasingly, children are targets, not incidental casualties of armed conflict... in some countries, conflicts have raged for so long that children have grown into adults without ever knowing peace." [8]

What drives people to go to such lengths to sell their family members for organ transplants, sell their sister's friends into prostitution, steal children out of orphanages and off the streets and sell them for sex films, and kidnap and train children to kill other children? Why would someone sell his or her body for a meal? Those acts are sometimes economically survival driven. In other cases, the greed and survival viewpoints depend on whether you are the victim, the supplier, or the customer.

Discrimination in this context is not just based on north-south hemispheric divides of color. It involves the treatment of those who have less standing in certain communities — poor versus rich, powerful versus unprotected, Gypsies in Europe, caste systems in India, Arab attitudes toward sub-Saharan Africans, and Latin American discrimination against those of African descent, and *children versus adults.*

In 2000, my initial investigation was focused on the exploitation of children emanating from the Balkan Crises, a conflict I covered in the 1990s. To accomplish this Endeavor, I started off in Western and Eastern Europe and went back to the Balkans, and then took the investigation globally for over the last two decades. It was a rude awakening to realize that slavery was alive and well at the cusp of the 21st century. It is more than alarming today — almost 25 years later — that slavery is growing in plain sight.

Every continent has its own stories of war, poverty, and discrimination. To begin with this saga in the Balkans, one must go back in history.

Before the fall of Communism in the Soviet Union and in Eastern European countries, there were jobs of some sort. Children were cared for by the Welfare State on some level. Some food was on the table. Granted there was a huge disparity in wealth between those who were in power and those who were not. Granted economies were poor, unemployment and starvation existed, but lack of jobs was not as rampant and prolific as it is today.

With the Fall of Communism — the Fall of the Welfare State, and governments in transition — and in some cases in near collapse — crime syndicate

leaders, in conjunction with small time criminal gangs replaced communist bureaucrats. Add to that, the feminization of poverty due to the lack of jobs, the lack
of social services because of corrupt governments, and a deliberate lack of consideration for women and children, what emerged was near chaos in most of these
countries. And, because of shifting from Welfare States to a Market economy, the
climate was ripe for women and children to become easy prey for ruthless predators.

In 2000, 50 percent of Russian adults were unemployed. Of the other 50 percent employed, only 25 percent were paid on a regular basis. Wage arrears were a
profoundly genuine problem. [9] In 2000, in Kyrgyzstan, 88 percent of the citizens
lived below the poverty line. Poverty increased more than 10-fold in Eastern European countries between 1990 - 2000. [10]

Add to this scenario, an ethnically charged and protracted Balkans Crises in the
1990s, which increased poverty in the Balkans and mayhem in Europe, and there
was an opportunity for callous operators, who lived by the cruel reality — *I will
survive and use you to do it!*

There have been four distinctive waves of human trafficking of women and
children on the street since the early 1990s across Europe. First, Thai, and Filipino,
then Dominicans and Colombians, then Ghanaians and Nigerians, and the fourth
wave included victims from Central and Eastern European countries, including
Russian and Ukrainian women and children.[11]

Paul Holmes, Inspector of Vice and Clubs, Metropolitan Police in London,
England, referred to this situation in 2000 as, "a global phenomenon, which
started in Eastern European countries with the Fall of Communism, and this *tidal
wave* has gradually reached the shores of the United Kingdom, and it is changing
the landscape of Europe." [12]

The 1985 Schengen Agreement, implemented in June 1990, added to the
nightmare of human trafficking in Europe. This Agreement is one of the legal
instruments, which enabled individuals to pass borders once they arrived in western European countries. The essence of the Agreement enabled individuals to
travel freely — without showing passports at borders — between Belgium, Germany, France, Luxembourg, and The Netherlands and the like. One moved freely
across Western Europe. [13]

The Russian Federation was comprised of 15 former republics. Because there was no centralized border control, passage was easy, and the republics served as transitory sites. The northern route through the Baltics was paved through the Lithuania and Polish border into Germany and Scandinavia, originating in Ukraine and Belarus. Once inside Germany, one could travel all the way to Amsterdam without showing papers because of the Schengen Agreement even if the papers were counterfeit.

In the southern region, there was an open border policy with Türkiye and Georgia, then onto Greece and other Mediterranean countries. If the immigrants travelled to Bulgaria, and further into the Balkans, the best destination to migrate west was through Albania, specifically Durres or farther south at Vlora on the Adriatic coast.

There, the fastest route was crossing the Adriatic Sea into the southern portion of Italy near Lecce, Brindisi, Ancona, and Bari on the coast, and from there, north into the heart of Western Europe. In 2000, the Adriatic Sea was akin to a rubber raft superhighway with hundreds of attempts, either by ferries, lorries, rafts, and in some cases, as stow aways in tankers.

The Chinese, on the other hand, in 2000 had an open-door policy since 1992 with Russia for tourists. The Chinese were willing to take unskilled jobs that Russians refused. Consequently, there were thousands of Chinese living in Moscow and Kyiv at that time. One of the primary migratory patterns from there was onto Prague and into Germany. Again, once inside Germany, the migration further west was easy due to the Schengen Agreement, especially with counterfeit passports.

According to Holmes in 2000, there were three basic reasons human trafficking was flourishing:

- A limitless supply of human beings from poor countries.

- A limitless supply of customers — some in their own countries, and some in economically developed countries, and

- A limitless supply of ruthless traffickers.[14]

In the middle of this migratory madness were the children. In transitory democratic states, children, who were once the babes of welfare, were then becoming burdens to families, who had little economic means to support them.

Consequently, the children were even more vulnerable. Their exploitation was a large and growing international business, and an underexposed issue.

The trafficking trade is not totally engulfed in sex, albeit the sex trade produced huge profits and the fastest cash. The demand for children had increased even for the youngest of children. Whether for child pornography, child prostitution, child sex tourism, or in other forms, millions of these children were fertile grounds of exploitation, even labor.

In the United States alone in 2000, the National Center for Missing & Exploited Children (NCMEC) received "on average, 500 cyber tips weekly regarding child prostitution, child pornography, child sex tourism, and sexual abuse outside of a family," according to John Rabun, Vice President, and Chief Operating Officer of NCMEC at the time. [15]

By 2020, NCMEC had received over 21.7 million reports to its Cyber Tipline. In 2021, it received 29.3 million, and in 2022, it received over 32 million. This barometer should not be ignored.

We are not winning this war against smut, and it is time for internet companies to be held accountable. The average age of children in America looking at porn in 2024 is eight years of age. Now, we have books in public libraries sensitizing young children to anal, oral, and vaginal sex and pushing gender dysphoria upon them as if this is normal. This shatters their childhoods' innocence.

Never in the history of humanity have agendas been pushed so consciously by institutions from federal governments, legislative bodies, politicians, doctors, schools, unions in the West, and especially, by the behavioral psychiatrists that have infected medicine, tech, governments, corporations, and international bodies. When these entities hire shrinks to change society's behavior, everyone should be concerned.

The impact of watching pornography upon children's brains where discernment has not fully developed was unknown in 2000. A quarter of a century later, we have brain studies that demonstrate that pornography images do impact the brain.

In 2000, Professor Louise Shelly of American University referred to the victims as "hidden." [16]

Whatever we think we are doing to protect children, is clearly failing.

Children are exploited on a multi-dimensional, multi-levelled, multi-faceted, transcriminal, cross-cultural, and transnational manner. It is a global phenomenon, which no international organization seems to fully understand. I personally believed in 2000 and every year after for a quarter of a century that trafficking human beings is far more profitable than the smuggling of drugs and weapons combined. I did not buy into the notion that human trafficking was the third largest business following drug and weapons, as some experts and politicians suggested in 2000 and said so at the time. Human trafficking produces the fastest cash with the least amount of risk. It produces the monetary foundation, which generates the money for the other illegal enterprises.

Those on the ground closest to the issue — law enforcement — are the most knowledgeable, but also the most vulnerable in terms of protecting the victims because they are under-funded, under-trained, understaffed, and there is no sustainable clearinghouse internationally for the volume of information surrounding this issue although there is more co-ordination in 2024 than in 2000. But the models created are not sufficient because the trade keeps growing. Those in the fight are not going upstream. When a society normalizes smut and trafficking, they only increase more dysfunctional and criminal behavior.

Traffickers are highly sophisticated on several levels and in most cases are steps ahead of good law enforcement officials logistically, legally, technically, and financially. Although amoral, the traffickers are creative, mercurial, and know how to pivot.

They have proven repeatedly that they are steps ahead of most law enforcement agencies. They have set the rules of the game. They know where legal loopholes and low risks exist, and where fertile ground for profits have potential. They are bold, brazen, and stop at nothing.

"In one case, we discovered a warehouse filled with kiddy boots. There was a shortage of these boots in Ukraine. The traffickers were going to ship them to Ukraine to sell them on the streets. They bought them in bulk in the UK. The remaining money was not going to be sent directly to Ukraine from the UK. That would be noticed and cause an alarm, so the money was transferred to Poland then to Ukraine," said UK Detective Paul Holmes in 2000.

"It gets more Kafkaesque. Some money was even sent through the Western Union. In one case, money was transferred in suitcases to Germany. In Germany, a Lada car is a status symbol. In Eastern Europe in Poland and Russia, suddenly in the last five years, everyone has a Lada. Ladas are manufactured in the west as well as the east. The ones manufactured in the west are fancier. Consequently, the status symbol in Eastern Europe is the western manufactured Lada," added Holmes.

"In Lithuania, there were two social groups — the poor who are dirt poor and the mob. In Lithuania, the status symbol is the western manufactured Lada. In Albania, boats are a status symbol, and they are practical because they are the business of trafficking people across the Adriatic. In refugee camps, the recruitment of prostitutes is at gun point in the camps," Holmes stated.

Then Holmes gave an explicit example of the trafficking game.

"In 1998, in Albania, there were 20 regional police stations. They appointed a new chief that the mob did not like because he was going to try to clean up the system. The mob burnt 19 of the 20 police stations overnight. These people are lawless," Holmes stated.

"One police chief in Albania confiscated all the rubber rafts in town. Then the next day, the boys showed up in his office touting guns and grenades and demanded their boats back. What is a police chief supposed to do in a situation like this?" Holmes asked.

"There was a Belgian who was appointed to help in Albania. When he was picked up at the airport, the Prosecuting General was driving a X600 with Frankfurt, Germany plates. When the Belgian did a run on the car plates, he discovered that the car was stolen. Furthermore, the Prosecuting General did not make sufficient money to pay for the X600. The Russians traffick rockets and machine guns through Poland. Every hooker is a potential courier," Holmes said.

"There have been three murders in UK, which can be linked to the trafficking prostitution rings. In the boot of Italy, 58 of the 59 murders of prostitutes have been linked to the Albanian mob. It is like what you Americans call the Wild West!" Holmes concluded. [17]

The exploitation of children involves slave workers, sex tourism, child pornography, both video and pictures, kidnapping, rape, gang rapes, and much more. With the onslaught of the internet by 2000, the volume of child pornography had increased, and the distribution was borderless. The volume of chatrooms on the internet for the exploitation and sexual solicitation of children was endless in 2000 and has only exploded in almost a quarter of a century with the onslaught of social media, online games, and apps, photos, and sextortion as a norm, and the normalcy of that which used to be sacred — one's privacy. And, of course, with the birth of the dark web.

Traffickers treat children like merchandise. They buy and sell them on the internet like ordering from Amazon.com. In some instances, the children are used for peddling drugs and killing the enemy.

The exploitation of human beings changed the landscape of Europe, as in Holland and Belgium, where the mafia and gangs were very violent. By 2000 in Frankfurt, Germany's suburbs transformed into machine gun war zones because of mob turf wars.[18]

The situation also changed the landscape of the globe. No longer could local law enforcement operate independently. Law enforcement then and more so today needs to be internationally linked because of the massive international migrations. Stand-alone law enforcement agencies are no competition for these newly linked transcontinental and transcriminal syndicates, which are more sophisticated than most law enforcement agencies. The "new" mafias surfacing by 2000 were more violent than the traditional mafias. Murder meant nothing to them. Before they got to that step, they would torture, and in some cases, burn the bodies to keep victims in line. Law enforcement officials dealing with international trafficking had to learn how to be culturally sensitive even 24 years ago.

"My squad has specific criteria to launch an investigation. We have top priority for investigations into commercial sexual exploitation of children — pimping. The number two criteria are trafficking of prostitutes. No one has a handle on the stats [statistics]. It is vastly different from the past. Prostitution is viewed as victimless. It is not like burglary, thefts, or murder. There are no standard techniques. This is a brand-new approach to the investigations. A lot of factors must be considered for a variety of reasons. The girl's safety is the most important. Victim consciousness is of primary importance," said Detective Holmes in 2000.

Holmes gave two examples.

"There was this Lithuanian girl who came to London and was eventually willing to talk. She was even prepared to testify but was concerned about the welfare of her grandmother back in Lithuania. I told the girl that we would — as we had in the past — contact the local police in Lithuania where the grandmother lived and have them protect her. She freaked out because the police officers in Lithuania were involved in trafficking," noted Holmes.

"A second girl was from Albania. Her auntie sold her, and then she was raped daily by her trafficker while he forced her into prostitution with other clients. Most of these girls from Albania are Muslims, so if they are deported, and their families find out about the prostitution, the girls will be sent to a worse place if returned because of the shame to their families. So, deporting the girls is not always the answer. You must have a philosophical approach. Prostitutes are victims of crime. Prostitutes are always exploited by somebody. There are victim issues concerning where they come from. The most difficult hurdle for the police locally — a hurdle which they cannot jump — is protecting the loved ones of the prostituted victim. The trafficking is done by deception — Debt Bondage. The traffickers are ruthlessly violent," emphasized Holmes.

Media stories have been written, law enforcement, government and non-governmental reports have been published, but no one had seemed to have a real handle on the magnitude of the ramifications worldwide in 2000. I do not believe they even do today although we in the civilized world think we have a handle on this.

The media has focused on local stories or sex stories because of the sensationalism of sex. Government reports have focused on specific counties or regions. NGOs have focused on their specific mission statements and love the publicity for their body of work and use that to increase their donations. Note that not all the NGOs' numbers are factual.

Since 2000, I have investigated not only trafficking cases across the globe, but NGOs who have claimed false numbers of rescues, how shelters are run, as well as those who have falsely accused innocent people of human trafficking, and institutional and policy-drive trafficking operations.

In 2007, I investigated a Spanish Catholic priest who made false trafficking claims against a wealth family in the Caribbean. Even after his statements were proven false, a U.S. judge refused to rule in the favor of the plaintiffs who had sued for defamation even though a documentary was produced which relied upon the priest's false statements. The U.S. court deemed the documentary a "point of view" production and basically, gave the producers leeway to push that false narrative to the public.

This arena brings out the worst and the best of humanity and attracts maggots because of the money one can make in trade and the money that can be raised to do good. It is the responsibility of donors to do their homework so that they do not give money to those who are only out for the money instead of truly protecting trafficked victims and taking measures that prevent the increase in the population of victims.

No donor should ever give a dime to an NGO unless they can prove their actions equate to the reduction in the number of trafficked human beings. If they are not also into prevention, they are not worthy of donors' money.

Although the exploitation of children is as ugly as it gets, and most of society does not want to know or speak about it, this topic must be addressed fully to eradicate it. The depths of the evil involved must be made known. It is only then that society will realize that this is truly *A Shared Global Shame.*

Organized Crime and the Traffickers

The Only Thing Necessary for the Triumph of Evil is for Good Men to do Nothing.

— Sir Edmund Burke

Organized crime syndicates across the globe have penetrated industries well before the onslaught of the internet, but even more so today because of hackers and the Dark Web. Corporate leaders are engaged knowingly in these black markets, as well as world leaders who claim to fight human trafficking but create domestic and foreign policies that facilitate an increase in human trafficking.

Elected politicians and corporate leaders and globalists who espouse freedom and claim they serve democratic values are indeed involved in this insidious trade.

By November 2023, a New York judge approved JPMorgan Chase's $290 million settlement with women who said the notorious Tier-3 convicted registered sex offender Jeffrey Epstein abused them.

U.S. District Judge Jed Rakoff called the proposal "a really excellent settlement" that could prevent sex trafficking in the future by alerting banks to potential consequences for facilitating financial transactions linked to sex trafficking crimes. Epstein's money in JPMorgan accounts enabled him to run his trafficking operations.

By 2000, in Latin America, the Colombia cartel had controlled the cities and a largesse of ranches throughout the country, and even some Venezuelan ranches. Colombians still control the drugs, which, are produced in Bolivia, Peru, and Ecuador.

Add in the production of Chinese fentanyl over the last decades across the globe that is distributed by cartels and trafficked victims used as drug mules, proves how insidious the drug and weapons trade overlaps with trafficking and smuggling.

Americans need to focus on the southern borders during the Obama administration and now, during the Biden administration. The co-ordination is purposeful. The policies are failures, and the inaction of this immorality is endless. American leadership is engulfed in human trafficking relentlessly. The U.S. domestic policy contributed to the increase of human trafficking on the U.S. border.

The falsified foreign policy reasons in Ukraine are morally unjustified when millions have been displaced. The U.S. and NATO should have driven all parties to the table in early 2022 for a diplomatic end to the Russian and Ukrainian conflict.

In 2000, there were about 9,000 criminal organizations in Russia as compared to 700 criminal organizations 10 years before that. The United Nations reported in 2000 that 40,000 Russian businesses had mafia ties. Russians sold arms, pornography, and human beings — anything that could be bartered or flipped into cash. They infiltrated the banking industry. The Russians and Ukrainian mobsters, many of whom were former security police, migrated across Europe, and even into the United States by 2000.

"This is what we call transnational corruption," stated Dr. Louise Shelley in 2000. [19]

One former National Security Agent stated in 2000, "I would not even go into Brighton Beach in New York" because of the Russian penetration into the U.S. [20]

The Russian criminal syndicates were *so out of control* that Russia's then Prosecutor-General Vladimir Ustinov gave a warning to the public.

"The bureaucratic system is riddled with bribe taking as never before. Everywhere, federal, and regional elites have become closely associated with financial-industrial and criminal groups," said Ustinov. [21]

In the Russian Federation, those in the Far East had worked with Japanese, Koreans, and Chinese mobs to transport commodities to those countries, including Thailand and other Pacific Rim countries.

The Southeast Asian syndicates and Chinese triads in 2000 represented the most sophisticated pirates of tankers on the open seas. They stole them and later used them for cargo and shipment of people. According to a 1998 report on piracy, published by the International Chamber of Commerce, these corporate-structured syndicates were impressive. These ships and tankers were "Hijacked to Order in the Philippines for about $300,000 and delivered in three days."[22]

The Turkish mob had worked with Russians in the South to move the contraband — humans and cargo — to Cyprus, Türkiye, Greece, the Middle East, and the southern Balkan countries. The Kazakhstan mob and other mobs in that region were linked to the Muslim mob for countries of origin such as Bahrain. The Russian mob had worked closely with the German mob for years.

By November 2000, Mikola Melnichenko was in hiding because he surreptitiously taped former President Leonid D. Kuchma of Ukraine. According to Melnichenko, he recorded Kuchma's conversations and claimed that Kuchma was not only corrupt then but was the kingpin of crime in Ukraine. Melnichenko claimed that legitimate businesses were shut down for political power and monetary gain for the Ukrainian inner circles, and that Kuchma was even implicated in the murder of a journalist who was working on stories exposing his corruption.[23]

Twenty-four years on, Ukrainian corruption is still at the top of global topics. Corruption has morphed into a new model. Now, it swirls around Volodymyr Zelensky.

In Hungary, by 2000, the Russians created businesses with the hopes of expansion once Hungary became part of the European Union and worked closely with different factions in the Balkans.

The late Slobodan Milosevic's son, Marko, one of the lead mobsters in Macedonia in the 1990s, was known for the illegal tobacco trade. In the Balkans, Milosevic, and his gang of "200" elitists allegedly wired millions of dollars into foreign banks. According to the German Intelligence Agency, a secret German government document claimed that Milosevic sent $100 million to Switzerland alone and was involved in drug smuggling. The report claimed that Slobodan Milosevic and Marko Milosevic sent a "three-digit million amount" abroad.[24]

Jeffrey Smith of the *Washington Post* reported that between 1998 and 2000, Swissair jets flew bricks of gold out of Belgrade to Switzerland. The gold came by trucks from the Bor mining complex. Yugoslav documents listed them as copper. After they were shipped, they were sold on the metals market, garnering $6.8 million. Much of that was transferred to a Cyprus bank account. According to the

Yugoslav Central Bank at the time, all of this was illegal because all the gold coming from Bor, which was state-owned, was to be deposited with the National Treasury.

By March 2001, the Yugoslav Central Bank launched a sweeping investigation. Evidence led to Milosevic and his gang of "200" elitists. Simultaneously, the Yugoslav democratic government, the UN International Criminal Tribunal, and the US Treasury tried to track down billions of dollars that were allegedly fanned out across the globe to France, Germany, Greece, Italy, Russia, China, Britain, Liechtenstein, and South Africa.

In 1997, Italian and Greek telephone companies paid $1 billion for the state-owned cell phone company. About $200 million of it was never deposited in state accounts. An additional $350 million of the payment was diverted to companies controlled by Milosevic's friends and has never been accounted for. It appeared that much of the money was funneled through bank accounts in Cyprus and Greece. [25]

This is an organized crime story. There are 30 to 40 Eastern European major crime rings. They are very systematically organized. They are different from the La Cosa Nostra [US Italian organized crime syndicate] in the sense that they will kill their own many times over for nothing. Some of the best organized crime racketeers come out of Hungary, the Czech Republic, and Ukraine.

Extortion is the name of the game with these guys. 'You want to do business — any kind — and you find yourself with new and unsolicited partners.' These guys are common gangsters on the one hand and organized crime experts on the other. Many folks are former secret police in Eastern European and Russia. They all have affiliations. This does not mean that all former secret police are bad guys though," stated an International Security Expert in 2000. [26]

In Italy, the stronghold was real estate and resorts. The Italian mob was heavily concentrated in the southern boot, which is less developed - Sicily, Campania, Calabria, and Puglia. The Sicilian mafia is best known for its connections to the American La Cosa Nostra.

The Calabrian Mafia, 'Ndrangheta,' or otherwise known as the "The Honored Society" consists of about 6,000 members in 155 families. The 'Ndrangheta are savvy enough not to advertise their wealth.

The Camorra originated from the Spanish Gardena when the Spanish took over Naples, Italy. They rented a quarter of Naples to the Nigerian mob for prostitution. Over 20 years ago, the Camorra had been linked to Russian gangs and were investigated for shipping weapons and nuclear arms. The Camorra consists of about 111 families in Naples, Salerno, Caserta, Benevento, and Avellino, Italy. They are also in Romania, France, Spain, Scotland, and the Dominican Republic.

And, then there is the *Sacra Corona Unita (SCU), which was formed around 1983.* The SCU has had a pyramid structure with distinct levels of membership with soldiers and enforcers. It is linked to other Italian crime syndicates and Russian and Asian criminal gangs.

The Sacra Corona Unita were considered the modern-day slave traders by 2000. They were responsible for smuggling and trading thousands of Albanians into Italy and then fanning them abroad. They were not as careless as the other Balkan mobs, but they were just as ruthless. [27]

Roberto, one of my drivers in Rome during the summer of 2000, told me, "You do not fool with them. You must be careful. They are not nice people. They are loco, you know, crazy." [28]

Thousands of Albanians have lived in southern Italy. They are Italian citizens of Albanian descent. Many of them came to Italy when Mussolini ruled. It is in this southern region of Italy where the Albanian and Italians mobs formed a union and began the serious exploitation of the Balkans people in the 1990s. Although they specialized in human trafficking, they always were involved in other criminal activities as well.

Traffickers adapt to risk. They do their best to avoid suspicion and escape arrest, but if caught, remain silent for fear of reprisals from other traffickers or even local police who are often involved in trafficking. Word of mouth is commonplace, especially in places like southern Italy and the Balkans.

By 2000 in Albania, everyone had a story about trafficking. If the stories were not about humans, they entailed arms, drugs, weapons, or toxic waste. Sometimes routes were changed, but not as much as suspected because some border patrols looked the other way. Some of the police were even involved in trafficking. Payoffs sealed the secrecy. The tools of the trade then included the internet, cell phones, and faxes, which automatically put the traffickers ahead of many police departments in those days.

In 2000, many rural law enforcement offices did not have the tools and training to address trafficking crimes. As the internet has expanded over the last two decades, and encryption and crypto currency has gained ground, traffickers and mobsters have become proficient with these tools also.

As complicated and twisted as this story is, none of the exploitation of children worldwide would occur if traffickers were not connected to local gangs with international contacts. If there were no markets, there would be no money exchanged. If there were no trafficking routes with lieutenants along the way, there would be no end products delivered. Everything is linked.

Border patrols are a significant link to organized crime syndicates. All commodities must be moved across the borders, and delivered to points of destination.

In 2000, the Russian Federal Border Guard Service, better known as the FBGS, in conjunction with the US Customs, confiscated contraband worth $2.34 million dollars. They confiscated 4.1 tons of drugs — 900 kilograms of heroin. The main routes were the borders between Russia and Ukraine on the west and Kazakhstan on the east. These were the same borders for transporting human beings and weapons. [29]

When asked if the boats coming from Albania to Italy traffick people and smuggle tobacco, Colonel Rizzo of the Gaurdia di Finanza, initially said to me in 2000, "There is no connection."

But then I asked him how much tobacco his Marine Unit confiscated coming across the Adriatic from Albania and Montenegro to Italy.

He proudly claimed that his men "confiscated 149,445,970 tons of cigarettes in 2000. In 1999, they confiscated 591,967,649 tons of cigarettes." Rizzo then handed me a copy of his confiscation records. [30]

"In Montenegro when you ship three containers of tobacco, it is worth one million dollars. Just times it by 1,800 and you are in the billion-dollar business," U.S. Customs Attaché Armando Ramirez stated in 2000. [31]

In a bar in the Red-Light District in Brussels, Alberto, a Kosovar trafficker, and drug dealer told me one night, "I buy and sell *everything. What is a price!*"[32]

Traffickers wear all kinds of masks. They are tour operators and travel agents, employment agents, bar madams, local women recruiters, parents, relatives and friends, teachers, village leaders, brothel owners, pimps, procurers, customers, and corrupt officials, who work in Customs, Immigration, Police, or Border Patrols with international ties. There are direct sales, such as kidnapping and bribes, and indirect sales, such as deceit and debt bondage. [33]

In London in 2000, a married refugee, drug addict, and former manicurist turned into a trafficker after getting addicted to heroin. He often transported girls from Vietnam to London. They were flown from Vietnam to France, and then driven to London.

Young girls were in high demand — as young as six years of age. It was common for 12-year-old Vietnamese children to be prostitutes. In 1998, it costs $20,000 to get a girl. By 2000, it costs $11,000; $3,000 was sent to Vietnam, $6,000 to France for delivery, and the last $2,000 was paid upon delivery in London. The trafficker's preference was for the girls to be hooked on heroin by the time they arrived because it was easier to control them. Once the girls arrived, the traffickers offered to get them a passport for an additional $5,000, which then kept them locked into the debt bondage game. [34]

Interpol officials claimed that drugs, specifically heroin coming from Türkiye, was forced on some of the trafficked girls to break them as they were forced into the sex trade. The new drug used in 2000 to break the children was called Thai pills. It was known to have effects like ecstasy. One US Customs Service official in Europe told me that the same routes for smuggling human beings throughout Europe were the same routes for smuggling tobacco and drugs into Europe.[36]

So how do you move human beings? The same way, you move drugs, toxic waste, nuclear arms, and weapons. Planning includes cars, boats, lorries, trains, trucks, airplanes, tankers, ships, forged documents with large, organized crime syndicates and small-town hoodlums. Sometimes this game is deadly.

The night before I met with Colonel Rizzo in Bari, Italy in 2000, an Albanian boat collided with one of his Coast Guard boats. The traffickers were so daring that they did not have their lights on, and neither did the Coast Guard boat, which had been keeping watch for them. Two Italians and two traffickers died. Rizzo was told about the fourth death as we sat in his office. [35]

The Italian Adriatic ports of Bari, Lecce, Brindisi, and Ancona, where many of the trafficked people arrived from Eastern Europe in the south, were also the same ports where drugs were smuggled from Türkiye and Macedonia. Some of the drug money was then deposited with the Kosovo Liberation Army. Albanian weapons were trafficked through Kosovo, and the Albanian coastal ports of Vlora and Durres, and in Albania's capital, Tirana. The commodities were different, but there was a distinctive pattern that emerged when traced to the ports of entry for contraband and the vehicles used. [37]

Even French Bishops weighed in on the debate of prostitution and the connection between drug trafficking and arms trading in 2000. They published "Slavery and Prostitution," and claimed the slave trade was controlled by gangs operating across Europe and found "prostitution as the first link in a chain of criminal activity that includes drug trafficking and arms trading."[38]

I decided that I wanted to have my own first-hand experience getting a visa at the Albanian Embassy in Rome in 2000, so I specifically did not get an Albanian visa before I left the U.S.

A couple of days before I went to Albania, I visited the Albanian Consulate office. It was packed. The Consul was alone. He was swamped and kept racing back and forth between his office and the embassy's main building. He was gone anywhere from 5 to 10 minutes three times in the hour I was waiting.

In the corner of the room stood a thigh-high wastebasket filled with hundreds of passports. Every time the Consul left the room, two young bandits would sift through the basket and stuff a bunch of passports into their knapsacks. When I asked if the passports were any good, one Albanian who spoke English said, "We recycle everything in Albania," and laughed.

When it was my turn and the Consul realized that I was an American, he told me that I did not need a visa.

"Americans at the Embassy say I need one. Are you sure?"

He smiled. "We love Americans. We want Americans. You do not need a visa!"

I never shared that I was an investigative journalist.

As I departed, I concluded that the Consul either did not notice that the barrel of passports was now half-empty, or he just did not care, or perhaps, he was on the take.

The Balkans

In 2000, the Balkans was a war-torn arena steeped in centuries-old biases, hatred, cultural, and historical differences. By 2001, the Fifth War of the Balkans was underway in Macedonia, which was preceded by the conflicts in Croatia, Bosnia-Herzegovina, Serbia, and Kosovo in the 1990s.

In the 1990s and by 2000, the Balkans was infested with corrupt officials stealing aid monies. Displaced and homeless refugees were numerous. Economies were replaced with black markets, and in some cases, nearly collapsed. War zones and post-war zones even on the throes of a comeback always have an underlying level of severe corruption where many are fearful of the next war.

Government officials and rebels were fighting over assets, and for all intended purposes, the population had little education and was emotionally and financially drained from the conflicts. In many cases, they were suffering from post-traumatic stress syndrome because of the entrenched centuries hatred of ethnic groups, and they were angry. In addition to the cross-cultural centuries-old hatred, which was rampant, this so-called "newfound freedom" had not improved their lot in life. Many believed in "The Myth of the West" — that life was better elsewhere- and for those who wanted to make money fast, they were frustrated. They were marginalized.

There were no jobs per se. The commitment to rebuild homes by the North Atlantic Treaty Organization (NATO) troops was not moving fast enough. And, as in most war-torn regions, everyone wanted to cut a deal just to survive in the short term with little care given to the ramifications or the cost of the deals they were about to make. Whatever put money in their pockets today was the short-term endgame. *Long-term was not part of the average Balkan psyche or culture at that time. The short-term prism was everything.*

The Balkan peoples were desperately trying to survive. They were very vulnerable, living on lost dreams, if they ever had any, and they were being swindled left and right by organized crime syndicates, petty thugs, multi-national corporations, and Superpowers. The Balkan people had no regard for the government. Some of them did not even understand the concept of government. There was a profound deep entitlement issue, which was blatant. It was called *corruption!*

Even the black-market money changers in Albania were visible on the boulevards. They would loiter all day in Skanderbeg Square with wads of US dollars, Deutsche Marks and the local Leik currency looking like bookies trying to place a bet or make an exchange. [40]

The most illustrative and visible story about Balkan crime had to do with the numerous Mercedes in plain sight. Every fourth car in Albania was a Mercedes with a Belgian, German, Italian, or French tag in those days.

Joseph Limprecht, the then U.S. Ambassador to Albania in 2000, boasted the following to me during an interview.

"Albania has more Mercedes per capita than any other country on the planet."[41]

Ten years before, the government would not allow the average person to drive a car, but Mercedes were everywhere in 2000 although donkey carts were still visible on the roads.

According to Albanians and ex-patriots working in Tirana in 2000, the Albanian mob in Germany bought the Mercedes, and then had them driven to Albania. The owner in Germany then would report the car missing, collect on the insurance, and the new owner in Albania paid him about US$3,000-$5,000.

Some Albanians saw nothing wrong with this transfer of goods because to them — no one was getting hurt — at least, no one according to their way of thinking. There was no connection to insurance fraud. There was no psyche for that concept. It had no value to them. [42]

Fabiola Laco-Ergo, then Vice-President of Useful to Albanian Women in Tirana, which educated rural girls on the risks of trafficking, and bragged of her meeting First Lady Hillary Clinton and showed me a picture of the two of them, was non-plus about stolen Mercedes.

"There is nothing wrong. No one is getting hurt." [43]

Francesco, a bartender at the Sheraton Hotel in Bari, Italy, who worked at a hotel in Tirana, Albania for several months in 1999 had a different take about Albanians.

"Albanians drove me crazy. They are such oppressed people. I would ask one of the workers to get an orange from the kitchen for the bar. He could not go alone to get *one* orange. He needed to take someone with him to witness that he was only taking *one* orange. Same thing happened if I asked for *one* plate. If I asked for *one anything, two always* had to go. The fear of being accused of stealing is too much — too much!" [44]

Yrii, my Albanian driver met me at the Tirana airport upon my arrival in August 2000. I had purchased an Albanian dictionary, and he had his "home-made" English dictionary. Neither of us spoke the other's language well, but somehow, we were learning to communicate fast, *so I thought.*

I was nodding up and down, yes, yes. He would sometimes smile and then flip into a bewildered facial expression. I could not figure out what I had said and was afraid I may have insulted him. Hours later at the Rogner Hotel in Tirana, a British contractor explained that nodding up and down means "No" to an Albanian, who has never left the country.

"You need to think the exact opposite here and you will be just fine," he said.

Albanian roads seemed parallel to the Albanian way of thinking 24 years ago. There were a few stoplights in Tirana. Most of them were inoperative, and drivers just ignored the broken ones. At intersections, it was customary to see four or five policemen in the middle of the road giving different command signals simultaneously. They were almost oblivious to the other's existence. The intersections were total chaos and seemed more like a Laurel and Hardy comedy skit.

John van Weeten, a British humanitarian who had led over 50 relief missions and was building and donating Albanian libraries in 2000 was resigned to the Albanian way of life.

"Albania is just chaotic." [45]

Driving to Vlora and back to Tirana in one day was a long drive, so Yrii and I shared the driving. It was quite an experience. To say that there were no rules is putting it mildly. Yrii, who was in the passenger seat, would tell me to "Slow... slow... slow!"

Then 15 seconds later, he would scream, "Go... go... go!" He was driving me crazy for the first 20 minutes. I could not figure out why Yrii was so emotional about slow... slow... slow and go... go... go.

The translator in the back seat woke up from a nap, and finally explained to me. "If you can see the road straight ahead you go fast. If you cannot see around the bend, you go slow."

"Why?" I asked.

"Because you will hit a car head on. It happens all the time!"

According to Fabiola Laco-Ergo, in the late 1990s, Albanians were "suckered" into a pyramid game. Everyone in the country went mad. The government encouraged people to play the pyramid game. A lot of people enthusiastically played the game. They even put up their homes as collateral. And then, the pyramid game collapsed as most do, and many people lost all their money. Those who did not were the ones who got into the game early and pulled out before the Ponzi scheme totally collapsed.

The swindled Albanians took the matter into their own hands. The government had bunkers of arsenals and ammunition throughout the countryside. Overnight all the bunkers were emptied, and the guns were distributed all over the country, and when the government ordered the return of the guns, Albanians stood their ground and refused.[46]

I met Kenn Underwood in Tirana. He was a very self-deprecating Brit, who worked for the United Nations back in 2000, and was one of the world's leading experts on Balkans weapons. He physically collected the weapons across Albania. He said that the newer weapons many times were not turned over. After crawling up a mountainside to get to a village, the owners would turn over the old ones and hang on to the new guns claiming the necessity to protect themselves. Underwood claimed that some of the Albanian weapons were showing up in other parts of the world. [47]

The root of any war always involves economics, and the Balkans conflicts were no different.

There was a kaleidoscope of assets involved in the Balkans. Most media stories in the 1990s concentrated on ethnic cleanses, self-determination, democracy, elections, human rights, and war crimes.

One of the truly under-reported stories was the financial stakes in the Balkans — the minerals and oil and gas pipelines — who owned them then, who wanted to own them, and who wanted to profit from them in the future?

Christopher Hedges, who covered the Balkan crises for the *New York Times* and Sara Flounders, who was the co-director of the International Action Center, had reported in the 1990s about the underlying motives of the Balkan Crises.

The Kosovar Stari Trg mining complex was estimated to be worth $5 billion. The Trepca mines, were considered "the richest lead and zinc mines in Europe and considered the "most valuable piece of real estate in the Balkans." In addition, there were 17 billion tons of coal reserves.

In 1998, Hedges wrote, "The Stari Trg mine, with its warehouse, is rigged with smelting plants, 17 metal treatment sites, freight yards, railroad lines, a power plant and the country's largest battery plant."[48]

And, beyond the wealth of the mines was the fact that they were "state-owned," and the State resisted privatization.

On August 14, 2000, 3,000 NATO troops descended upon Trepca's mining complex, and seized the lead smelting plant in Zvecan in the early morning hours. The *stated excuse* was that it was emanating pollution. Bernard Kouchner, one of the Founders of Doctors Without Borders, who was then head of the United Nations Mission in Kosovo released a statement.

"As a doctor and chief administrator of Kosovo, I would be derelict if I allowed a threat to the health of children and pregnant women to continue for one more day." [49]

The truth is that the complex, which was the leading source of jobs in the region, had been shut down after the NATO bombings in 1999, and this plant had only been back in operation for a few months before the seizure. Immediately after NATO troops seized the plant, it was turned over to a consortium of private mining companies. The parent company was ITT Kosovo Ltd., a joint venture of U.S., French, and Swedish companies. One of the U.S. partners was Morrison Knudsen International, which merged with Raytheon Engineers and Constructors, the supplier of Patriot missiles in the Gulf War and a supplier of radar equipment to the U.S. military. [50]

This seizure was interesting then considering the later reports about NATO troops wanting to return home from the Balkans in the 1990s because there were so many leukemia cases among their troops. The United States long ago acknowledged their bombing of Kosovo in 1999 was with uranium-depleted warheads, otherwise known as D.U. Some suspected a link between the D.U. and the increasing cancer cases showing up in the Balkans. Approximately one-third of the Greek forces had demanded to be returned home also. Portuguese and Italians were demonstrating to bring home their troops also, and the Belgians even held a conference in March 2001. [51]

Kosovo was not alone when it came to a toxic environment in the Balkans. As we drove around Albania for nine days in 2000, I witnessed garbage everywhere. On Sundays, families hosted picnics and played soccer on the outskirts of Tirana in what was considered a park on top of one of the mountains. The area was filthy. Trash was all over the place. Underneath the park was toxic waste.

The air in areas around Durres and Vlora on the Albanian Adriatic coast was too thick to be near the sea. The port of Vlora was filled with oil. Albania had been used as a toxic waste dump for decades. In the 1990s, Germany was forced to take back tons of toxic pesticides after it was delivered to Albania and found to be harmful.

Considering all of this, Kouchner's statement hardly made any logical sense whatsoever. It did not make any more sense than former U.S. Secretary of State Madeleine Albright's statement on August 23, 2000, when she held a joint press conference with Albania's Prime Minister Ilir Meta in Washington, DC.

"Meta's government has restored public order, fought crime, worked with the country's neighbors and modernized the economy," said Albright.

This statement was made on the same day that she pledged an additional $30 million to Albania.[52]

I do not know what "Albania" Albright had visited, but it was not the same one I saw.

The Balkans oil pipeline project also involved the Albanian-Macedonian-Bulgarian Oil Pipeline Corporation LLC (AMBO), which was based in Pound Ridge, New York. In June 1999, AMBO announced in a press release that the U.S. Trade and Development Agency (TDA) had signed an agreement with the Bulgarian government to build an east-west oil pipeline across the Balkans.

The TDA was to supply one million dollars' worth of technical engineering support, which would supplement the original 1995 feasibility study for the $825 million AMBO project. Brown & Root, a subsidiary of Halliburton, which was based in Texas, wrote the feasibility study. Brown & Root had been providing logistical support to the U.S. Army in Albania, Croatia, Bosnia, and Macedonia.

At the U.S. Embassy in Albania, there were numerous Root & Brown notices plastered on the embassy doors entering the inner security checkpoint. Some of the men hired for this contract were staying at the same hotel I stayed at while in Tirana, Albania. The TDA announced separately that it would give an additional $588,000 to the Bulgarian Ministry of Regional Development.

The AMBO proposal was to build a 913-kilometer pipeline from Burgas, on Bulgaria's Black Sea coast to the Albanian port of Vlora on the Adriatic Sea. The pipeline would be used to ship Russian, Azerbaijani, Kazakhstan, and Turkmen oil transported across the Black Sea onto European countries and North America. The target capacity for financing purposes was 750,000 barrels of oil per day, which could be expanded to one million barrels per day, or 35 million metric tons per year. The trans-Balkan pipeline was then part of the Transport Corridor #8 plan, which had already been sanctioned by the European Union's Council of Transport Ministers. Corridor #8 which was to include a highway, railroad, gas pipeline, and fiber-optic telecommunications line, as well as the AMBO's pipeline.[53]

AMBO stated in a June 1999 press release the following.

"We are delighted to be the beneficiary of this funding because it signifies priority support of our project by the U.S. government.... It also confirms our belief that this development fits the U.S. government's strategic thinking concerning the transport of Caspian oil. In addition to strongly supporting the Baku-Ceyhan pipeline project, support of [AMBO's] project by the U.S. government takes significant long-term pressure off the Bosphorus Straits and is a natural extension of American's overall policy for multiple east-west oil and gas pipelines.... "[54]

TDA emphasized the following.

"American companies stood a good chance of securing contracts for the AMBO pipeline because there were to be $580 million worth of CALM buoy systems, electrical cabling, line pipe, oil storage tanks, pigging stations, pipeline coating, pumps, SCADA communications systems and vehicles over the life of the project."[55]

So much for the human rights' argument!

Humanitarian workers are concerned with the *human hell holes*, as disaster relief workers refer to war zones. Multi-nationals and governments involved in war, historically, are concerned with economics. And, the Balkans had plenty of these ingredients, but this was not a story about the politics of the Balkans.

This investigation was about the exploitation of children emanating from these conflicts over so-called democracy, human rights, but also the obvious, the war about natural resources. What was of tantamount importance was that to grasp the situation in the Balkans, it was necessary to understand the Balkan mentality, its cultures, and why they were fighting and why vulnerable, poor, and disadvantaged people in the Balkans were still suffering in 2000, and barely hanging on, and, simultaneously, why children were being killed and exploited going *into* and coming *out of* the Balkans and trafficked through the Balkans.

Everyone in a war zone is at risk. That is what war is. The women and children in the Balkans were no more protected than women and children in any other war zone.

In 1992 in the Balkans, children were kidnapped and raped in Foca, Bosnia. The town sits on the Drina River in southeastern Bosnia. Here the Bosnia war of 1992-1993 changed the lives of Muslim girls and women, who were repeatedly raped, brutally beaten, tortured, and some murdered. Foca was a rape center for Serbian soldiers. When the Serbs took over Foca in 1992, non-Serbian men were imprisoned. The women and children were housed in motels and schools, and in a sports hall.

Repeatedly, women and girls, some as young as 12 and 13 years of age, were removed from these dwellings, taken to "quasi brothels," and gang raped. One witness testified that when she was 15 years old, she was locked up with her sister, who was four years older. and their mother in a motel. Four men raped her.

Later, she was taken to a house where she was a domestic servant and sex slave for other soldiers for prolonged periods of time. Eventually she escaped, but only after she and another girl were sold to Montenegrin soldiers for 500 German marks each. Later, when some of these soldiers stood trial, the most shocking argument was made by the Chief Defense Counselor, Slavisa Prodanovic.

"The rape in itself is not an act that inflicts severe bodily pain," said Prodanovic.

Others were raped along the Arizona Highway between Sarajevo and Tuzla, behind closed doors in brothels, in rural shacks along trade routes, and in refugee camps. [56]

Luxembourg Socialist Lydie Err, in preparing a report for the Parliamentary Assembly of the Council of Europe, claimed in the 1990s that there were "conditioning camps" in Albania, Italy, and the countries of the former Yugoslavia, where according to statements gathered from victims then, women were sequestered, raped, tortured, drugged, and starved. Retaliation measures ranged from simple financial sanctions to assassination. They were sent on to "training camps where they are forced to have 50 to 60 relations per day." [57]

These victims were tossed into the sex trade industry as easily as flipping fries. They were sold into prostitution and indentured slavery, and even found servicing those who were there to protect them — the UN peacekeeping soldiers. One Romanian victim, who was trafficked all over the Balkans, showed me a picture of a U.S. soldier from New Jersey who visited her in a Macedonian brothel.[58]

In January 2000, U.S. Staff Sgt. Frank Ronghi, a member of the Third Battalion, 504th Parachute Infantry Regiment of the 82nd Airborne, pled guilty to rape and murder of Merita Shabiu, an 11-year-old Albanian girl in Kosovo. He was sentenced to life imprisonment by a military court. During the investigation, more names emerged. In March 2000, the 82nd Airborne disciplined five other enlisted men and four other officers for their involvement.[59]

On March 9, 2001, Helga Konrad, the former Austrian Minister of Women, offered her assessment of the situation in the Balkans. Konrad was later appointed the O.S.C.E. Special Rapporteur in Vienna overseeing human trafficking policy.

"The situations are even worse in districts where the United Nation's peace-keeping force is stationed... About 30 percent of those who go whoring are staffs of UN Troops, and 80 percent of the income of prostitution are paid by soldiers of NATO-led Multinational Stabilization Forces (SFOR)," said Konrad.

In early April 2001, Radhika Coomaraswamy, the United Nations Special Rapporteur on Violence Against Women, spoke to the United Nation's Human Rights Commission in Geneva, Switzerland. She admitted that cases of direct violence against women by peacekeeping forces did occur, but that the number was not high. She told the commission that there had been "a vast increase in trafficking activity" in Bosnia-Herzegovina and Kosovo.

"It is essential that all UN Forces are held to the same standards of international human rights law as are nation-states. To do otherwise creates a climate of impunity in which offenses proliferate. Now especially when the UN is running administrations such as in Kosovo and Timor-Leste, we feel it is essential that some kind of structure be in place to deal with these kinds of issues," said Coomaraswamy. [60]

Even those from the Balkans who immigrated to the United States, and still had family back in the Balkans had heard from family members first-hand what had been going on in the Balkans.

Nick, a waiter at Le Steak restaurant on Third Avenue in Manhattan, told me in 2000, "You *must be careful."*

Nick was originally from Pija in Kosovo. He is Albanian and one of eight children and had been in the U.S. since 1989. One of his brothers remained in Macedonia. His sisters were back in Kosovo.

"The rape stories I am hearing are wild. I heard that the KLA [Kosovo Liberation Army] is very much involved with prostitution," Nick exclaimed. [61]

It is a fallacy to think that wartime *rape camps* though — as opposed to Ho Chi Minh City brothels during the Vietnam War — originated in the Balkans. In the early 1990s the world was aghast that rape was used as a wartime weapon ethnically in the Balkans Crises. It took a decade to bring to trial some of those who were strategically instrumental in orchestrating rape camps, where girls as young as 12, and women as old as 70, were repeatedly gang-raped in front of their family and neighbors, and some even impregnated by their rapists.

Before and during World War II, girls as young as 12 up to young women in their 20s were kidnapped, lured, deceived, sold, and forced into prostitution for the Japanese soldiers in their occupied regions.

Then the camps were called *Comfort Stations,* and the women and girls were referred to as *Comfort Women.* From the beginning of the 1930s, comfort stations were established in Manchuria, China. The first station was set up in Shanghai in 1932. An extensive deployment of comfort stations occurred around 1937. The Japanese referred to them as *nigyuichi,* meaning "29 to 1." This was the ratio of how many men were to be sexually serviced by each woman or girl daily.[62]

According to a 1944 U.S. Office of Information Report, the comfort girls numbered anywhere from 80,000 — 200,000, and were found anywhere the Japanese Army was stationed. Comfort Stations were in China, Borneo, Myanmar, Hong Kong, Indonesia, Korea, Malaysia, New Guinea, Okinawa, Philippines, Singapore, Thailand, Vietnam, and the South Pacific Islands, such as Papa New Guinea. The women and girls came from Japan and Japanese colonies in Korea and Taiwan, as well as from Japanese occupied territories in China, Myanmar, Indonesia, Philippines, and Vietnam. Dutch Indonesian girls and women were also victims, but Korean girls and women comprised 80 — 90 percent of the victims. The reason for this is because in 1925 Japan ratified the International Convention for the Suppression of Traffic in Women and Children. Women and girls from a signing country's colonies were intentionally excluded from protection.[63]

In 1948, the Batavia Court punished only 13 Japanese soldiers for forcing 35 Dutch women into prostitution. The Indonesian women who were raped were totally ignored. The Tokyo War Crimes Trial, better known as the International Military Tribunal for the Far East, never brought a charge against any Japanese soldier for this sexual enslavement before or during World War II. In 1965, the first post-war bilateral treaty was signed between Japan and Korea. It was to ignite industrialization projects. The women beyond the 35 Dutch women were never even acknowledged in the treaty.[64]

The biggest difference today is that rape can lead to AIDS. So, for every sexually exploited child, AIDS is not just a risk, it is a reality. The increase in AIDs started showing up among the peacekeeping forces in the Balkans. During the summer of 2000, the Finnish government claimed that their peacekeeping forces returning home were a factor to the increase in AIDs in Finland. In July 2000, the UN Security Council admitted that UN peacekeepers had been spreading AIDS.[65]

During the 1994 Rwandan genocide, rape was a common occurrence, far more common than ever reported in the press. President Paul Kagame of Rwanda stated that rape during the 1994 genocide was a consequential and "contributing factor to the current increase in AIDS in Rwanda" years later.[66]

Rape is that silent secret that the world does not address and realize is a contributing factor to the spread of AIDS worldwide. It had occurred on an ongoing basis in Sierra Leone, Guinea, Liberia where at least, 300,000 individuals were displaced refugees, as well as in Uganda, Sudan, and other countries, where they were migrations and war zones.

The Balkans mafia was linked to organized crime syndicates across Russia and Europe. In the 1990s, Eastern Europeans and Russian mobsters fanned out across Europe. They established themselves in pocketed communities and found that the long- term ways of making money were not as lucrative or as fast as trafficking human beings. They found that the quickest way to make money was in the sex trade industry.

Trafficking human beings is easy cash, and it is minimal risk to the trafficker. Penalties are still minimal in most countries. Hence, there is a huge cast of characters internationally linked with one motive in mind — money. The goal of the mobsters is to not only traffick human beings *into* the Balkans by coercion, kidnap, or deceit, but to also traffick them *out* by the same means. [67]

Except for Hungary, most of the former Soviet bloc countries and eastern European countries were extremely poor in 2000 with high unemployment rates. People were barely surviving. Even though they had so-called freedom for the first time, some were very vulnerable and willing to risk their own lives or their neighbor's life or a relative's life for a better life financially. Coupled with this ambition and the myths about the West, and the will to survive, the landscape became fertile ground for trafficking.

And, when it came to organized crime syndicates, some who would be fighting at home, laid down their swords of prejudice to make a dollar. The goal of the trafficker is to flip the vulnerable human condition into a commodity and, better yet, serious money.

"Serbians and Albanians lay down their arms to make money in trafficking. They traffick everything —tobacco, guns, people," said Yrii, my Albanian driver.

"We traffick Black Africans from West Africa. They [Eastern Europeans] traffick their own. It does not matter where they are from or who buys them. In the end, we make money," boasted Marcos, a self-proclaimed Nigerian pimp in Vienna. [68]

According to Marcos, Nigerians in his line of work deposit their monies in Swiss, Liechtenstein, and Austrian banks. Marcos claimed that his brother in Brussels was also a pimp and trafficker. [69]

Some Europeans' own racism about the Balkans fueled the trafficking narrative about the Balkans' trafficking situation. It was not then uncommon in 2000 to find western Europeans, who believed that all eastern Europeans in their backyard were Albanians.

It was remarkably like how many white Europeans referred to all black prostitutes in Europe as Nigerians. The truth is that the African prostitutes in Europe were from West Africa, but not all Nigerians. They also stemmed from Sierra Leone, Ghana, Gambia, Senegal, and Cote d'Ivoire. The so-called Albanians were from Moldova, Macedonia, Kosovo, Serbia, Bulgaria, Bosnia, Albania, and the Czech Republic, Ukraine and other parts of the Russian Federation and Eastern Europe.

How real were the widespread rumors about the Eastern European mobs in 2000? Were they *everywhere* as law enforcement officials and experts told me?

What I discovered was that not only were they everywhere, but the local traffickers whom I met were petty thugs filled with a lot of ruthless bravado, and in some cases, with more nerve than brains, although very resourceful and violent.

In 2000, the illicit trade was dangerous. Smugglers and traffickers used more powerful weapons and moved with bodyguards. By 2000, European law enforcement was confiscating weapons from the Balkan gangs in Amsterdam. They seized grenade launchers, explosives, firearms disguised as portable telephones, pens, attaché cases, and umbrellas. Authorities believed that Yugoslavs moved the weapons, while the Turkish Mafia moved the humans and drugs. Officials believed that the arms were headed to the terrorists.

In the Netherlands, rival groups were claiming each other's territories. Three fatal gangland-style attacks occurred in and around Amsterdam. One occurred in a restaurant where two men and a woman were gunned down. Four men were killed in a brothel, and two other men were killed on the outskirts of Amsterdam. Police raided 30 sites and confiscated cash, counterfeit currency, stolen jewelry, heroin, automatic weapons, and ammunition.[70]

One night in Brussels during the 2000 soccer game celebrations, I decided to venture into a bar in the Red-Light district. Some of the local law enforcement officials, who were staged outside of my hotel for soccer duty, told me that it was filled with Kosovar boys — meaning traffickers.

Paul-Louis de Gendt, one of the managers of a restaurant in the Grand Place in Brussels, arranged for his Turkish friend to accompany me for a couple of hours. The corner bar was rundown and operated by a couple from the Balkans.

The first person, who came up to me, was a British chap, who was casually dressed. He leaned over and quietly said, "Lady, do you have *any idea where the hell you are? This is dangerous.*"

I smiled, *"Yes, meet my friend from Turkey, and let me buy you a drink, and then you can tell me what you're doing here!"*

My new friend just looked at me in total bewilderment. He never really had a chance to fill in the blanks because Alberto, who was in his early thirties, and no more interested in the soccer game on the big television screen than I was, inserted himself in the middle of our conversation. He was from Pristina, Kosovo.

With great confidence, Alberto announced loudly, *"How much you cost?"*

To which I replied holding my Nikon camera, *"Oh, you don't have to pay to have your picture taken."*

The conversation began to go downhill from there. I acted like I did not know what he was talking about. He called the other girls in the room, "my whores."

I told him, "You should not call women whores."

He repeated it again but this time, he was swinging his arms, showing some frustration.

Finally, to try to add some levity, I said, "I am far too expensive for you. You could not afford *me!* I am not a hooker. I am a photographer, but I bet you are a pimp!"

And, then we went back and forth about what a pimp is. In the end, he smiled, I laughed, the Brit was gulping, and my Turkish friend was gesturing, wanting to know if everything was *okay or did, I want to leave?*

Alberto settled down a bit, and we continued.

Because I was intentionally carrying cameras, I kept insisting that I was taking pictures of Europeans celebrating the soccer season, and clicked away, and just kept asking questions.

At this point, the Brit was on his third pint and just shaking his head.

Finally, Alberto admitted that he was a trafficker. He does it for the quick money. He had been doing it for two years. He moved his "stock" between Antwerp, Brussels, and Bonn. Most of the girls he trafficked arrived in Brussels by train.

When asked, if they have documents, he said, "No, that is why they arrest." Alberto said that young girls bring "high prices," and when I asked how young, all he would say was, "very young, very young."

Alberto claimed that he learned English during the war in the Balkans. He said that he learned it from the peacekeeping forces, and when I asked why he spent time together with peacekeeping forces, he said, "They buy from us."

He would not tell me how many other traffickers were in his operation.

I asked him, "Do you deal in drugs?"

He quickly responded, "What you like? I get for you."

And, when I told him that I did not want any drugs, he got edgy.

And I knew it was time to leave.

So, the Turk and I climbed back into his car, and headed back to Paul-Louis' restaurant.

About 45 minutes later, Alberto and a few of his friends swaggered into the restaurant. We had no idea that Alberto followed us. Alberto did not seem to want to take No for an answer, and I certainly was not going to risk finding out otherwise.

Paul-Louis told me to leave through the kitchen. He would manage the situation. So, I slipped out the kitchen door, and went back to my hotel.

It was a fact — Albanian, Kosovar, Macedonian, Ukrainian, Czech, Moldovan, Bulgarian, Polish, and Russian children were being exported and imported into the Balkans and across Europe for sexual trafficking.

In London in 2000, prostitution was legal if done alone. Brothels technically were not legal, but so- called prostitution flats — one prostitute to an apartment, and three or four to a building was legal. These flats clustered in Soho, Notting Hill, Kensington, and other neighborhoods were visible in 2000.

The old days of Hyde Park Street prostitutes were gone. The street action in 2000 was in certain train stations in the city, and on the outskirts of London. The most visible sign throughout London in 2000 was in the red telephone booths. The insides were plastered with pictures, numbers, and solicitations for any kind of sex that suits one's fancy. Single Red-Lights in windows for a prostitute operating alone were common in certain areas. The younger children spent time together at train stations, but every now and then you would find a young child in a flat.

In the Soho flats, I met Kosovar and Bosnian prostitutes. One girl, who looked about 15 years of age, and claimed to be 18, did not have any papers with her. She said that she was from Kosovo and had only arrived in London a month earlier. She crossed on a raft to Italy and then came by ferry across the English Channel. Another, who was bruised on her legs and thighs, and without papers, initially claimed she was from Milan.

When asked where she went shopping in Milan, she drew a blank. A bit later, she acknowledged that she was from Bosnia. Both girls came to Bari, Italy, across the Adriatic from Albania.

When I made these rounds with Paul Holmes, head of the Vice Squad in Central London, and one of his detectives, I felt like I was on a movie set. The buildings were run down. Pipes were exposed. Steps were narrow. Men were lurking outside of doors. Signs advertising "new girls" were glued on the walls. It was surreal.

Inside every flat we entered, there were two rooms; one was the sitting room with a blaring television, and the other was the bedroom. There were two people in each flat — the prostitute and an older woman, whom the police officers called the "Mum." They were present to protect the girls if something went wrong. The cockney-accented Mums looked older than their years as if they too had had tough lives.

At one point when we were speaking with an older prostitute from Malta, a customer banged on the door. The Mum opened the door and shouted, *"She's busy!"* and slammed it shut.

Holmes piped up, *"There is no need to lose business!"*

So, the Mum swung the door open, and the customer was invited in and waited in the bedroom.

As we were leaving, I lingered and looked in the bedroom.

Black leather boots, some with spiked heels, were lying on the floor. Chains and collars were dangling from hooks. And there was this chap sitting on the bed, which was draped with a *Donald Duck* bedspread.

I looked at him.

He looked at me.

I can only imagine what he was thinking.

Although London brothels were outlawed in 2000, it did not mean that they did not exist. Some after-hours clubs and discos were sometimes covers for brothels. There was an after-hours club across from the Ritz Hotel in Piccadilly Square called Rois des Cave. The night I went to the Rois des Cave, a band was playing on stage with some dancers in the main room, where there were long tables where groups of five or six young girls from Africa and Eastern Europe sat together. The place was filled with Arab men.

Seque, one of the African girls sitting at the table, claimed that she was 15 years of age and came to London with her sister who was three years older. Together they had worked at the clubs. Seque was charging about $50 for oral sex. First, she claimed that she was from Nigeria and finally admitted that she was from Senegal.

"I do not want to be here. I wish I were back in Africa," confided Seque.

Two young Nigerian girls I met at the Dorchester Hotel one night said that they came over by ferry from France and that they had no documents, no money, and they, too, wanted to go home.

The Nigerian mob controlled the African sex trade into the United Kingdom. Once inside, the British pimps took over. The girls were trafficked into Europe from West Africa.

The girls were coming from Nigeria, specifically Benin City, where one of the tricks was to use voodoo to get the victims trapped into prostitution. Wealthy Nigerian men, and even women, who are former prostitutes, and now madams, offered the girls jobs.

The traffickers would approach their parents and lie to the parents. They would tell them their daughters would have legitimate jobs overseas. Everyone would sign a contract, and then a voodoo high priest or high priestess blessed the contract by taking something of a personal nature from the victim in front of the parents. Sometimes, it was a nail, or pubic hair. It was only when the girls left home and found themselves in Europe that they realized that they had been tricked into the sex trade.

At that point, their passports had been confiscated and even if they had wanted to get out of the trade, they feared reprisals against their families and shame if they had not produced money. As bizarre as this is, the voodoo rituals used was a highly effective tool to coerce these African trafficked girls.71

Nigerian prostitution had been a hot issue in Italy by 2000. The girls were posted all over the boulevards in Milan, Rome, Naples, and even on the hillsides of Tuscany. Two days after I was driven all over Rome for a couple of nights, about 100 girls were collected by the police and loaded on a plane bound for Nigeria. This was not the first time that the Nigerian government and the Italian government worked together. There had been several flights returning African victims to Nigeria prior to that.

The Nigerian prostitution problem was so vast that Amina Titi Abubakar, the wife of the Nigerian Vice-President, founded Women in Trafficking and Child Labour Eradication Foundation in the late 1990s. She claimed then that trafficking in human beings was one of the "most pressing and complex human rights issues in the world." They were not human rights violations. These were crimes in plain sight that involved a systematic criminal syndicate of kidnapping Nigerian children.

African girls were not just in London and Italy though. They were in the Red-Light districts of Brussels and Amsterdam. Brussels had a huge contingency of "Nigerian so-called prostitutes," and the incredibly young were behind closed doors. They were not in the windows.

There is an area in Brussels, where the Nigerian children were housed. The African girls could be found on the border of Italy and Switzerland as well.[72] They were in the clubs in Vienna, Austria. In Paris, there was a club named Ruby's, which was an extremely popular disco/brothel for the African girls. It eventually closed.

West Africans arrived by boat into Spain or by plane into Paris first and then flown to Italy, or into Paris by plane and by train to Brussels or Amsterdam, or by ferry into England. In some cases, the children were flown into Gatwick airport in the UK.

The traffickers would order them to tear up their documents in flight, and upon arrival, claim to be under 18 years old so UK officials would host them in public housing. That was what the law required then if they were minors. Once there, they contacted a trafficker, or were contacted by a trafficker, and then often just went missing. It had become such an issue in the United Kingdom that British authorities attempted to crack down on the situation by 2000.

David Gaylor, who was with the Sussex Police Department said, "The situation in Brighton [England] is out of control." [73]

In Brussels, the eastern European children could be found at the train stations and in the Red-Light Districts under streetlights. The younger children were more covered up than the older ones, who often wore thigh-high boots and noticeably short skirts. Some of the younger ones dressed in pants and jackets with pimps lurking often in a corner.

Christian Van Vanssenhoven, a Brussels police officer, claimed that more than 50 percent of the foreign prostitutes on the streets of Brussels were from Albania.[74] Again, my suspicions were that this is a cultural confusion. Many of the Balkan children were trafficked through Albania, but not all of them were Albanian.

Alberto — the boastful trafficker I met in the Brussels bar — confirmed that most of those who arrived from the Balkans or other Eastern European countries beyond Albania were told by their pumps and traffickers to tell anyone who asked where they came from to say "Albania."

The reason for this then was because if the victims were returned to their home-land — allegedly Albania — the local traffickers there would be able to get them right back into the sex trafficking arena quickly and transport them across the Adriatic to Italy and beyond.

In Amsterdam, the Eastern European children were visible in the train stations, but not so much in the Red-Light Districts. On the outskirts of Amsterdam, they roamed the streets. In a place called Theemsweg, cars lined up and just pulled into corrals for sex. Theemsweg, a thriving carport, was jammed until 3am.

According to Marjan Huls, an Amsterdam Vice Squad detective, "It is a horrible situation."[75]

In Geneva, the sex trade was linked to the hotels and conventions. There was an influx of prostitution when a convention came to the city. When the automobile industry descended upon the city, an unusual influx of younger children was shipped in as "fresh meat."[76]

It was akin to the publicity later focused on the Super Bowl in the US as a sex trafficking event several years later. American NGOs have had it all wrong though.

Conventions of any kind — political, business or sports — are fertile grounds for sex trafficking. What some johns would not do in their backyards, they may partake in on the road.

In Italy, the child sex victims from the Balkans and Eastern European countries were everywhere. Part of it was because Italy was the first stop on their journey after crossing the Adriatic. Another reason was that once the children were moved farther into Europe, a new group arrived. So, there was a constant shifting market. Some of the Eastern European girls lined the Via Salaria, which is north of Rome. In the Eor District, the Albanian pimps were out on the street at night after 10pm. While the girls strutted up and down the boulevards, the pimps gathered at drive-by cafes with guns tucked under their jackets.

Girls from Bucharest, Romania, and Budapest, Hungary were trafficked into Montenegro and then transported across the Adriatic into Italy in the north. According to the International Organization for Migration, 300,000 women and girls were trafficked from Eastern European countries into Western European countries. Eighty percent of them were forced to work as prostitutes and were treated as slaves.[77]

Children trafficked into Europe in the north were trafficked across Romania, Ukraine, Poland, and then into the Czech Republic and Germany. In this area, incredibly young children were the largest markets, but the victims were not only girls.

Many young boys in Germany were trafficked from Berlin to Hamburg to Munich and Bonn and back. Many of these children found their way into The Netherlands and were traded from one city to the next within The Netherlands.

In Albania, the two primary points of trafficking back in 2000 were Durres and Vlora, both seaside ports, where owning a boat or a raft was a status symbol.

Arriving in Albania only days after the July 2000 fatal Italian boat accident in the Adriatic, that event turned into a major political incident. The Italians demanded that the Albanian government crackdown on the traffickers instead of ignoring the situation.

Three days later, while in Vlora and Durres, I was told, "The boats are back in the water."

When I asked a trafficker if he was going turn on his lights, he said, "No, No, never. Then they will shoot us!"[78]

The Balkans then was not just a haven for trafficking Balkan children. Kurds, Turks, Iranians, Iraqis, and Greeks used Albania's coastline as a point of entry into Europe. Moldovan and Romanians were trafficked north as well as south across Albania. In Albania then, the people were so poor that trafficking was not even looked upon as a crime by some. It was just a way to make money.

Berat, Albania, is an Ottoman town. First time I visited it in 2000, I felt like I was in another world. There were no sounds of birds. I could feel the tension in the air walking the streets and back alleys.

Unlike Skanderbeg Square in Tirana, where chaos and the hustle and bustle prevailed, Berat's Square was empty. Not only were there hardly any people walking around, but there was no traffic. In the late 1990s, over 1,000 young girls were trafficked out of Berat. As I was taking pictures of the empty square, a man started yelling at me and walked briskly toward me.

"Do not speak," piped up Yrii, my driver.

"Who is he?" I asked Yrri.

"He is a Kurd - a Kurd mafia," added Yrii.

So, I retreated inside the street café and just waited, and we eventually headed out of town.

According to Yrii, criminals in Albania get angry if you take their picture.

This was the same reaction I received when I started to take pictures in the bar in Brussels. On that occasion, one of the "boys" grabbed my camera and Alberto, the trafficker who wanted to "buy" me, stepped in, and exchanged angry words with him and then he backed off.

In terms of the Balkans conflicts, human rights and international law experts in Sarajevo claimed that every third child in post-war Bosnia suffered serious psychological and emotional problems, and that did not even consider the number of children who lost limbs. UNICEF claimed that between 1992-1994, approximately 16, 000 children were killed in Bosnia.

Muhamed Sestanovic, author of *Crimes Against the Psychological Integrity of Children*, and an expert on the psychological effects of war on children, claimed that war crimes in fact have psychological effects on children that are long-lasting. He surveyed children and found that after the disastrous attacks in Sarajevo in 1993, and Srebrenica in 1995, and Tuzla in 1996, the children demonstrated disorders. Sestanovic claimed that these traumas not only affected their present day lives and predicted they will affect the next generation.[79]

Balkan Profiles – 2000

ALBANIA was a Country of Origin, Transit, and Destination.

More than 8,000 Albanian girls were trafficked in Italy, and more than 30 percent of them were under 18 years of age. [80] Albanian Mafia trafficked hundreds of illegal immigrants from former Yugoslavia to the UK. Women and children were hidden in Belgian ports of Ostend and Zeebrugge and then ferried to British ports of Hull and Purfleet in Essex, where they applied for political asylum. [81]

In Milan, Italy, 80 percent of the trafficked victims were foreigners. There were 19,000-25,000 so-called prostitutes — really sex trafficked victims — in Italy by 2000.

In Milan, women and children who were abducted from eastern European bloc countries were auctioned naked for $1,000. Some 75-80 percent of the trafficked females in Italy were on the streets, and violence was used to keep them in line.

By 2000, children and women trafficked were typically aged 14-18, and less frequently, 19-24. Italy had been a holding location for Asian children trafficked by Chinese and Japanese criminal gangs.[82]

It was not unusual for girls who were forced, coerced, or kidnapped in countries of origin to be taken to an auction, where they were forced to strip while men fondled them, and then bid on them. Italian gangs sent "orders" to Albania, and the Albanian gangs rounded up the girls. Auctions were held throughout the Balkans. Girls from the Balkans who were trafficked in Rome were paid about seven dollars for oral sex. Some of them were sold for $900 and told that they had to repay that debt to their pimps. Even in Italy in 2000, there were newspaper stories about Albanian girls' who were burned or beaten to death if they stepped out of line.

Young Kosovar women and girls were lured or abducted from refugee camps in Albania during the Balkan crises, and then sold into the sex trade in western countries such as Italy, Belgium, and the United Kingdom. Since their return to

Kosovo, local NGOs reported several instances of young women and girls being abducted or recruited again by traffickers believed to have been linked to Albanian criminal groups. [83]

In 1999, Vlora police detained 1,212 illegal immigrants, including 745 Kosovars fleeing the war in Yugoslavia. Police arrested 15 smugglers, confiscated 15 boats, impounded 25 cars and smuggling buses, and shut down three secret mills that produced rubber boats. The department also fired 18 percent of its force.[84]

BOSNIA-HERZEGOVINA was a Country of Origin, Transit, and Destination.

There were four major trafficking and smuggling channels in Bosnia. Sarajevo was a major regional center. Iranians and Kurds arrived by plane from Teheran and Istanbul weekly. They were then transported to Srebrenica, Velika Klausa, Mostar, and Teslic. Not needing visas and allowing them to stay for three months without registering with the police enabled the trafficked to move about the republic.

From Mostar, the route continued to Zadar and Sibenick in Croatia, and then by ship to Italy. From Srebrenica in the north, the trafficking route was by ferries or boats to Croatia. Once at Teslic, the border crossing was at Bosanski Kobas. [85]

In March 2001, there were night raids across Bosnia. Five hundred local police, in conjunction with UN, Bosnian migration officials, and NATO peacekeepers busted nightclubs. As a result, 177 victims were freed bringing the total enslaved victims to 400 over a two-year period in Bosnia alone.[86]

The U.S. military camp, Eagle, was on Highway Arizona.[87] According to Philipe Boudin, a former journalist, who ran a Paris-based NGO, focusing on children involved in migrant work and domestic slavery, Highway Arizona between Tuzla and Sarajevo was a "rape highway," where kidnapped and trafficked victims were taken to be "broken" by violence, torture, gang rapes, and drugs.[88]

The UN Mission in Bosnia, in conjunction with police, broke up prostitution and smuggling rings involving about 170 young women, including children. Many were forced into the sex trade. Of those 170 victims, 93 of them worked in bars in Brcko, a northern district of Bosnia in the Muslim-Croat sector known as Arizona. The rest were in Serbian areas. About 64 of the girls were from Moldova, 60 from Romania, and 37 from Ukraine, and the rest were from other Eastern European

The victims were sold for $1,000-$2,000 in the Arizona area on the military access road between Tuzla and Sarajevo. [89]

Spanish secret services accused Italian NATO peacekeeping soldiers in Sarajevo of organizing a child exploitation network for girls between the ages of 12-14. Their report claimed that the girls were brought to the Sarajevo suburb of Ilidza in 1996 and taken to the Croatian coast, where NATO troops went to relax. The Italians denied it. [90]

One in four women raped during the Bosnia Crises became pregnant. Raped women and girls all suffered from rape trauma — constant fear, anxiety, withdrawal, loneliness, suicidal tendencies, reliving their traumas with flashbacks, phobias, and feelings of shame and guilt.[91]

In addition to the rapes and trafficking, escaping was a nightmare. There were one million landmines across Bosnia-Herzegovina. Six years after the war, people were still being maimed and killed by the landmines. The landmines were even planted in the homes of returning refugees.[92]

BULGARIA was a Country of Origin, Transit, and Destination.

Women and girls from Bulgaria were trafficked to Greece, Türkiye, Cyprus, Italy, the Czech Republic, Poland, Germany, The Netherlands, and France. As a transit country, the girls came from Ukraine, Russia, Moldova, and then were trafficked onto Greece, Macedonia, Albania, and into Western European countries.

For the first time in 50 years, female unemployment had soared in Bulgaria by 2000. Trafficking was recognized as "organized crime."

Although prostitution was legal in Bulgaria, trafficking and profiting from trafficking, whether it be for sex or any other trade, was illegal. Penalties then were more severe for trafficking of minors whether it be inter-country or across borders. Approximately 80 percent of trafficked female victims interviewed were rape victims. [93]

As of March 1999, Bulgaria had no refugee law. At the time, it hosted 460 refugees and 3,000 registered asylum-seekers. Most came from Afghanistan, Iran, Iraq, the former Yugoslavia, Armenia, and Ethiopia. [94]

In Sofia, there were about 90 clubs set up for prostitution. [95]

CROATIA was a Country of Origin, Transit, and Destination.

Due to the employment of international troops, as well as the opening of Eastern European borders, prostitution had flourished. Trafficking was punishable for up to one year in jail, but ten years if done to a minor. Prostitution was not illegal, but the act of soliciting was penalized with a fine and up to one year in jail. Coercion or force increased the jail time to three years. Prostitutes were not protected under the Criminal Rape Act in 2000. [96]

Croatia had been a traditional heroin route from the Middle East into Europe. The political turmoil closed the route for a while back in the 1990s. By 2000, the international gangs were back in business with a flow of illegal immigrants and drug smuggling. [97]

Levels of corruption in Croatia were staggering and found to be in the billions of dollars by 2000. The late President Tudjman's plan to create a wealthy conclave of 200 rich families added to the corruption. Hundreds of state companies went bankrupt. Experts estimated that $2-6 billion dollars had been stolen. Unemployment stood at 20 percent, and if the bankrupt companies could not pay the workers, then the numbers then were expected to rise another 25 percent. People were helpless and hopeless with their government and their judicial system. The government was overwhelmed by its incapability of fighting the crimes.[98]

In February 2001, Tihomir Blaskic, a Croatian General was found guilty and sentenced to 45 years in prison for crimes against humanity under the UN War Crimes Tribunal. Although he was not charged with any of the killings, he was charged with overseeing the killings of Muslims in Bosnia from 1992-1995.[99]

A Croatian daily newspaper, *The Vecernji List*, reported that Croatian police arrested more than 30 people suspected of smuggling illegal immigrants from Eastern Europe and Asia. The police arrested 34 suspects in the Medjimurje region, which bordered Hungary and Slovenia.

The police had claimed that this group has been involved in smuggling immigrants from Bosnia and charged them $460 each. Polic had claimed that they have made over $360,000. Croatia's 600-mile mountainous border with Bosnia was uncontrolled. It was estimated that 50,000 people entered Western Europe through the Balkans. About 10% came from Bosnia. In late 1990s and turn of the century, Croatia did not require visas for citizens of many Islamic countries.[100]

KOSOVO was a Country of Origin, Transit, and Destination.

Although this republic of Serbia was run by the UN and NATO-led troops in 2000, it was extremely dangerous. Armed Albanian militants were infiltrating Serbia and killing police officers. There was an explosive sex trade industry in Kosovo, which was believed then to be run by gangs, and driven by the demand of international troops and aid workers.[101]

The Italian Carabinieri officers, who worked in the Multinational Special Unit (MSU), were fighting the organized crime syndicates connected to Italian, Turkish, Russian, and Serbian gangs. The MSU claimed that tour/travel companies guaranteed to their customers that they would get them to their chosen destinations, whether they be by dinghies across the Adriatic into Italy or traversing Albanian landmine fields. The MSU checked 29 travel agencies around Kosovo and discovered that 19 of them arranged illegal transport to EU countries. Some provided them with fake documents. The MSU was collaborating with British peacekeeping forces and MI6 agents, as well as UNMIK, the UN Mission in Kosovo. The experience of the MSU was invaluable because they had been waging wars against the Italians for years, as well as against the Sacra Corona Unita in the Apulia district in Italy.[102]

Presevo Valley in Kosovo was located next to the area where the US troops were then housed. It was in the very region where the ARIZONA Rape Camp was located. [103]

According to the Caza Alliance in 2000, there were over one million children living in Kosovo.

In 1999, more than 800 US soldiers were sent from the 82nd Airborne to Kosovo. A military report found that many of the soldiers were not trained for their mission, and that Army leaders in Kosovo and in the U.S, failed in their duties.

In January 2000, Merita Shabiu, an 11-year-old Albanian girl, was raped and murdered by Staff Sgt. Frank Ronghi, a member of the Third Battalion, 504th Parachute Infantry Regiment of the 82nd Airborne. He pled guilty and was sentenced to life imprisonment by a military court.[104]

During Ronghi's investigation, officials found that others in Ronghi's unit, Company A, mistreated civilians in the town of Vilina days and weeks leading up to the murder. Albanian men and women were assaulted and beaten by U.S. soldiers. By March 2000, the 82nd Airborne had disciplined five more enlistees and four officers for their involvement in misconduct.

Officials involved in this portion of the investigation included Battalion Commander, Lt. Col. Michael D. Ellebe and Company Commander Captain Kevin J. Lambert. The report found that soldiers received little peacekeeping training before deployment and had not even conducted a peacekeeping mission exercise. The report found that there was a propensity of favoritism towards Serbs and an overly hostile display toward Kosovo's Albanians.[105]

The Organization for Security and Cooperation in Europe (OSCE) reported that sex trade in women and children, illegal adoptions, sexual exploitation, had exploded in Kosovo since the influx of NATO Troops, UN officials and NGOs. "Clients" paid anywhere from a few hundred to a few thousand dollars for the victims.[106]

When the United Nations Forces took control of Kosovo in 1999, more than 500 murders had occurred in Kosovo. [107]

The population in Kosovo had increased since the United Nations forces arrived in 1999.

Fifty percent of Kosovo's population of 2.3 million was below 25 years old. There was no age restriction for alcohol, and the younger generation flocked to bars and discos. Drugs use was rampant. Kosovo's economy was at a standstill. Unemployment wavered between 60-80 percent. [108]

Scottish Marines brought the much-needed muscle to take on the Albanian and Serbian mobs when they arrived in Kosovo in the fall of 1999. Within five months, they got the reputation of busting the mobs.

Operation Norfolk, waged by these Scottish-based commandos, began fighting sex slavery in Kosovo, in conjunction with UNMIK, the international police force, and Kosovar Police Service. Their target was the Albania Mafia in Kosovo. What Operation Norfolk's investigation discovered was that the Serb and Albania gangs had put their hatred on the shelf when it came to the sex trade.

The Scots busted a Pristina "bar" and freed 26 girls. They were from Moldova, Bulgaria, and Ukraine. They found one girl who was chained to a bed and forced to service clients every 40 minutes. The girls were sold for about $800 each.

The Scots also busted a caravan in the Presevo Valley, which was notorious for crime and found a 13- mule caravan loaded with one million contraband cigarettes. In 2000, the Scots found one million cigarettes stowed in a petrol tanker. The cigarettes were being smuggled by Ekrim Luca, an Albania Mafia group in the region. He was a close friend with Milosevic's son, Marko, who was running the Macedonian mob. The Scots also seized about 100 illegal weapons.[109]

MACEDONIA was a Country of Origin, Transit and Destination.

In a German documentary, released in December 2000, a German soldier claimed that soldiers visited brothels in Tetovo, Macedonia where young girls were housed as sex slaves. The soldier claimed the German military superiors were fully aware. A brothel owner stated during an interview that since she had arrived in Macedonia in 1998 the number of brothels had increased dramatically since the troops arrived. A 16-year-old had been interviewed and she claimed that she had sex with hundreds of German soldiers. [110]

MONTENEGRO was a Country of Origin, Transit, and Destination.

Montenegro's population back in 2000 was about 650,000 and just over 51% were women. They made up 35% of the workforce. Wage discrimination and domestic violence were quite common. Although prostitution was illegal in 2000, sex trafficking was exploding.

The Montenegrin Women's Lobby was established.

Below is an excerpt from their report.

Many young women from the countries in extensive economic crisis (e.g., Eastern European countries) see employment abroad. They respond to job advertisements for babysitters, hairdresser, maids, waitresses, models, or dancers. Employers visit families of these women and girls, [under 18], promising good employment abroad, easy jobs, high wages, and monthly support sent regularly to the families. It is important to note that some of these women and girls are aware that they are going to work in the sex industry, but unaware of the unbearable conditions. The ones who come to work as erotic dancers and strippers are forced into prostitution as well. Others agree to work as prostitutes until they earn enough money to live normally in their home countries. They rarely reach their goal. As [for] the others, they are sold several times in[a] few different countries or cities to fulfill the demand of the clients and nightclub owners for the new, fresh women and girls (fresh meat, as they call it). At the very moment of their arrival, their passports and all other documents are taken away. To "break" them psychologically, individuals or groups starve, drug, beat, and rape them several times a day.

When they succeed or exhaust the women so they can no longer defend themselves, women are forced to workday and night, sometimes having 15 or 20 clients per day. Middlemen or "trafficants," often cooperating with the local authorities or police, buy and sell women over the border. They rarely use the actual border- crossings. They do it over illegal crossings, hills, lakes, or rivers. It is common that some women have student, tourist, and legitimate working visas. "Used" girls are usually sold again in Albania, or they lose every trace.[111]

The trafficked girls could be found in Ulcinj, Bar, Podgorica, and Rojaje. Bar was known as a port for trafficking humans, tobacco, and arms. Visas were not required for visitors who stayed only one month. Bar owners used to employ five women dancers with a working permit for three months.[112]

ROMANIA was a Country of Origin, Transit, and Destination.

"This decade [1990s] has been punctuated by inflation, unemployment, and corruption…. over half the population lives below the poverty line…. the country's inhabitants make up a cultural kaleidoscope. To the north, Hungarians, and Germans, to the south and east, Turks, Croats, Serbs, and Ukrainians. Inter-spread throughout the country are the Romas, the world's largest Gypsy population… ."[113]

Bucharest was also known as a mecca for paedophiles. [114]

By 2000, Romania had a significant problem of 9,000 children with H.I.V., and malnourishment among pregnant women and infants. About 30% of Romanians then lived on $1 a day. About 60,000 children lived in shelters. Romanians saw that number as a success because a decade earlier there were 170,000 children living in shelters. Until the late 1990s, foster care did not even exist. About 29,000 children had been placed with families.[115]

Because unemployment was high, young girls sought their dream in the West as students, dancers, and waitresses. The Romanian "liberalization" visibly showed up in pornography first. The second wave was prostitution, which was intricately linked to organized crime, trafficking, and violence. Prostitution in Romania was tightly bonded with brutality, physical and psychic torture, sexual violence, and servitude.

Romanians were trafficked to Albania, former Yugoslavia, Italy, Austria, Germany, Türkiye, and Hungary. Fifty percent of those trafficked were under 18 years of age. The most common recruitment was through bogus job offers. Romanian prostitutes were cheaper than Russians or Ukrainians. [116]

Under Romanian Criminal Code, prostitution was only an offense if a full-time job and with more than one partner. Pimping and buying prostitutes were against the law, although men were not usually prosecuted because of legal corruption.

Trafficked women and girls forced into prostitution risked punishment if they pressed charges against their traffickers. The victims risked being charged for prostitution. Trafficking was only an offense if it was connected to pimping.

Otherwise, trafficking could not be prosecuted. [117]

SERBIA was a Country of Origin, Transit, and Destination.

While the Islamic immigrants entered through Sarajevo, Bosnia, the Chinese entered through Belgrade, Serbia. Approximately 70,000 smuggled Chinese lived in an area in Belgrade, known as "Little Shanghai."

After the NATO bombing in the 1990s, Slobodan Milosevic worked out a deal with the Beijing government and sold them fake passports. Serbia served as a passageway for the Chinese going onto Germany and the UK. The 58 Chinese migrants, who died on a truck in Dover, England during the summer of 2000, were transported through Serbia. In September 2000, Yugoslav police were caught smuggling 25 Chinese into Montenegro. Officers were paid approximately $400 for looking the other way.[118]

Slobodan Milosevic was arrested on April 1, 2001, in Serbia for corruption and criminal conspiracy. As interrogations of cronies increased, charges were expected to widen to orders to commit murders against his opponents.

In April 2001, Dr. Daniel O'Brien, formerly of Medecins sans Frontieres (Doctors Without Borders), testified in Paris before the National Assembly which was inquiring into the murders of 7,564 people at Srebrenica, the safe United Nations protection zone taken in 1995 by the Bosnian Serbian Forces. The Inquiry was called to discover why there was no attempt to save Srebrenica and whether there was a deal struck with Milosevic who by then had admitted that he had secretly funded the massacre.

Colonel Tom Karremans, who was then the Commander of the Dutch battalion in 1995, repeatedly asked for airstrikes. The UN Protection Force headquarters, which was under the command of French General Bernard Janvier, ignored Karremans' repeated requests. As the Serbs took control, the Dutch offered no resistance. Rumors in Paris had swirled around the possibility that at the time of the massacre, a deal was struck between French President Jacques Chirac and Slobodan Milosevic so that French soldiers, who had previously been taken hostage, could be released.

"I remember the fear, the crying, the hysteria. They knew they were being taken to their deaths. I remember the 350 UN soldiers — pimply-faced teenagers on their national service — who were scared and did not know what to do. There were children playing in the park and one boy was decapitated. I remember the stench with all the people crowded up together and the sewage flowing between them, the mothers desperate because they had no milk for their babies. Some of the people there were completely losing their grip and having to be sedated. Then suddenly 80 buses just appeared from nowhere. All the locals were saying they were going to be killed, but you just did not want to believe it — out of naïve faith in humanity, I suppose. But they were right. After Auschwitz, they said something like that could never happen in Europe again. But it did, and what is more — UN Troops were there to watch it," said Dr. Daniel O'Brien. [120]

SLOVENIA: In 2000, there was not enough trafficking into or from Slovenia for it to be considered a Country of Origin, Transit, or Destination.

"The law on "enslavement" prescribed criminal prosecution for a person who "brings another person into slavery or a similar condition, or keeps another person in such a condition, or buys, sells, or delivers another person to a third party" or brokers such a deal.

Sentences for enslavement convictions ranged from 1 to 10 years' imprisonment. Individuals could be prosecuted for pimping or pandering "by force, threat, or deception," and the penalty for that ranged from 3 months to 5 years imprisonment or, in cases involving minors or forced prostitution, 1 to 10 years imprisonment. There were no prosecutions for trafficking in persons in 1998; in 1997, three persons were successfully prosecuted." [121]

The Ages

It is a myth that only children in their teens are sexually exploited. By 2000, there was a growing demand for younger children — children as young as 9 and 10, especially if they were virgins, and even a demand for infants and toddlers. The demand for children was increasing as the ages were decreasing.

This market has increased exponentially over the last quarter of the century because of social media and apps engulfing the internet, and the fact that the civilized world refuses to discuss the depth of depravity among us regarding normalizing the sexualization of children that leads to child abuse, which is child rape, which is a fertile ground for sex trafficking.

The expanding market was no longer the 12 to 15-year-old girl with makeup, who looks 21, or the 14-year-old boy sexually seduced by an adult in authority like a priest or Boy Scout leader.

On the first leg of this investigation through London, I met with Paul Holmes, who was initially introduced to me as Head of Vice, Central London, Charring Cross with the famed UK Police Force. He had a successful career with the New Scotland Yard.

"How old are the victims?" I asked Detective Holmes.

"As young as infants," Holmes stated emphatically.

I had to ask him to repeat what he just said.

He did and then, Holmes proceeded to tell me a story that seemed too bizarre, far too shocking and horrifying, and beyond my imagination and experience.

A white South African man had arrived in London years earlier. He had visited a sex shop, and as is sometimes the case, according to Holmes, he struck up a conversation with the sex shop operator, and eventually got around to asking for what is termed "child pornography."

According to Holmes, sometimes sex shop operators not only sell child pornography out of the backroom closets because it is illegal but refer some of these blokes to other parties.

The South African man eventually got around to asking the sex shop operator where he could find a child.

The owner started to ask the South African bloke, motioning with his hand *vertically*, "How old are you looking for?"

The South African man started motioning with his hands *horizontally*.

After a few moments, the owner realized that the South African wanted to rape an infant.

What happened next demonstrates the reality of how difficult it was then to put perverts behind bars.

The sex shop operator was so disgusted — *even by his own standards* — that he called the London Vice- Squad and reported the South African man.

The police were prohibited from arresting the South African because under the UK law "intent" was not enough to arrest someone. The pervert would have had to been caught with a child.

The next best decision, according to Holmes, was to put the South African under surveillance for as long as he was in the UK. So, for the duration of his visa that is exactly what British law enforcement did.

The South African never found an infant.

Thank God.

Technically, there was no crime in the UK, but upon his departure from the UK to South Africa, the London Vice Squad called the South African police, who in turn, met the man at the airport when his plane landed and questioned him.

The South African lost his temper, assaulted one of the police officers, and was arrested on the spot. There was no other charge.

When Holmes told me this story, I was stunned, and could not wrap my mind around the age of the victims or this story.

I kept thinking…

This must be an oddity. Surely, there are few with these perverted proclivities.

I was about to find out how dead wrong I was.

Two weeks later while in Amsterdam, I was advised to meet Jola Vollebregt, a Dutch detective. We had dinner with Carlos Schippers and one of his colleagues.

Over dinner, I told my dinner guests about my meeting with Paul Holmes in London and shared how I was having an extremely challenging time wrapping my brain around the fact that trafficked victims were as young as "infants, toddlers and very young children."

At this point in time, I thought I was experienced, well-educated, well-travelled, and seasoned. The conversation at dinner that night changed my perspective completely, and I was humbled beyond words.

They all agreed that what Paul Holmes told me was true. I told them that if that is the case, then you need to educate me because clearly, I do not know the depths of this evil and depravity because what you are telling me is that this is "among us."

What followed next changed my life forever.

The next morning, Jola called me.

"You passed the test, Christine," Jola said gleefully.

"What test?" I asked laughing.

That is when I learned that Jola Vollebregt and Paul Holmes were colleagues and co-founders of the Interpol Trafficking Committee in Lyon, France. Carlos was a renowned forensic profiler and not knowing me professionally or personally they were curious whether I was a journalist interested in the "tabloid" angle of this story, or genuinely interested in diving deep and getting the full story.

They determined I was the latter, and interested in getting the truth wherever the facts and evidence led me. In short, I was profiled. I laughed with Jola and Paul over this for years.

At this point in time, I had no idea where this investigation was leading, but clearly, somewhere I had never experienced.

In war zones, the worst is expected, but to imagine this was embedded in what we refer to as "civilized" society seemed unfathomable to me.

"Tom Erents wants to meet," Jola said next.

"Who is Tom Erents?" I asked.

"He is Head of the National Pornography Unit at The Hague," explained Jola.

So, I got on the train.

Next stop was The Hague.

The Hague

After talking with Tom and Jola for a while, Tom asked me if I wanted to see the "evidence."

"Not really, but I guess since I'm investigating this — I guess I must," I said bewilderingly and reluctantly.

At this point in time, I did not even realize what I was agreeing to, but it hit me like a brick shortly thereafter.

This day was a pivotal tipping point in this investigation. Since then, I have had my sights on Silicon Valley, its corporate TECH leaders, board of directors, investors, and those financial investors, who boast of owning TECH stock and watching their stock values increase. I know of the smut that increases their financial coffers.

First, Tom and Jola showed me a large room that stored a collection of child porn images. The voluminous collection from floor to ceiling had belonged to a Dutch Senator, who had died. The collection had been housed at his foundation. When this pervert died, the foundation's employees discovered the collection, contacted the authorities, and told law enforcement to get the smut off the property.

That collection proved invaluable to law enforcement over time and was marked as an "ongoing open investigation." I was asked not to talk about this and did not for decades.

When I was shown this collection in 2000, it was well before Myspace, Facebook, Twitter, the explosion of online games, online gambling, online pornography sites, phones with cameras, cell phones in children's hands, and in the hands of billions across the globe who are now addicted to social media, which has created one of the largest cesspools known in the history of mankind and one of the most unregulated social human experiments in history.

This is well before anyone asked what are the long-term effects of internet and social media? This was before the average age of 8-year-old children were looking at porn on the internet. It was before Backpage, but not before Craigslist, which was created in 1995. It was well before what we know as the "dark web" emerged and certainly well before I learned that there was a movement to decriminalize paedophilia worldwide and normalize gender dysphoria to legalize the mutilation of children.

To put this into context, in the U.S. alone where the population in 2024 is estimated to be around 330 million, 75- 80 million Americans have been born in 1990 and the following decades. Translated — that generation has no idea what the world was like before the internet implosion.

Let that sink in because what I learned at the Hague Porn Unit in 2000 was a tipping point moment that needs to be digested.

For the next several hours, Jola and Tom showed me what was in the dead Dutch Senator's collection and on the internet, and what had been confiscated regarding babies, toddlers, and incredibly young children — both boys and girls.

It is my personal belief that the average person then and now has no earthly idea that this very dark violent perversion even exists, but what I know to be true is that perverts in western society are now trying to normalize this smut while targeting children.

The photos that Jola and Tom showed me that day went beyond the scope of crimes. Words cannot even express these evil and vile images. Every image was evidence of a crime scene. Child pornography is the wrong terminology. These are images of pedo-criminality. They are child rape images.

As a professional photographer, I was drawn to the eyes of the victims in the images, but you do not need to be a photographer to see the terror in these young victims' eyes.

One image of a toddler about 16 or 18 months old still haunts me. Her little ankles were shackled to a bamboo stick. Her little hands were tied to the stick. No one could miss the terror in her eyes. She was obviously scared of the man standing next to her with his penis angled toward her little face in the image.

What was even more frightening was the increasing volume of this smut on the internet that Tom and Jola told me about that day in 2000. There was an ever-growing demand for images of infants, babies, and toddlers being raped.

There was a very logical reason for keeping the collection an "ongoing open investigation." According to Tom, approximately 85 percent of the images on the internet in 2000 had been recycled.[122] US Customs Officials in the ICE Cyber Crime Unit, which was opened by former New York City Police Commissioner Ray Kelly, confirmed this as well.

What was referred to as child pornography had been circulating for decades in the preliminary stages of what we know today as the internet, but now that internet has expanded over the last two decades there has been an ever-growing appetite and demand for *new images.* [123]

At this point in time — almost a quarter of a century ago — according to Tom Erents, law enforcement covering this cybercrime beat was hit with volumes of "evidence." As the internet expanded, it had become a tsunami of smut and barbaric perversion.

International cybercrime law enforcement officials had found themselves entangled with identifying whether the image of a baby being raped or a young, but still older victim being raped, was a recycled image or an image of a new victim who had to be rescued.

The Hague Porn Unit used the dead Dutch senator's collection to compare the internet images at that time with his collection to figure out if the victims needed to be rescued, or if the images were recycled from prior decades.

John's explanation was perfectly logical to me. I had been trained as a criminal investigator years before while in law school. Law enforcement was a few years off from developing a more advanced technology for internet image comparisons.

What I learned that day was that once someone posted an inappropriate image on the internet, the image remained online. There have been attempts through the last decades to remove this smut. Nothing used to date has sufficiently done the job of removing all.

There are cases of child rapes, prosecutions of the rapists and traffickers, and still justice has not been found to be fully served because the images have remained on the internet. There are cases of survivors, who have been re-triggered when their images re-surface and they become aware that the images are still in circulation.

By the end of session at The Hague Porn Unit, I was *blown away and absolutely disgusted.*

"How are you feeling," asked Jola as we were leaving.

"I am just too disgusted for words."

My head was spinning.

After talking back at Jola's home, I took the train back to Amsterdam that night thinking, *Who the hell are these monsters who rape children?*

That day was a life-changing experience. My life has never been the same.

By the time I entered my hotel, I was emotionally drained.

I woke up early the next day, took a run, cancelled my trip to Paris, and went to church.

This investigation was turning into a story that needed to be told and I had just given my word to these law enforcement officials not to talk about this collection for now.

I knew I had to go deeper into the story.

From that day onward during this investigation, I slipped into churches — did not matter to me whether it was Catholic — my heritage — or another denomination. I needed to pray because this was very dark.

I had walked into what was pure evil and needed the strength not to quit.

The only person I was in touch with during this period was a former colleague at CNN — Ed Turner, the consummate news man.

"Ed, there is a market for raping infants, babies, and toddlers," I told Ed after meeting with Paul Holmes in London.

"CD — get the story. This is a potential blockbuster."

Ed's advice to me when I decided to do this story was to make it clear to those who had commissioned me that they had no say in how I ran the investigation and no say editorially.

After that day with Jola and Tom, I called Ed again. His advice was repetitive.

"Do your magic, keep your head down and just follow the facts and keep in touch."

Child predators are secretive, clever, twisted, narcissistic, self-serving, and vicious. Law enforcement officials who have investigated paedophiles told me that it is not unusual for paedophiles to keep souvenirs that belonged to their victims.

They groom older victims with pornography. Every law enforcement official and every investigative journalist on this beat knows this is called grooming so when anyone on a school board or anyone in government, who objects to the term grooming, take it to the bank, that person is lying. "Grooming" is a criminal tool of the trade by child rapists.

They are hunters for prey. Predators can read who is a potential victim. They know how to manipulate, lie, coverup, and excuse their behaviors. They are very broken human beings, and emotionally detached cowards.

Ninety-nine percent of paedophiles were thought to be men when I first embarked upon this investigation. 124 They would join online chatrooms and clubs, exchange tapes, and bounced from one chatroom to another all over the internet. They even exchanged codes so that these like-minded perverted colleagues could look in each other's computer libraries.125

I concluded early on that these perverts just like the traffickers on the street believed their own hubris. The internet was a game changer for them because it allowed the perverts to go online and find other perverts and those relationships validated the others' perversions.

I was ignorant, and I mean ignorantly unaware — situationally brick braindead about this topic at the beginning of this investigation. Hence, I had to rely on the experts in this field, who turned out to be law enforcement and forensic profilers.

Jim Reynolds, a retired Scotland Yard official and a recognized paedophilia expert in the United Kingdom was one of my teachers.

When I met with Reynolds, I had just landed in London and was staying at Claridge's Hotel. I was jet-lagged when we met in the restaurant.

Ours was a most unusual conversation. This was before I even met Paul Holmes or Jola Vollebregt weeks later. I was drinking coffee trying to stay awake while Jim was explaining to me the difference between paedophiles and hebophiles. I knew nothing about a "fixated paedophile."

A "fixated paedophile" is someone who likes 8-year-olds, but has no sexual attraction to 13-year-olds," said Reynolds.

I clearly remember thinking and saying this at the time to Jim, "What the hell — What in God's name have I gotten myself into?"

Again, these paedophiles were all men as the law enforcement officials explained to me at the beginning of this investigation. They told me there were isolated cases, where women have in fact run off-line pornographic libraries that included child pornography. Law enforcement raided one such club in Asia in 2000.

Around 2003, I was brought in by Scotland Yard again to view photos of the women discovered in a major internet bust. I was curious about who they were and how they looked and what ages. It was across the board on looks, ages, ethnicities, and races.

Another case was that of Marc Dutroux, an infamous Belgian predator and murderer. Dutroux's sentence was life behind bars. His wife, his accomplice, was jailed. She filmed Dutroux raping children. Their caged victims died of starvation. His wife eventually was paroled from prison and entered a convent. 127

Other paedophiles travelled to exotic locations in Thailand, Cambodia, Costa Rica, even Australia and Brazil just to rape young children. These crimes are called sex tourism crimes. Traffickers rent the children for the night, and for a week. Children were forced to have sex with other children and then the perverts film them. Then the paedophiles add these new images to their libraries and exchange them with other perverts for money or barter for other images with their fellow criminals, either through the internet or through the mail. The exchange has been accomplished by word of mouth, but, by 2000, it was exploding over the internet.128

Paedophiles were surfing the web looking for children in chatrooms. By 2000, U.S. Customs Cyber Crime officials had identified thousands of internet chatrooms. Jim Nagle and Jim Gibbons, two U.S. Customs veterans, showed me how easy it was to join a chatroom and perverts target children.

When I was initially commissioned and before I went overseas in 2000, Ray Kelly had moved over to ICE to create the agency's Cyber Crime Unit. He got wind I was investigating and advised Nagle and Gibbons to bring me in on the inside.

They had just moved to an undisclosed location and were barely unpacked, but their computers were up and running. I had never been in a chatroom.

Nagle and Gibbons logged into one of these chatrooms known for trolling for children. They identified themselves as "Heidi 13."

In a *nanosecond*, the response jumped on the screen.

"Hi Hon, how are you? Are you alone?"

The name of the chatroom was identified as *"Fathers/Daughters."*[129]

Law enforcement officials told me there were plenty of internet discussions about adults who rape prepubertal or pubertal children. Many times, paedophiles are considered prepubertal molesters, and the clinical term for pubertal molesters is ephebophilia. Having said all of that, the term — *hebophile* — is used more on the street than ever because by 2000, there was a growing market for younger children. These were men who rape girls in the initial stages of puberty, and according to law enforcement, do not necessarily consider themselves paedophiles.

Some "hebophiles" over 20 years ago justified raping a younger girl — 11 or 12 — because of AIDS. They stated that they believed that there was less risk having sex with younger children. Some even believed, so they said, that if they had AIDS and had sex with a virgin, they would be cured. Some even believed, or so they said, that if they had sex with someone younger, their sexual potency would increase. As bogus as these arguments were then and are today, they were proffered by clients, traffickers, and pimps. So much so, that there was in 2000, and still today, a higher price for a younger child, and even more so for virgins — both girls and boys. Some wealthy clients in 2000 would pay $5,000 for a virgin for a night.[130]

Over 20 years ago, I was told the demand for children had skyrocketed, and it had even affected some markets negatively. Colleen, a Madam in Paris, who had been in the business of supplying high-class escorts for 20 years, expressed frustration to me over tea at the Hotel de Crillon in Paris.

Colleen was "losing some business" because she refused "to supply children to some of her wealthy clients."[131]

Who are these people?

A US Customs Service Agent in London said that one of the leading convicted paedophiles in England would come across as being "charming" if you did not know his history. [132]

Gary Salt was a renown paedophile among the perverted. I almost interviewed him behind bars, but his legal team shut that down. He was so sick that he would allow paedophiles to have their pictures taken with his own children as if it were a Christmas card.

Paedophiles and hebophiles can be homosexual or heterosexual. Some have sex with adults and children. Some are even married with children. In the real world, they can look like monsters and saints.[133]

In 2000, younger children were being used for other types of exploitation other than sex. In Germany, it was not uncommon for younger children to be used as drug peddlers. That is what the term "drug mules" means.

Marcos, the Nigerian pimp I met in Vienna said, "*Who is going to prosecute an eight-year-old?*"[134]

One night in a club in a Vienna club, I met young girls in their late teens from Eastern European countries. They were drug mules into Western Europe, sexually trafficked on the street and in the clubs in Western Europe and brought the Euros back to Eastern European countries and the cycle just repeated itself.

In Africa, Central Asia, Middle East, and Latin America, children have been used in war as child soldiers. Children, as young as 10, have been trained to kill other children.[135] Overall, the demand has been increasing for varied reasons — sex trade and non-sex trade industries — all harmful and risky human behaviors.

In Türkiye in 2000, there were stories about illegal adoptions of babies for organ transplants. There were even people posing as potential adoptive parents, who were in the sex trade business.

In Plain Sight

In early 2004, UK journalist Jeffrey Picket and I travelled to Guatemala to investigate the international adoption arena, which was presented to us as a fertile ground for trafficking adoptive children to America.

We believed Bruce Harris was a sincere advocate for children at that time. Harris was the Executive Director of Casa Alianza, an international non-profit organization, and the Latin American branch of Covenant House, which was created in New York City years earlier to protect homeless street children.

Harris was partners with NGOs associated with the U.S. State Department's Trafficking in Persons Office. (TIP). The U.S. federal law shepherded by Congressman Chris Smith, the late Congressman Tom Lantos, who was a Holocaust survivor, and former U.S. Senator Sam Brownback created that office.

I have always found it disingenuous that the U.S. TIP office recommended that foreign countries establish their federal trafficking office in their judiciary department while the U.S. kept its trafficking offices initially housed at State Department, and later expanded to the U.S. Department of Labor.

President William Jefferson Clinton signed this anti-human trafficking federal law in October 2000. I first began this investigation earlier that spring.

At the time, I thought how ironic, considering Clinton's own intern scandal inside the White House a couple of years earlier, and through the years, how hypocritical that he hooked his sail and the Clinton Foundation to Jeffrey Epstein and Ghislaine Maxwell, who preyed upon young girls.

Harris led Casa Alianza from 1989 to 2004. This NGO had been recognized for providing shelter, food, and immediate care to homeless and runaway youth across several Central American countries. It had received awards and accolades for years. It received the 1996 Swedish Olof Palme Prize, the 1999 International Award for Children's Rights from the International Bureau for Children's Rights in Montreal, Canada, the 2000 Conrad N. Hilton Humanitarian Prize, which rewarded one million dollars, and the 2002 Jorge Angel Livraga Award. Harris even received a 2000 Order of British Empire (OBE) award from Queen Elizabeth in England.

But, in the fall of 2004, Homayra Sellier, President of Innocence in Danger in Europe, rang me exceedingly early one morning, "Wake up — we need to talk."

Harris was alleged to have paid a teenage boy for sex in a hotel after picking him up on the street. Harris had left Central America, and no one seemed to know where he was. I needed to find him. He was in the U.S. Harris was married at the time and a father of two teenagers. Harris had gone radio silent.

I tracked Harris down in Florida and demanded he tell me the truth. He admitted to me that yes, he had had sex with this kid, but he did not even see the young man's face. Harris found his victim on the street and took him back to his hotel room.

When I asked him about the "rumor" at that point that the young man had been a resident at Caza Alianza up to 2002, Harris said the most shocking statement.

"Had I known that he had been a former resident of Caza Alianza, Christine, I never would have had sex with him."

My jaw dropped.

"Bruce, you are finished in this field of protecting children." I was emphatic. This was non-negotiable.

Silence was his response.

I then called two individuals: Jan Eliasson, the then Swedish Ambassador to the U.S., who later served as Deputy Secretary General of the United Nations, who was a champion against all forms of human trafficking.

I reiterated my conversation with Bruce Harris.

The second phone call was to John Miller, the then Ambassador of the U.S. State Department's Trafficking in Persons Office. Miller was a former Congressman from the state of Washington.

Both agreed with me.

Harris was "done."

I share these stories now considering what is happening in the U.S.

The world needs to grasp just how sick the internet is and how sick our society is, especially when there is a movement to decriminalize paedophilia, and a multi-layered attempt to sexually normalize incredibly young children about anal, oral, and vaginal sex through library books and sex education and health classes in school districts. Now, we have morphed into legalizing and promoting the mutilation of children without the parents' consent.

As of June 2022, President Joe Biden via one of his numerous executive orders, threw the entire weight of the US federal government behind LGBTIQ+ policy. The + stands for decriminalizing paedophilia and any other unimaginable sexual fetish.

It is not a theory or conspiracy that there is a movement. It is a fact.

I first became aware of it circa 2011. By 2019 I became a witness in the room of this movement as an investigative journalist.

The late Dr. Judith Reisman informed me of a group that wanted to decriminalize paedophilia in the United States. She had attended a conference where Dr. Fred Berlin had been speaking. I knew of Berlin because his name up in my global Catholic sex scandal investigations in 2002. He was one of the psychiatrists on the team that made the decision to recycle perverted priests.

When Reisman told me that there was a movement to decriminalize paedophilia in the US that seemed nuts to me at the time.

But, lo and behold, in 2019, I discovered the same group Judith had spoken to me about a decade earlier. Although their conferences were never open to the media, in 2019, they invited therapists and social workers.

As a result, I asked Carolyn Ewing, who has experience in behavioral psychology and was then head of a mental health association, to sign us up and use our real names.

She did, and received an email but it did not offer an address. Later, she received an email from the Executive Director of B4UAct that was hosting the event, explaining they did not tell us the location of this conference initially to avoid "attackers" because of "stigma" and "media."

I reminded Carolyn that in the reservation page there was a price for the media, which was the same price for the therapists and social workers. In the final confirmation email, the Executive Director noted that usually after the conference, the attendees get together for dinner. We had no intention of attending that dinner.

Before we attended the all-day conference, I asked very trusted intelligence, law enforcement, and military sources to find me someone who had infiltrated NAMBLA — North American Men Boys Love Association.

NAMBLA is a group of men in the U.S. connected to other paedophile groups worldwide, who prey upon little boys and teenage boys for sex.

I thought it a tall order, but in the end, our colleagues delivered.

Within a day, Del Wilber, who had been a law enforcement official in St. Louis years ago, and later worked for the CIA, introduced us to our next mentor.

Bob Hamer is a lawyer, a Marine Corps veteran, and a renown FBI Special Agent, who served 26 years undercover. Bob's career involved posing as a variety of unsavory characters — drug dealers, terrorists, gangsters, and the like.

The most difficult character Bob ever played, according to him, was a paedophile when he infiltrated NAMBLA for three years.

While I was investigating the Catholic Church sex predators following my first global human trafficking investigation, Bob Hamer was posing as a paedophile as he went undercover at NAMBLA's group meeting at Grand Central Station in New York City in plain sight of the public arriving and departing from one of the most iconic buildings in one of the most bustling cities on earth.

Bob sent us his book, "The Last UNDERCOVER," which I highly recommend. It is a head-snapping revelation.

The story he wrote in his book is riveting and very enlightening and every parent should read it. I cannot say enough to express our appreciation and gratefulness for Bob's courage, analysis, and mentoring.

When we first spoke, Bob mentioned to me how surprised he was not to run across a Catholic priest when he infiltrated NAMBLA for three years circa 2003/4. I thought so too because a Catholic priest named Paul Shanley, who had been convicted of raping children, was a promoter of NAMBLA.

"NAMBLA is the most paranoid group of all groups I've infiltrated," Bob shared.

That registered with me. I had witnessed that with traffickers.

Then Bob shared, "But, paedophiles like *to talk and share.*"

I too had found traffickers, pimps, and rapists very chatty, and boastful, and completely detached from situational awareness.

Bob educated us.

But, as prepared as we thought we were, Carolyn and I never expected to witness what we did as we walked through the doors of the conference.

First, there were more women than men in attendance.

According to the face of this group — those who do not understand or accept that sexual attraction to minors is normal and should be decriminalized and accepted as a normal sexual orientation are ill-informed.

What Carolyn recalled from that meeting is poignant.

"Everyone there, except for the two therapists at our table, were MAPs. There was a more compelling reason than money that motivated their desire to normalize paedophilia. Having it included in the Diagnostic and Statistical Manual of Mental Disorders (DSM-5TR) was merely a stopgap before normalization. How many times did we hear that day that people are sexual from womb to tomb, that sex is fluid, that minors can agree to sexual behavior? Hence, they are not victims," wrote Carolyn reflecting upon that day.

One woman in attendance stated several times, "Sex is fluid."

Those in attendance were in the community of MAPs — Minor-Attracted Persons - and this conference was organized by B4UAct.org.

We sat with two therapists who appeared not to be part of the MAP individuals in attendance. At least one goal of the meeting was to convince therapists to become advocates for MAPs to change the laws in the U.S.

Asking the therapists to advocate on behalf of MAPs to change the laws was a transparent financial carrot stick to therapists and social workers. *You change the law, and you could make money because B4UAct has clients in need of counselling.*

Under U.S. law, teachers and those in the health industry are required to report child abuse to law enforcement. Therapists also are required to report paedophiles to law enforcement.

The leaders of the group wanted the therapists to advocate that the U.S. adopt the German model which does not require that therapists report paedophiles to law enforcement.

The German Prevention Project Dunkelfeld began in Berlin in 2005 with a large media campaign to offer paedophiles and hebephiles who wanted help from therapists to manage their sexual abuse of children. It was initially funded by the Volkswagen Foundation and has been financially supported by the German government since 2008.

The community was arguing that they are misunderstood. They do not harm children and they need access to mental health counselling ostensibly because they suffer so much from being stigmatized and they need help before they act out on their sexual attraction to minors.

But what was revealed in the room was quite different from that position.

One middle-aged man stood before the audience and admitted he was a convicted sex offender and that he spent 10 years in jail. He stated that he believed he had a "relationship" with his "friend" and that if any psychiatrist wanted to be a B4UAct counsellor, they needed to come to *him directly*.

His name was Michael Harris. He hails from Indiana. He said to the therapists in the room that BFUAct is receiving 3 referrals a day — meaning they need counsellors.

I asked questions about research and lo and behold he made a beeline to our table during a break and started talking with me.

Immediately, he told me, "We need media."

At first, I thought, the group googled me, but then he started to repeat his story and I realized he had no idea who I was.

"How did you meet *your friend*," I asked Harris.

The friend was a son of a woman he knew who was going through a tough divorce.

"How old was your friend?" I asked.

"Eight years of age," he replied *nonchalantly*.

Harris then went on to admit that he had "other relationships with minors," but that relationship was the only that ended up in a prosecution. Harris was a self-admitted MAP, otherwise known as a "Minor Attracted Person,' which means he is sexually attracted to minors. He was married with two children.

"How does your wife deal with this," I asked.

"She knew before getting into the marriage," he replied — again, *nonchalantly.*

One of the therapists sitting at our table got up and walked away when he mentioned "eight." Harris' admission triggered her. She has shared with us earlier that she was in attendance to learn more and to see if she could manage a MAP client.

After Harris moved on, the therapist seated next to me turned to me.

"You ask good questions. Who are you?"

"I'm an investigative journalist," I replied.

She smiled and gave me a thumbs up.

A court asked her to counsel a convicted sex offender. She wanted to learn more to see if she could "handle" even dealing with a second child sex offender client.

Following the interaction with Harris, an older man clearly near his 70s came over to our table during lunch and focused on me. He started to share the importance of being able to seek counselling. He shared that years ago a therapist told him he liked "chickens."

I could feel my eyes popping. I did not know what was going to come out of his mouth next, so I excused myself to return to the buffet in the hallway, and he just kept following me and talking as if we were the only two people in the room.

He was excited his prior therapist was able to "label" his sexual proclivities.

Finally, I turned to him and said, "What does that mean about chickens?"

"I like them very young," as he motioned with his hands horizontally.

I looked him at him and could feel my disgust rising. I told him *nonchalantly* I needed to go back to the table inside the conference room.

As the day ended and Carolyn and I were heading toward the car in the parking lot, a group of about three attendees were outside. "Are you going to advocate for us?" one guy yelled out.

I turned to him and said, "I do not think so."

Flippantly, he said, "You do know everyone in that room is gay?"

I just nodded and said, "But, not everyone," and smiled.

What we heard at the conference was disturbing.

In retrospect, it was a very clever lobbying tactic to invite therapists and hold the financial carrot in front of therapists to get what MAPs wanted.

One of the men in the room who identified as a MAP was originally from Germany and was living in California. During the conference, he claimed that George Soros' money was funding university curricula for courses on paedophilia. He never stated which universities or whether the funding was direct or through a cut-out organization.

After we left, I reported back to Bob.

"You hit the potential motherload," wrote Bob Hamer.

I pulled up open records on Michael Harris because of his actions later at the conference.

He returned to our table and handed each of us his cards. One of Harris' cards read that he is an Indiana Advocate for NARSOL.

A file anyone can find on the internet about Harris I found interesting.

"On or about February 26, 1999, Harris pleaded to one count of child molesting, a Class B felony for his sexual contact with a ten-year-old boy. On April 29, 1999, the trial court sentenced Harris to ten years in the Indiana Department of Corrections for his child molesting conviction. While incarcerated, Harris earned an associate and a bachelor's degree in general studies. On November 6, 2002, Harris was released on parole."

Prior to his release, Harris executed his "Conditional Parole Release Agreement." Part of the agreement included that he "shall not use any computer with access to any "on-line computer service" at any location (including place of employment) without the prior approval of your parole agent. This includes any internet service provider, bulletin board system, e-mail system or any other public or private computer network."

"You shall not use your employment as a means to acquire new victims. Your parole agent may contact your employer at any time. You will not work in certain occupations that involve being in the private residence of others, such as, but not limited to door-to-door sales, soliciting, or delivery. Your parole agent must first approve any employment in which you do engage." the agreement reads.

"You shall not possess any items on your person, in your vehicle, in your place of residence or as a part of your personal effects, which attract children, or that may be used to coerce children to engage in inappropriate or illegal sexual activities. You will not engage in any activities that could be construed as enticing children," the agreement further reads.

Harris also agreed that he would "have only one residence and one mailing address at a time."

Harris' file stipulates what happened next on parole after his release.

"Harris began working as a casting director at "Michael L. Harris Productions" ("MLH Media"), a film and video production company that he had incorporated prior to his molestation conviction," reads his file.

Harris was developing video production scripts with a cast of characters that included parts for minors as actors. He reached out to another party who was a casting director. He told her he was producing a film that called for "(approximately) 90 child actors." According to the case file, Harris never disclosed to the other casting director that he was a convicted sex offender. The casting director sent seven actors to Harris before she discovered Harris was a convicted sex offender. Two of the actors were under the age of 18.

The file can be found at: **https://caselaw.findlaw.com/court/in-court-of-appeals/1150073.html**

The NARSOL card lingered with me. The statements in the room that day have resonated with me since.

NARSOL stands for National Association for Rational Sex Offense Laws.

For more than a decade, NARSOL has hosted national conferences. On their website, they have posted that "NARSOL opposes dehumanizing [sex] registries by working to eliminate all laws, policies and practices that propagate them."

In June 2024, NARSOL will host another one of their national conferences in Atlanta, Georgia. NARSOL claims to represent 800,000 registered sex offenders. The organization claims to be working with the American Civil Liberties Union (ACLU).

NARSOL's Chair is Robin Vander Wall, the former Director of Faith and Family Alliance, a political advocacy group.

He has been active in republican political circles and has been associated with major conservative politicians and political players on the national scene from convicted lobbyist Jack Abramoff to Ralph E. Reed, Jr., and Grover Norquist, who were entangled in what has been known as the "Jack Abramoff Indian lobbying scandal" in 2005. It involved bribery, extortion, and fraud.

When the *Washington Post* reported on that story on October 16, 2005, they described Vander Wall as "a former Regent University Law School student and Republican operative," who "was later convicted of soliciting sex with minors via the internet and is serving a seven-year term in Virginia state prison."

In 2004, Vander Wall was convicted on five counts of computer solicitation of a minor and one count of attempted indecent liberties with a child.

At the time of Vander Wall's conviction, the Virginia State Attorney General's office issued a press release.

Vander Wall's conviction was "a result of an undercover investigation that involved Virginia Beach Police officers pretending to be three different 13-year-old boys in internet chatrooms between November 2002 and January 2003," read the news release.

Today, Vander Wall not only sits on NARSOL's Board, but founded Vivante Espero, the foundation that financially supports NARSOL. He has been the recipient of a fellowship with Just Leadership USA, another non-profit organization, "dedicated to cutting the U.S. correctional population in half by 2030."

Vander wall is also associated with North Carolinians for Rational Sexual Offense Laws (ncrsol.org).

On that website, the group makes one of their objectives well known in an article authored by John Covert, a member of the Arizonans for Rational Sex Offense Laws Executive Committee.

As a result of the U.S. Supreme Court's 2003 decision to have sex registries available to the public beyond law enforcement officials, these groups want to change the law because they feel discriminated against — the same mantra that we heard in the 2019 B4UAct.org conference in the Baltimore area. Some of these registered sex offenders claim they are stigmatized for sex crimes because they are required to register. MAPs stated that they feel stigmatized for their sexual orientation and want their sexual attraction to minors to be officially recognized as normal and legal.

"Policy makers around the country took it as an invitation to pile on new regulations and requirements, vastly expanding [sex] registries that had once focused on a narrow spectrum of serious crimes to include an ever-growing list of offenses, even including such things are public urination and sex among underage teenagers," wrote Covert.

The current Vice-Chair of NARSOL is Michael Shimkin, the Founder of the non-profit Global Village Engineers (GVE), which is an affiliated organization of the World Economic Forum's Disaster Resource Network.

GVE "recruits and manages a volunteer corps of civil engineers, environmental scientists and other technical experts to work with rural communities and non-governmental organizations in the developing world," reads one of their internet postings.

Shimkin's NARSOL bio states that in 2002, "he was selected as one of the World Economic Forum's 100 Global Leaders for Tomorrow." He is also a member of the Sex Offender Policy Reform Initiative Executive Committee of Massachusetts and serves as a member of the Vivante Espero Investment Committee.

Vivante also publishes NARSOL's bi-monthly newsletter, "the Digest," which has been in circulation since at least 2014.

These newsletters are interesting to say the least as they serve as a roadmap to what NARSOL's state chapters are focusing on for their judicial reform in state legislatures for over 10 years.

At the 2019 B4UAct.org conference, Michael Harris also handed us his card for Indiana Voices. This organization was founded in 2002. It is an affiliated chapter of NARSOL.

According to their website, "Indiana Voices is an official contact point for NARSOL (National Association for Rational Sex Offense Laws). As such we work to combat new and currently existing laws which make it difficult for persons required to register as Sex Offenders to reestablish themselves in the community and to lead normal productive, offense-free lives."

"For Minor-Attracted Persons (MAPs) whether you have been legally involved or are just learning to deal with your own sexuality, if you need a therapist to help you on your journey, B4U-ACT offers therapists referral service. All therapists are pre-screened by B4U-ACT Volunteers who are MAPs themselves," reads the Indiana Voices website.

Interesting — perhaps, MAPs are screening therapists to see if those therapists will report "sexually active" paedophiles and minor-attractive persons to law enforcement, or advocate for MAPs desired legislative changes?

Indiana Voices' focus for the 2024 Indiana Legislative Session was tracking specific bills:

HB 1307 banishes serious sex offenders from visiting public parks when a child under 18 years of age is present. It also dictates that sex registrants moving to Indiana from others states or moving back to Indiana are Lifetime Registrants. Indiana Voices states it is opposing this bill.

SB 12 and HB 1057 prohibits sex offenders against children from establishing a residence within 1000 feet of a pool, beach, clubhouse, playground, or park owned, leased, or operated by a homeowners' or property owners' association. Indiana Voices states it is opposing this bill.

"There are multiple bills proposed that will eliminate the statute of limitations for prosecution of sex offenses. We oppose these bills… " reads their website.

Some of the other bills Indiana Voices has been tracking include video voyeurism, public voyeurism, child seduction by an authority, and age verification on adult websites, which is obviously, Adult "PORN" sites.

Colorado had been a conservative state, but almost twenty years ago, a conscious plan was put in motion to turn the state liberal. By 2024, Colorado is one of the more progressive states in the U.S.

In the last 20 years there has been a concerted effort to not just defund the police in creative ways but elect or appoint state prosecutors who are lenient on crime.

In recently years, there is a trend in Colorado to give mild reprimands to those parties who buy the very youngest of children or traffick them for sex.

As a result, Colorado State Representative Brandi Bradley of Littleton, Colorado introduced a bill, HB24-1092, entitled "Minimum Sentence Crimes against Prostituted Children."

The summary of the bill reads:

"Under current law, various crimes related to child prostitution are class 3 felonies. These crimes include soliciting for child prostitution, one type of pandering of a child, procurement of a child, keeping a place of child prostitution, pimping of a child, inducement of child prostitution, and patronizing a prostituted child. The bill requires a court to sentence a person convicted of one of these crimes to the department of corrections for a term of at least the minimum of the presumptive range for a class 3 felony, which is 4 years."

The bill further states:

"Under current law, the crime of pandering of a child is either a class 2 or class 3 felony, depending on the conduct involved. Pandering that uses menacing or criminal intimidation to induce a child to commit prostitution is a class 2 felony. The bill requires a court to sentence a person convicted of this type of pandering to the department of corrections for a term of at least the minimum of the presumptive range for a class 2 felony, which is 8 years."

Seems reasonable on the surface, right? Punish those who rape, pimp, or prostitute children. It is after all 2024. Not exactly in the now very blue state of Colorado.

Representative Bradley introduced this bill after attending a human trafficking session by Colorado's Douglass County commissioners. Bradley had found in her research "most of all the perpetrators of these crimes were getting off with only probation, unless the crimes were stacked up."

"We had witness testimony from several different counties, giving statistics that showed the majority of these perpetrators were only getting probation," said Bradley.

Three individuals testified against the bill.

"One said that Bradley's bill would cause harm to the LGBTQ kids that get kicked out of their home because they couldn't sell their bodies for sex," wrote Bradley.

Politicians debated the bill before the Veteran Affairs Committee, which is known as the "kill" committee in Colorado state political circles.

Of those on the committee, eight democrats voted against Bradley's bill while three republicans voted for it.

According to Bradley, one representative stated that she could not vote for the bill because she could not vote to send an abuser to jail to be further abused. Another representative stated that the bill does not count for mitigating factors like trafficked children doing these crimes as an adult. Another claimed that the bill does not allow judicial discretion when in fact the bill calls for 4 — 8 years, which is a range for judicial discretion. In Colorado, most perpetrators serve less than 50% of their sentences.

"The only thing I can justify from their vote is that they do not want to put paedophiles in jail, and they do want to jeopardize the safety of our children," wrote Bradley after her bill failed.

"I know that there has been a push to make minor attracted persons legal in several states, and in Colorado there has been talk of changing the age of consent to the age of 11. I can only imagine who pulled the strings to make eight people in the same party vote against my bill," wrote Bradley.

"The bill was going to make a mandatory four-year minimum sentence for people who buy children to rape them and have sex with them and the Democrats voted against it," wrote Colorado State Representative Pastor Scott Bottoms.

"They came up with every excuse, including that the buyers of the children are the victims, and that passing this bill would put children in harm," Bottoms further noted.

So, what is happening on the state level with those who are ignoring protecting children in America?

"The democrats in the Colorado House of Representatives have declared all-out war on children, parents, and life. They have voiced their desire to make Colorado the most liberal leftist state in America. The democrats continually vote to protect paedophiles and sexual predators while voting against babies and women," wrote Bottoms. "They do not think parents have any rights over their own children - that is their words. Criminals are given rights every week in the legislator while rights are intentionally taken away from children. The next obvious step for democrats is to make paedophilia legal. This is coming in the next two years in Colorado. We need everyone' help to combat this evil that is consuming Colorado," wrote Pastor Bottoms.

How far-fetched is this reality that American politics is on the verge of decriminalizing paedophilia?

Look at the trans movement in America where President Joe Biden, via an Executive Order in June 2022, has thrown the entire weight of the US federal government behind LGBTIQ+ policies, and keep in mind, there is a definite movement to normalize paedophilia. Now, President Joe Biden may deny that is his intention, but that is the goal.

In March 2021, President Joe Biden issued the first-ever national gender strategy to advance "gender equity and equality."

This moment in time "requires that we acknowledge and address longstanding gender discrimination and the systemic barriers to full participation that have held back women and girls," reads the White House website.

Hence, the Biden-Harris administration's justification to establish the White House Gender Policy Council, headed up by Julie Klein, is tasked with setting "forth an aspirational vision and a comprehensive agenda to advance gender equity and equality in domestic and foreign policy — and demonstrates that families, communities, and nations around the world stand to benefit," reads the White House document.

Look at what is happening at school boards across America with sexualized cartoons in books. Decades ago, *Playboy Magazine* published paedophilia cartoons, but in those days, *Playboy* wrapped the magazines in brown paper covers in the mail. Today, the sexualized books in children's libraries are not covered. The cartoon porn is explicit in the books for the youngest of children.

The sex education classes that school districts, teachers' unions, and some of the LGBTIQ+ community, are pushing target children. Some activists are attempting to normalize Drag Queen reading sessions for young children.

Even legislators and parents who challenged these explicit sexualizing books are vilified.

Children are being swayed to believe that there is a difference between sex and gender and those who do not agree with that position and with the onslaught of pronouns use are deemed to be out of touch with reality.

In some states, children can be removed from their own parents' custody if the parents do not agree with gender-affirming programs. The trans movement leaders, in conjunction with other benefactors, are targeting children.

Just like B4UAct.org wanted therapists to advocate for them, the medical industry and WPATH, which is a TRANS activist organization, is pushing puberty blockers on children.

Jamie Reed, a whistleblower who worked in a St. Louis gender-clinic as a case manager, went public with what she witnessed first-hand in 2023. She alleged negligence and mistreatment of children at the pediatric gender clinic. Now, the ACLU is targeting her.

In her February 7, 2023, affidavit, Reed wrote that the clinic was advertising services but not offering them. She also stated that the parents and clients were not told that puberty blockers had an FDA black box warning as of July 2022.

"In July 2022, the FDA issued a "black box warning" for puberty blockers, the strictest kind of warning the FDA can give a medication. It issued the warning following evidence in patients of brain swelling and loss of vision. Despite this warning, doctors at the Center continued their automatic practice of giving kids these drugs," wrote Reed.

"In hundreds of cases, Center doctors automatically issued puberty blockers or cross-sex hormones without considering the child's individual circumstances or mental health," Reed further wrote.

It is interesting how the marketing threat given to American parents is that your child may commit suicide when the puberty blockers have a warning that the very medicine a doctor might prescribe can make a child's brain swell or make the child blind.

With the concerted effort to sexualize children and to normalize the sexual trafficking of children, we need transparent conversations across the country to counteract this insidious effort to reduce parental control and to normalize transsexuality.

This has nothing to do with left or right politics.

It is time to listen to those who understand what is going on here.

Jeff Cleghorn has been a gay-rights activist since the 1990s. On March 4, 2022, he submitted his testimony to the Connecticut legislature. He has now come out of retirement to save children.

"Gender ideology and queer theory are causing medical, physical, and mental health harm to kids. Groups like *The Trevor Project* and *GLSEN* spend tens of millions of dollars each year targeting school children of all ages. *GLSEN*'s mission statement boldly touts its "K-12" programmatic work. From Connecticut to Georgia, my home state — and all over the United States — children are being damaged by this dishonest ideology," attested Cleghorn.

Cleghorn was a closeted gay young Army officer working at the Pentagon. He became a gay-rights activist after attending the 1993 March on Washington for Gay and Lesbian Equal Rights. His focus then was on changing America. His focus was on sodomy laws, adoption, marriage, security clearances, military, workplace discrimination, hate-crimes, AIDS, and police raids.

After honorably retiring from the U.S. Army and graduating from law school, Cleghorn served on staffs and boards of several gay-rights groups.

As a result of his history and experience, Cleghorn is now speaking out "to warn against what has happened since."

"I have watched with dismay, as the apparatus of the former gay-rights movement was taken over by far-left activists and retooled for a different mission: to promote Queer Theory," attested Cleghorn.

"Queer theory is about changing society to believe that sex and sexuality can mean anything anyone says they mean. Loosely put, they believe our understanding of sex (which they substitute with the words "gender" or "gender identity") is a problem because that understanding was formed in past times (and a problem because white heterosexual Christian males created these understandings)," further attested Cleghorn.

He continued with examples — "sex is now "assigned at birth," instead of determined at conception; kids can be "born in the wrong bodies;" and a heterosexual man with a wife and kids can become a woman by simply declaring he is a woman. Hence, the proliferation of new "LGBTQ+" genders, sexualities, and identities — each taken as seriously as the other. Newly invented "identities" like "nonbinary," "pangender," "demisexual," and "genderqueer" have taken hold among the young. Eunuchs (males with castration fetishes) are now an official "gender identity," according to WPATH — The World Professional Association for Transgender Health (a far-left activist group masquerading as a medical association)" Cleghorn testified.

The obvious question is "How the hell did we get here?" and who put this latest into motion.

Back in 2015, President Barack Obama was the first U.S. president to ever mention the word, "transgender" in a State of the Union Address. Shortly thereafter, the president created an office within the U.S. State Department to incorporate his vision for LGBT rights. It was akin to what President William Clinton did back in the 1990s when he incorporated human rights into the U.S. foreign policy within the U.S. State Department. The significance of both was to incorporate those messaging signals into US foreign policy.

Between the time, Obama announced the appointment, he added "I" to LGBT. I had to ask a colleague what the "I" stood for because I was clueless.

"Hell, if I know," said my friend.

That stood for "intersex" which I learned meant one is neither a male nor female. Go figure.

Furthermore, we have a PHARMA PIMP president named Joe Biden continuing Obama's border trafficking policy. Obama's policy expanded the immigration trafficking operations on the U.S. Southern border. Today, the southern border policy is off the rails.

Obama's Arab Rising policies during his first presidential term involved BIG TECH training those Hillary Clinton as Secretary of State called *civil societies to hold their governments accountable*, but was in fact, an operation that *trained foreign civil dissidents on social media in foreign locations how to overthrow those so-called despots and leaders that the Obama administration wanted to take down from Libya's Gaddafi to Egypt's Mubarak.*

Today, Joe Biden has expanded those "trafficking" policies to include not only mandated vaccinations that indeed cause harm, but medical treatments forced upon children and parents who have no say that have life-altering changes.

It is time to listen to de-transitioners, victims of sexual abuse and sex and labor, organ, and internet trafficking victims. None of them over the last twenty-four years has ever told me their experiences were good and healthy.

Raping a child messes up their lives. Raping them medically and putting anyone at risk is medical trafficking without informed consent.

Those of us who are non-victims need to stand up and protect every child regardless of race, religion, nationality, or ethnicity.

This is *A Global Shame* that insults the dignity of humanity.

Romanian Rambles

It becomes evident early in our explorations that we should focus on the dire dilemma of children. The problem of children is so critical that it forms one of the stumbling blocks for Romania's entry into the European Union [EU]. Like the dogs wandering Bucharest's streets, orphaned and abandoned children are commonplace. It is said that there are 60,000 orphans in institutions; no statistics are offered as to the hordes of orphans or abandoned children outside of government institutions or street-children, which one sees plentifully in the capital.... . He [the late dictator Ceausescu] ruled that fertile women under 45 are to have at least 5 children. Economic conditions, however, prevented parents from supporting large families... . We are told of a 36-year-old mother who in 1997 abandoned her 14th child. Her parents were raising three of her children; four were in orphanages while the remaining seven died of malnutrition and lack of medical care.

Early in his 24-year tenure, Ceausescu declared states 'willingness to assume responsibility for its children. A vast network of orphanages blossomed, staffed by untrained and over-worked personnel. The story of child neglect, abuse, and suffering was legend. With the dictator's fall in 1989, international pressure forced the government to take steps to rectify the situation. A program of child protection system [child protection services] was implemented, the thrust of which was a decentralization of institutions. The reform program continues and although conditions have ameliorated significantly, much is wanted. In fact, it is abysmal.

A disturbing element of the overall problem is youth [who] grow up as street-kids... . These youngsters possess minimal education. Manual or vocational training is an exception, and they lack an appreciation of such rudimentary matters as personal responsibility and hygiene. The discharged orphans have no "street smarts" and are quite simply lost.

Frequently, they turn to prostitution and crime.

— Letter written by Alexis S. Troubetzkoy November 1999

The Victims

Fertile grounds for trafficking are not limited to poverty, economic disparities, globalization, international migration, erosion of family values, civil and military conflicts, growth of international transcontinental crime, weak and under-staffed, under-paid, untrained law enforcement, the export of labor, and even AIDS.[136]

Toss in a massive amount of societal indifference, willful ignorance, a massive shift to a narcissistic society that consciously and without a conscience forever commodifies human beings, it is no wonder the global society now is engulfed in an explosion of slavery in the last 25 years with all its faces from sex to labor to sex tourism to child soldiers to medical to organ to ritual abuse torture to internet trafficking and child mutilation and medical experiments in violation of the Nuremberg Code.

That is why I have concluded that not addressing slavery in the 21st century is *A Shared Global Shame.*

Shame on those of us, who now focus on reparations while willfully ignoring what is occurring across the global currently.

Victims are trafficked for sex, but there are more victims trafficked for labor. People are trafficked to work in sweatshops, in the illegal adoptions arena, for organ transplants, forced marriages, mail-order brides, domestic work, forced labor, drug trafficking, begging, medical experiments, and within the entertainment industry.

Victims trapped in this nightmare become marginalized and isolated. Victims enter through this door and end up in a pit of fertile grounds that snag them further into human trafficking arenas. Those first steps may be heading to a war zone to make money because the economies in their own countries are failing. The lure to improve one's lot in life is strong. Individuals believe that they will be able to support themselves and their families in other countries and hence, they take the steps to migrate.[137]

Human trafficking victims do not know all the risks involved. They range from deplorable working conditions, no access to health and medical facilities, lack of documentation, long hours, low or no wages whatsoever, prolonged indebtedness to the traffickers or brothel owners, and overwhelming physical, and sexual abuse. They risk AIDS, rape and gang rape, drug addiction, emotional and psychological abuse, prosecutions, deportations, and in some cases, murder. [138]

If they survive any of this — if they are arrested, rescued, and then deported, they still face the difficulty of reintegration in their homelands. Reintegration is complicated.

In many cases, reintegration can be extremely dangerous. By the time the victims have escaped the clutches of the traffickers, many of them have faced threats of violence to their families which is one of the traffickers' tools of intimidation. The traffickers know where the victims have lived, and even know the names of their families. Going home is more than just getting your documents and taking a train or plane. [139]

Children are easy prey. They are kidnapped, coerced, sold, leave home voluntarily with a firm belief that life will be better elsewhere hoping to find a job, or agreeing to be prostituted for a brief time to make easy money. They do not understand the isolation factor. What faces them is tremendous physical, psychological, emotional, sexual, and even financial abuse. The violence surfacing in 2000 was so overwhelmingly more violent than in earlier decades that in some places even willing prostitutes had turned to their communities, when possible, but not every community was willing to help. [140]

According to Max Guido, the Secretary General of Caritas Diocesana in Rome in 2000, the prostitutes had asked the Catholic Church to establish an office specifically for the prostitutes because the violence was so gruesome. They felt that they had no one to turn to and they were terrified of the police.

In Northern Italy, one Catholic priest paid off a pimp to stay away from one of the girls, who later met with the Pope John Paul II to discuss this matter. But that was not the response of all communities. Some do not offer to help because they fear retaliation.[141]

Roberto, my Rome driver, took me to where the trafficked girls walked along specific boulevards during the summer of 2000.

"These girls work long hours" said Roberto with great exasperation.

"These girls work 25 hours 8 days a week. They go to church... then boom, boom, boom! The Italian mob and the Albanian mob kidnap girls and even hold them for ransom. The Albanians supply the girls. The Italian Mafia supplies the neighborhood. It is a mess... a huge problem — a huge mess," shouted Roberto in exasperation.

The Albanian mobsters murdered four policemen in southern Italy in 1999. Children were involved... not just younger women — children — *young children.* These mobsters trafficked *little boys and little girls.* Many of the victims lived on the streets. They did not have papers and did not have jobs. [142]

Some of the victims I interviewed corroborated Roberto's story.

Another night when Roberto and I were driving up and down the boulevards, we stopped at an outside café, and sat at one of the tables. Young men were sitting at another table.

They were Italians.

"Pimps in Italy are Albanians *and* Italians," said Roberto.

"We must leave. This is an extremely dangerous place," he abruptly whispered.

As we were leaving, two girls walked by. The older one was named Lea.

"How are you?" I asked.

Lea just shrugged her shoulders and tilted her head.

"So so... okay," she said with a noted sadness.

She was from Benin City, Nigeria. She said that she had no papers and that living in Italy was "*very hard.*" She said she had no money and had been in Rome for one month.

Very quickly, she spotted a man.

"I must go" snapped Lea and quickly moved back to "her station" in plain sight of her pimp.

She walked swiftly to the other side of the road.

Lea's girlfriend, who accompanied her, could not have been more than 14 years old.

I glared at her pimp as Roberto pulled my arm encouraging me to leave.

A Dutch documentary titled "*How 10,000 Bulgarian Women Are Being Screwed by Western European Animals*" [143] tells the tale of one Eastern European girl, who was kidnapped, gang-raped, and forced into prostitution. At one point, she claimed to have begged some clients to help her, but they claimed not to understand. When she finally escaped, she begged other people in the village to help her, but no one came to her rescue. She claimed that part of the reason was that the village was profiting from the brothels in the town.

The victims have no say whether condoms are used. The decision is strictly up to the customers. If a victim argues or displays any resistance, the girl could or would be tortured or beaten up by her pimp. In most cases, the prices increase if condoms are not used. [144]

Almost all girls I interviewed during my first trafficking investigation in 2000 had been repeatedly gang raped to break them emotionally and psychologically. Their trauma was forever compounded.

The safe houses, where children waited for documentation before returning to their homelands, usually did not include counselors, especially in rural and impoverished areas. Funds went to the guards who protected the safe houses from the traffickers and pimps, instead of counselors.[145]

Physical and psychological isolation is essential for controlling the victims. Traffickers would steal their victims' passports and documentation, and if the victims were to get out of line and threaten to go to the police, the traffickers would often tell them that the police were working with them. The victims would believe them because in many instances, some of the police in their homelands were involved in trafficking. [146]

By 2000, some European communities had become outraged with the throngs of eastern Europeans immigrants begging on their streets.

"You could not walk down the Champs Elysees without stepping over children. Adults would lay the babies on the sidewalks. Many of the children did not romp like normal toddlers or even wiggle. Eventually, the public outcry was heard, and the immigrants moved on to Madrid, Spain.

Yet, no one knew how thousands of immigrants were moved logistically from the boulevards of Paris to Madrid. Later, it was discovered that the children were fed cough syrup to put them to sleep while their mothers — or traffickers — begged," said one American living in Paris.[147]

The victims were not just victimized by their traffickers and pimps. Their own families victimized them. If a Muslim girl had returned home and her family discovered that she was sold for sex, even if she had been kidnapped and forced into sex trafficking, it was highly likely that her family would ostracize her for shaming the family.[148]

Their Stories

Nothing brings reality closer to the truth than hearing the stories from trafficked victims themselves across all the faces of trafficking — sex, labor, child soldiers, organ, medical, internet, ritual abuse torture.

It does not matter whether the victims were coerced, kidnapped, or initially chose to prostitute themselves to survive, or chose to leave their homes because life there was unbearable.

The late Susanna Angelli, who befriended me in 2000 was someone who cared deeply about children. Susanna was a woman of substance and wealth with a career that spanned decades. In the 1970's she was mayor of Monte Argentario, Italy, as had been her father and grandfather. She was involved in Italian politics for over 20 years. She was the first woman appointed as the Italian Minister of Foreign Affairs and Under Secretary of the same ministry.

Susanna established The Il Faro Foundation in Rome in 1997 to help both boys and girls under 18 years of age, who had immigrated to Italy. She hired staff to teach skills to the children so they could survive, such as making pizza and cutting hair. Her foundation's goal was to help the children find jobs after they completed their training and help them socially integrate into Italian society.

Susanna invited me to meet with the children at her Il Faro Foundation.

"We are not to ask their stories, but I invite you to hear their stories. They know you are a journalist and care about children," Susanna told me over tea.

And, with a wink and nod, Susanna said, "Come back to me, Christina, I am very interested to know who is living at my foundation too."

The day I visited the Il Faro Foundation, only boys were present.

When I met with the boys, it was a small group, all under 18 years of age.

From Their Own Voices —

Ylli was a 16- year-old Albanian from Pristina, Kosovo. He took the ferry from Durres, Albania, to Bari, Italy, in 1999. He was sick of the war. He spoke Italian and German. His goal was to get to Dusseldorf, Germany, because his cousins and friends lived there. He made it to Milan by train, then onto Genova, Strasbourg, and then Dusseldorf, where the police stopped him. Because he had no papers, they asked him what his first place of entry into the European Union was. When he told them Italy, they sent him back to Italy and he ended up in Rome, where he lived with 129 boys at Boy's Town. Then, he decided to take his training at the Il Faro Foundation.

Ligon was 17. He was from Tirana, Albania. He made his way to Vlora, Albania on the Adriatic coast. He paid $250 to go on a rubber raft to the Italian coast of Brindisi. They left at 8am and arrived at the Italian shores about two hours later. He had no papers. Twenty-seven people were on the boat. When they arrived, they were taken to an abandoned house, and then the train station. From Brindisi, he took the train to Bari, and from there, to Rome.

Sazan was 16, and came from Tirana, Albania. He was the most relaxed of the group. He did not speak a word of English except for **"America is It! America is It! Take me to America. I work for you!"** He smiled, joked, and laughed.

His mother was a homemaker and his father made cheese but was also doing odd jobs to put food on the table for his family. They were extremely poor. His brother, Louie, was 21, and had lived in Rome for six years. His other brother, who was 18, had been in Rome for 30 months. Both worked in restaurants. His parents would never leave Albania because their parents were still alive.

First, Sazan went to Kavaja on the Albanian coast. He paid $250 to go on a rubber raft with 30-35 other people and headed toward Lecce on the southern Italian coast. They left about 9pm. The trip took about one hour. On the boat, there was an Albanian who collected everyone's money. They never saw any police. They made it to shore at Lecce safely and were met by an Italian. The group was taken to an abandoned house, where the lead Albanian counted heads and called for private cars. The cars arrived and took them to another abandoned house in Bari, where they were told that they must be ready to leave by 4am. Sazan's oldest brother met him in Bari and took him by train to Rome. At Il Faro, Sazan was learning how to make pizza. He dreamed of owning a pizzeria. Sazan had two sisters still in Albania with his parents. They were 10 and 13 and he "worries" about them because of all the "kidnapped girls."

Elrado, 17, was also from Tirana, Albania. Sazan and Elrado did not know each other in Albania. He spoke Italian very well and a little English. In 1997, at the age of 14, he took a rubber raft with 40 or 50 other people. It was a 'mixed group" — "babies and older people." Elrado paid $250. Some on the raft paid $500. Elrado said that the Albanian and Italian mob worked together. Their raft crossed at night from Vlora. It took about an hour. The boat landed somewhere near Lecce. They also were met by Italians when they reached shore, and then taken to an abandoned house. Once there, the leader took a head count to determine how many cars were needed. The next morning men in private cars took them to the train station. Elrado came to Italy to make money because there were no jobs in Albania.

Three 15-year-old boys from Addis Abba, Ethiopia, were also at the Il Faro Foundation. Two were from Addis Abba proper and the other one was from the outskirts. They came to Rome for an education. Their parents just put them on a plane *bound* for Rome. These children did not know anyone there. **Mohammed and his two friends were** soft-spoken and gentle. Two of them came at the age of 13. The third arrived in Rome at the age of 12. They lived at Boy's Town with the other boys and attended classes at Il Faro Foundation.

When asked what the eastern European boys were like to live with, one of them said sheepishly, "They fight a lot. They are violent and angry. We leave them alone. Like now. We do not eat with them."

The most stunning story was from **Peter, a 17-year-old,** who tried to come to Italy from Albania 17 times. The last time he was finally successful. The first 14 times, Peter had hidden under the trucks on the ferry. Because he had no documents, he was sent back to Albania. Then his family paid $250 to get him a place on a rubber raft with a trafficker. If Peter failed the first time, he was given a free second try. If he failed a second time, he had to pay another $250. Peter paid the full $500. My initial reaction was that Peter was tenacious. I told him that was admirable and smiled at him. Everyone in the room laughed.

Peter, in a very self-confident and stern voice, reprimanded me and the boys.

"You should not laugh. It is a tragic experience. When the police show up, the traffickers will throw women and babies overboard. I saw it happen. I have seen people who cannot swim die in front of me. I had to leave Albania," Peter said in exasperation.

I felt his pain.

"How old were the children, Peter," I asked.

Peter replied sternly.

"Two- or three-month-old babies."

The room fell silent, and the mood changed immediately.

All the other boys had successfully made it over from the shores of Albania on their first attempt. None of them had heard Peter's story before now.

I still wondered though why Peter was so committed to leaving Albania.

"Why did you have to leave? Did you rape or kill someone?"

Peter looked me dead in the eyes.

"I never *raped anyone*."

"What was the conflict, Peter?"

And then Peter slowly proceeded to tell his story. Three years earlier, when he was 14 years old, he was with his Father and his cousin in his Father's "fancy" car on a road just outside of Durres, Albania. Masked men stopped them because they wanted his father's car. Peter was shot in the leg. His father was murdered. His cousin was shot five times in the back and was still in a Greek hospital.

According to Peter, the masked men were Albanian mobsters. Peter's family took revenge against the criminals after this incident.

"Seeking revenge in the Balkans is part of my culture. That is why I had to leave," said Peter emphatically.

Except for Sazan, the Albanian boys were stern, cautious, and protective of themselves. They did not show a lot of humor. According to Susanna Agnelli, one visitor to the Foundation said that she was "scared to death of the boys." Sometimes the boys argued and started throwing insults and fists, and the Foundation demanded respect and reprimanded them for fighting. Attending classes at Il Faro was a prize to these children, and they knew it, but their emotions still ran high.

After meeting these children in Rome, I travelled to Albania.

There, I had the opportunity to meet with 20 girls, who had been coerced, kidnapped, or forced into prostitution, and in most cases, repeatedly raped. None of them had any documents as they waited in a safe house in Tirana, the capital. All of them wanted to go home. None of them wanted to be in the sex trade.

I spent seven hours with them. They lived in two barricaded houses among a dusty cluster of buildings with blown out windows. It looked more like a war zone than a safety net for trafficked victims. Nestled behind the buildings were two Alpine three-story homes — new and clean with back-to-back doorways crossing over an alleyway protected by guards with automatic weapons. The girls range from 16-24 years of age.

My contact told me that Ledia, the "Mum" of the House, would meet me at my hotel. I was not allowed to bring Yrii, my Albanian driver, for security reasons. After we left the hotel, Ledia told me that she did not know if the girls would share their stories with me. A British journalist had met with some girls a few months before, and the girls did not feel comfortable with him.

"Let's just give it a try," I said.

When we arrived, the guards smiled politely brandishing their weapons, and ushered me into the small courtyard where some of the girls were sitting on the patio. We walked into the living room as Ledia and Alma, another woman who cared for the girls, called for the girls to come over from the second house. They filed into the room, some boldly, others quietly, some sheepishly. Others joked, whispered, and demonstrated their own curiosity about me. They were all shapes and sizes, many of them short, young faces with pain seared into their eyes. Many of the girls had been arrested, either in boats off the Adriatic Sea heading toward Italy or picked up by the police for having no passports and documentation, or for prostitution.

They were in these safe houses because when the police interviewed them, they claimed that they wanted to get out of the sex trade and wanted to go home. Ledia and Alma were then called and conducted their own interviews. The agreement that Ledia made with the girls was that she would help them, but they had to agree to stay out of the sex trade, stay in the safe house, have no contact with their pimps or traffickers, and wait for their documents to return home. They were allowed to call home, but they were never allowed to give the location of the safe houses. This was all before the advent of iPhone so tracking locations was never an option.

One girl was from Ukraine. The others were from Romania and Moldova. Ledia was the translator. She was Albanian by birth, went to school in Romania, and the only obstacle for language was that she spoke no Russian or Ukrainian. There was a victim who spoke Russian, so when we spoke to the Ukrainian girl, we had to translate three times, instead of twice. The Ukrainian spoke Russian.

I began by telling them I was an American journalist and had crisscrossed Europe interviewing everyone and anyone who would talk with me about trafficking and the exploitation of children. I shared some of my observations and emerging patterns and asked them if they would tell me their stories because the world needed to know what happened to them.

Immediately, one feisty girl piped up emphatically.

"No one cares about us."

I knew instinctively this was going to be a hard conversation. My eyes started to swell up. I could feel her pain and hopelessness. I tried to hold back my emotions and did not want to repeat my mistake of misunderstanding as I did with Peter in Rome.

"I do, and the people I know care. We want to help. And, if no one tells us their stories, we will not be able to help as much as we can, but we are determined to help, and you need to tell your stories to the world. You tell me your stories and I promise you I will take them to the world stage."

I went around the room asking them where they were from and how old they were. I asked them if any of them had been beaten, raped or tortured. Their eyes started to swell up. Their pain was real. Too many arms went up reluctantly. One girl had razor marks on her left arm from her elbow to her wrist. I kept looking at her. She was overwrought with sadness. Some were very defensive. Some were Mothers. Some were married.

"Where are your husbands?" I asked.

"Back home with our babies," they answered.

"Let me get this straight. Do you mean your husbands are home safe and you are out here trying to make some money and are getting raped? Explain this to me," I said in horror.

That broke the ice. At that point, the bonding began.

It became clear to me that the stories I had heard throughout the summer were all the same. There was no money in what we in the West called Democratized Countries in Transition. There were no jobs. When the girls reached 14 or 15, the parents wanted them to get jobs to contribute to the family income, and since the jobs did not exist, they became easy prey for the traffickers, who either kidnapped, deceived, or coerced them. In some cases, they willingly succumbed to prostitution for economic survival although not one girl or woman I met enjoyed prostitution.

One may assume these children and young adults on the streets were streetwise. This could not be farther from the truth. These victims, like the boys at the IL Faro Foundation, were very naïve and traumatized. Some believed that they had no voice because that is what pimps and traffickers had grilled into them. The traffickers cancelled their voices, manipulated their thoughts, demeaned them, and commodified them. They were psychologically and emotionally abused as well as sexually traumatized. Before they arrived at the safe houses, many of them had already tried to get out of their situations but found themselves helpless and hopelessly intimidated by their pimps and the traffickers.[149]

At one point during our initial two hours when I met with the girls in a group, a truck drove by in the alley. It made a lot of noise and backfired. Several of the girls jumped with fear. They believed that the traffickers would find them and kill them. It was a constant fear.

The Ukrainian girl had a baby. When asked if she was going to tell her mother what happened to her, she shook her head, "No, no, no. She can never know. She would kill me."

As she began to tell her story, I sensed from looking at the other faces that her anguish was not alone.

One girl's eyes swelled up in tears.

"I was a virgin a month ago. I was raped. I am a Muslim," said another.

Then, she ran out of the room in shame. There was real pain in the room.

I even found myself swelling up in tears. After a couple of hours, I asked them if they wanted to meet with Ledia and me to talk privately. They all nodded yes.

So, for the remaining five hours, Ledia, Alma and I heard their stories for the first time.

Just like Susanna Agnelli, Ledia and Alma had been advised not to ask questions these children about their traumatic experiences.

I learned that day this was the first time that any of them had ever shared their stories in a group.

Jrina, the Ukrainian girl and her friend, who spoke Russian and two of their friends stayed behind first. Jrina, 24-year-old, was a seamstress in Ukraine. She had been married for five years and had a three-year-old daughter. Her unemployed husband was living in Ukraine. Jrina had a girlfriend in Ukraine who was in love with a young man, who wanted to go to Yugoslavia in 1999 to work and make enough money in three months to return and buy a home.

So, Jrina decided to join them. That was over a year ago. They left Ukraine for Hungary and then went onto former Yugoslavia. The boyfriend took them to an apartment in Zava, took away their documents, and locked them inside the apartment. He brought clients to them. When they did not perform, he beat them, and allowed the clients to beat them as well.

Jrina was prostituted in bars, sold to a strip bar, beaten by a man named Sali, who was Yugoslavian, and another man named Sombor, who was Serbian, who were both in their early 30s. They raped her every other day in between clients. They gave her no money for five months and sold her to a Serbian man in Belgrade. He kept her in an apartment and told her, "No one will help you."

She was kept for five more months. Then an Albanian man bought her. She never knew the prices as she was sold from one man to the next. Jrina was then taken from Belgrade to Podriequez, Montenegro, where she lived in a fifth-floor walkup apartment. From there, she was illegally transported by boat from Montenegro to Albania, where she had four to six customers a day.

"Was the sex always violent and kinky?" I asked.

Jrina shuddered.

"What kind of things happened to you?" I asked.

With tears in her eyes, she said, "A woman like you would never understand." Then she burst into tears.

"All kinds of horrible things… all kinds," she whispered.

Jrina said that at one point, her arms were shackled in chains, her legs spread apart, and she was hoisted up off the ground and tortured.

Jrina said that she saw too many young teenagers in the bars and in the brothels. Far younger than she.

"13, 14, 15," Jrina said.

On July 23, 2000, Jrina and other victims were on a boat headed for the Italian coast. The police stopped them. Jrina had no documents. She was arrested and Ledia was contacted. Jrina told her that she wanted to go home so she was placed in the safe house.

Elena, a very petite shy **17-year-old** girl, was from **Romania**. At the end of April 2000, her girlfriend asked her to go with her by train to her boyfriend's house. They took the train all night, and the boyfriend was waiting at the station when they arrived. He took them to a dormitory type of apartment. There, the boyfriend said that two men from former Yugoslavia called and said that they were going to Italy, and that he, his girlfriend, and Elena were going to go too. Elena had absolutely no plans to go to Italy whatsoever and was told that she could not go home.

The two Yugoslavian men showed up brandishing dragon and snake tattoos with flames coming out of their mouths. The men said that they would take Elena's friend, but not Elena.

"I was small. I was told I had to remain," Elena said.

Then the boyfriend told the traffickers, "If you cannot take us all, you take no one."

So, the men agreed to take them all. They went by car to the Romanian border. Then they took a long dark walk near a river and took a boat across it. Then, a car met them and drove about 30 minutes to a village, where they stopped at the second house in the village. At 6am the next morning, they took a bus to Montenegro.

"I did not know where I was," said Elena.

Then they were taken to a hotel. The next day two other men showed up, one from Albanian and one from Montenegro.

"You are coming with us," ordered the men.

By car, they were then taken to a lake, and told that they were in Albania. The house they were taken to had five girls from Moldova. Two men had bought them.

Then the police raided the house, and Elena was arrested for not having any documents. Elena is the only girl I interviewed who was not raped.

After she told me her story, she told me that she was very worried about her other Romanian friend in the safe house. She told me that Meidani, who was also 17 years old, had no family or friends or job back in Romania.

Elena, again with tears in her eyes, begged me.

"Please, please can you help her? She has no one to return to. They will kidnap her again."

Olesea was 17. She kept taking deep breaths as we sat on the sofa. Ledia kept stroking her arm to console her. Olesea was from **Moldova**. She was a waitress at a pub in Salto Preita. The owner accused her of stealing $500US. Olesea said that she did not steal the money. The owner met with Olesea's Mother and told her that her daughter "must repay the monies or else." The owner informed Olesea and her mother that he was going to bring Olesea to Albania and then onto Italy to get a job to repay this bogus debt.

Unbeknownst to Olesea at the time, she was sold for $500.

"A man named Alberto bought me. He raped and beat me. He told me, I will kill you and force you into prostitution. I will throw you into the sea," Olesea said with tears in her eyes. It was obvious to me she was still traumatized.

Alberto was 44 years old, married, had a 6-year-old child, and his family allegedly lived in Italy — at least that was what he told Olesea. Alberto raped Olesea three times and strangled her each time during the rapes. Olesea was a virgin when she met Alberto.

"Why didn't you leave after the first rape?" I asked.

Olesea said that she could not get away because Alberto locked her in his house in Durres, Albania and when he would leave, he locked her inside. Once, he took her to the beach.

Alberto told Olesea "not to talk with anyone and that if you go to the police, the police will help *me — not you.*"

Olesea believed Alberto.

When they returned to the house from the beach, Alberto fell asleep and accidentally left his keys in the door key. Just when Olesea thought Alberto had dozed off, Olesea ran out the door and jumped on a bus. Alberto chased her on foot. Then Olesea jumped off the bus, ran to a house, and banged on the door until an elderly woman answered it. Oleasa spoke no Albanian. She tried to communicate with the woman and the woman's neighbor. They brought her inside, gave her some water and something to eat, and called the police. While they were waiting, the neighbor went outside and saw strange men in "fancy" cars. When the neighbor told her friend, she reached for the closet doorknob and pulled out a gun.

"If he enters this house, I will shoot him," said the elderly woman.

Olesea was turned over to the police and then the safe house. Olesea had been one of the girls who jumped when the truck went down the alleyway.

After our interview, Olesea started to cry and said something. When I asked the translator what Olesea was saying, she looked at me,

"Olesea says I do not know why women leave their home countries. It is better to stay there and starve to death."

Daniela, the girl with the razor-scared arms was **22 years old**. She was from **Erse, Romania.** She had lived with her fiancée for five years. Her friend asked her to go to another town in Romania. The next day her friend said that they "had to go" because they were going to go to Italy. In late 1999, they entered Yugoslavia by car. They made it to Montenegro by bus, and then two Albanian men transported them by car to an apartment. A man named Gramos informed them that they were in Albania. Then the victims were driven to a hotel in Durres on the Albanian coast.

Gramos got into a fight and was arrested. As a result of that, Daniela was arrested for prostitution and for not having legal documents. She was thrown into jail in Durres with eight other girls. One night, the Chief of Police in Durres, told the girls that he and another police officer were going to take them by van to the Romanian Embassy in Tirana where they should wait until morning.

They waited all night. Daniela and the girls panicked. They took two taxis back to the Durres police station. Then the police arrested them again.

During this incarceration, Daniela tried to commit suicide by slashing her arm. Her scars went from her elbow to her wrist. About a week later, the police told the incarcerated girls that they were going to take them to the border and release them.

They were driven from Durres to a place where there were "mountains, railroad tracks, and the sea" Daniela said. The police told them to get out of the car and walk straight for 100 meters. As the police pulled away, they shot off their guns. Within moments, a white van pulled up.

Marcos, who was about 25 years old, told them to get in the van. He spoke Italian. He was with two other men. One had an AK47. Marcos was constantly on his mobile phone as they drove to an abandoned house. Marcos then told them that the Chief of Police sold them for 1,000 Deutsche marks each.

"You work for me," boasted Marcos.

Later, Daniela was arrested again for prostitution and for not having documents. This time, Ledia was called.

Valentina was from **Moldova.** Valentina and her girlfriend, **Natalia**, left Cahul, Moldova, because there was no work for them. Valentina's parents had no work and no money. Some of their friends told them that if they went to Albania, they could find jobs in Vlora, Albania.

At this point during the interview, Ledia and I smiled a little. Valentina was curious why we were smiling, and we told her because there are "no jobs in Vlora. It is one of the ports for the traffickers." Valentina had not known this.

Together Valentina and Natalia went to Serbia and then onto Tirana, Albania. They had no visas and went to the train station to beg for food. They were paid $50US dollars for sex. The police arrested them because they had no papers.

Gabriela lived with her fiancé in **Erse, Romania.** Her friend asked her to help her go to another city — Timişoara — as a favor. **She eventually learned that her friend lied to her.**

They arrived in Timișoara at an apartment and spent the night. The next day, her friend told her that they "must go."

Gabriela asked, "Why?"

Her friend said, "We must go to Italy."

In November 1999, they entered Serbia illegally by car, and then travelled onto Montenegro by bus. Two Albanians offered to give them a ride to Albania by car. They arrived in Durres at a hotel, where they were raped, beaten, and chained. They were later arrested for prostitution and for not having any papers.

Florina was from **Cluj, Romania. She** was **21 years old.** With an illegal passport, Florina left Romania five years ago looking for work. Initially, she wanted to go to Hungary, but she never made it. She arrived at the Bulgarian border, where a trafficker offered to take her to Greece to do some agricultural work. She signed a contract and then he took her to a hotel where he sold her to a man from Moldova for $3,000 Deutsche marks. She spent five weeks in Bulgaria when she was sold to Makx, a brothel owner in Velesti, Macedonia.

Makx was 59 years old, married, living with his wife, and his five children ranging in age from 13 to 24 years old. His youngest was a boy. His wife, Mia, was 50 years old. Makx owned two houses in Velesti.

Twelve prostitutes were there when Florina was at Makx's brothel. His wife, Mia, mingled with the girls and knew what was going on. From 7pm — 4am every night, customers arrived at the brothel. They drank while the girls danced and stripped. They were never paid and often beaten by Makx and his customers.

"Makx is a horrible man," said Florina.

She said that NATO troops and German soldiers came to Makx's brothel. There were four Romanian girls, three Moldovans, four Russians, and one Bulgarian. At one time, there were two boys.

Makx was violent and often beat the girls with his fists. Another man in the village bought Florina and some of the other girls from Makx.

"He tried to help us. He paid for us, and we had to work for him at his bar, but we were not sold for sex."

Eventually, that man let Florina go. Two Albanians came to this second bar and offered to take her to Albania. By boat, they arrived in Albania. The police arrested her because she had no papers.

At the end of the interview, Florina handed me the pictures of the girls at Makx's brothel.

"Please, please help these children. They are too many young children in these brothels," begged Florina.

The Laws

Excellencies, Sirs, Members, and Officials of Europe,

We have the honorable pleasure and great confidence to write this letter to tell you of the objective of our voyage and of our suffering, We the Children of Africa.

We appeal to your kindness and solidarity to come to the rescue of Africa. Help us, we are suffering enormously. Help us, we have war, disease, not enough to eat. There are schools, but a great lack of education, of teaching.

— A Note found with Yaquine Koita (14) and Fode Tourkana (15), two boys from Guinea, who were found frozen to death in the landing gear of a Sabena Belgian Aeroplane, after attempting to smuggle themselves to Belgium. August 5, 1999.

Human trafficking, otherwise known as the term for slavery in the 21st century, is not a new notion or a new business. International bureaucratic bodies have confronted the issue of human trafficking before now, but since the 1990s, the numbers of those who have been trafficked have snowballed. Human trafficking has evolved into a multi-billion-dollar business with no boundaries and even fewer constraints than before.

At the 2000 International Seminar on Trafficking in Human Beings, the United Nations Office for Drug Control and Crime Prevention (ODCCP) announced that "the international trafficking of human beings represents the world's third largest area of organized crime business." [150]

I disagreed with that conclusion then as much as I have disagreed with that conclusion today. The commodification of human beings whether it is in the sex, labor, internet, medical or with PHARMA experiments is the largest organized crime business in the world.

For purposes of simplification, human trafficking, and the exploitation of human beings, are not just violations of human rights, but crimes.

Society has dealt with this issue in the course of history over centuries, but sometimes with different labels depending upon how the issue of the day had come to manifest itself during different eras.

The following is a compilation of selected Human Rights Documents excerpts and legal conclusions for purposes of understanding the legislative and legal evolution of how society has dealt with the issue of the exploitation of humans internationally.

Many are not even binding, but they do illustrate some international standards and definitions by which to judge those definitions, which are currently under consideration, and which are much needed on State and National levels today.

Through the course of modern history, legal definitions are much-needed tools to eradicate violations of human rights and crimes. They are not the answer, but they are a beginning. They should never be under-emphasized. Words and definitions can be immensely powerful tools to guide civilized societies, which must protect those who are exploited.

Bad actors use words to deny, deflect, distort, and defame whistleblowers to destroy the truth or their reputations to hide evil. That is what censorship is.

1) International Agreement for the Suppression of the White Slave Traffic of 1904.

2) League of Nations: 1920

When the League of Nations was designed, there were two committees: one on slavery and one on trafficking. Slavery addressed what we would call labor trafficking today. Trafficking then focused on what we called sex trafficking today.

3) Slavery Convention (1926):

The 1926 Slavery Convention was an agreement among member states of the League of Nations that obliged signatories to eliminate slavery, the slave trade, and forced labor in their territories.

Article 1: (1) Definition of **Slavery**: status or condition of a person over whom any or all of the powers attaching to the right of ownership are exercised; (2) Definition of **Slave Trade**: all acts involved in the capture, acquisition, or disposal of a person with intent to reduce him to slavery; all acts involved in the acquisition of a slave with a view to selling or exchanging him; ... every act of trade or transport in slaves... ."

4) Supplementary Convention on the Abolition of Slavery, the Slave Trade, and Institutions and Practices Similar to Slavery (1956):

"Article 1: Definition of **debt-bondage**: status or condition arising from a pledge by a debtor of his personal services or those of a person under his control as security for a debt... ."

5) Forced Labour Convention (1930):

"Article 2(1): Definition of **forced or compulsory labor**: all work or service which is exacted from any person under the menace of any penalty and for which the said person has not offered himself voluntarily... ."

6) Universal Declaration of Human Rights (1948):

"Article 4: No one shall be held in slavery or servitude; slavery and the slave trade shall be prohibited in all forms... ."

7) Convention for the Suppression of the Traffic in Person and of the Exploitation of the Prostitution of Others (1949):

"Article 1: The parties to this Convention agree to punish any person who, to gratify the passions of another: (1) Procures, entices, or leads away, for purposes of prostitution, another person, even with the consent of that person; (2) Exploits the prostitution of another person, even with the consent of that person."

"Article 2: The parties to this Convention further agree to punish any person who: (1) Keeps or manages, or knowingly finances or takes part in the financing of a brother; (2) Knowingly lets or rents a building or other place or any part thereof for the purpose of the prostitution."

8) Convention for the Protection of Human Rights and Fundamental Freedoms (1950):

"Article 3: No one shall be subjected to torture or to inhuman or degrading treatment or punishment."

"Article 4: (1) No one shall be held in slavery or servitude. (2) No one shall be required to perform forced or compulsory labor."

9) European Social Charter (1961):

"Article 1: The right to work... .

Article 2: The right to just conditions of work... .

Article 3: The right to safe and healthy working conditions... . Article 4: The right to a fair remuneration... .

Article 19: The right of migrant workers and their families to protection and assistance... ."

10) International Covenant on Civil and Political Rights (1966):

"Article 8: (1) No one shall be held in slavery; slavery, and the slave-trade in all their forms shall be prohibited; (2) No one shall be held in servitude; (3) (a) No one shall be required to perform forced or compulsory labor."

11) International Covenant on Economic, Social, and Cultural Rights (1966):

"Article 6: (1) The States Parties... recognize... the right of everyone to the opportunity to gain his living by work which he freely chooses or accepts, and will take appropriate steps to safeguard this right;"

"Article 7: The State Parties...recognize... the right of everyone to the enjoyment of just and favorable conditions of work... inter alia minimum remuneration, safe and healthy working conditions, reasonable limitation of working hours;"

"Article 9: The States Parties... recognize the right of everyone to social security, including social insurance."

12) Convention on the Elimination of All Forms of Discrimination Against Women (1979):

"Article 6: State Parties shall take all appropriate measures, including legislation, to suppress all forms of traffic in women and exploitation of prostitution of women."

13) Special Rapporteur of the United Nations (1982):

Special mention of child work as prostitution as one of the principal categories to be considered in the campaign against child work.

14) Special Rapporteur on Trafficking of Persons and the Sex Trade presented a Report to the Economic and Social Council of the United Nations (1983):

Special mention of specific problems of children subjected to sexual exploitation.

15) Resolution on the Exploitation of Prostitution and the Traffic in Human Beings (1989):

Suggests a common strategy of legal and non-legal measures to "combat trafficking in women for forced prostitution."

16) Convention on the Rights of the Child (1989):

"Article 32: ... Protection from economic exploitation and from performing any work that is likely to be hazardous or to interfere with the child's education."

"Article 34: ... Protection from all forms of sexual exploitation and sexual abuse... ."

"Article 35: State Parties shall take all appropriate national, bilateral, and multilateral measures to prevent the abduction of the sale of or traffic in children for any purpose or in any form."

17) International Convention on the Protection of the Rights of All Migrant Workers and Members of Their Families (1990):

"Article 11: (1) No migrant worker or member of his or her family shall be held in slavery or servitude. (2) No migrant worker or member of his or her family shall be required to perform forced or compulsory labor."

"Article 68: (1) Measure to impose effective sanctions on persons, groups or entities which use violence, threats, or intimidation against migrant workers or members of their families in an irregular situation."

18) United Nations Commission for Human Rights — Programme of Action for the Prevention of the Sale of Children, Child Prostitution, and Child Pornography (1982):

This document is a governing principle that creates goals and objectives for Member States.

19) Vienna Declaration. Vienna World Conference on Human Rights (1993):

"Section 18: Gender-based violence and all form of sexual harassment and exploitation, including those resulting from cultural prejudice and international trafficking, are incompatible with the dignity and worth of the human person, and must be eliminated."

20) Resolution of Trade in Women (1993):

Urges the need for international co-operation and for the improvement of the position of trafficked persons.

21) United States Federal Law (1994):

Established fines and/or imprisonment of up to 10 years for anyone convicted of traveling abroad with the **intent** to engage in sex with a minor.

22) Beijing Platform of Action (1995): Fourth World Conference on Women

"Article 113: The term "violence against women" means any act of gender-based violence that results in, or is likely to result in, physical, sexual, or psychological harm or suffering to women, including threats of such acts, coercion, or arbitrary deprivation of liberty, whether occurring in public or private. (b): Physical, sexual, and psychological violence occurring within the general community, including rape, sexual abuse, sexual harassment, and intimidation at work, in education institutions and elsewhere, trafficking in women and forced prostitution."

"Article 122: The Special Rapporteur of the Commission on Human Rights on violence against women… is invited to address, within her mandate and as a matter of urgency, the issue of international trafficking for the purposes of the sex trade, as well as the issues of forced prostitution, rape, sexual abuse, and sex tourism."

"Article 130(b): take appropriate measures to address the root factors, including external factors, that encourage trafficking in women and girls for prostitution and other forms of commercialized sex, forced marriages, and forced labor in order to eliminate trafficking in women, including by strengthening existing legislation with a view to providing better protection of the rights of women and girls and to punishing the perpetrators, through both criminal and civil measures."

23) Convention based on Article K.3 of the Treaty on European Union, on the establishment of a European Police Office (Europol Convention) (1995):

"Article 2 (2) … Europol shall initially act to prevent and combat unlawful drug trafficking, trafficking in nuclear and radioactive substances, illegal immigrant smuggling, trade in human beings, and motor vehicle crime."

24) World Congress Against Commercial Sexual Exploitation of Children (1996):

In Stockholm, Sweden, ECPAT (End Child Prostitution in Asian Tourism), UNICEF, and the Swedish government and numerous children's rights NGOs convened this World Congress. Twelve countries initially signed a declaration and action plan against commercial exploitation of children.

25) Resolution on Trafficking in Human Beings (1996):

The European Parliament calls upon the European Commission and member States to provide a clear definition of trafficking in human beings and to identify trafficking as a violation of human rights and a serious crime.

26) Communication from the Commission to the Council and the European Parliament on Trafficking Women for the Purposes of Sexual Exploitation (1996):

This document takes the recommendations of the European Conference on "Trafficking in Women for the Purpose of Sexual Exploitation" into consideration and focuses on a restricted definition of trafficking in women.

27) Plan of Action Against Traffic in Women and Forced Prostitution (1996):

Focuses on trafficking in women for the purpose of forced prostitution and sexual exploitation.

28) The Report on the Promotion and Protection of the Rights of Children:

Impact of Armed Conflict on Children. Graca Machel authored this report.

29) The Hague Ministerial Declaration on European Guideline for "Effective Measures to Prevent and Combat Trafficking in Women for the Purposes of Sexual Exploitation (1997):

The EU member states reaffirm their commitment to maximize co-operation in the combat of trafficking in persons, and in the combat of trafficking in women.

30) Treaty of Amsterdam (1997):

Article 29 requires EU member states to co-operate in police and judicial matters in criminal cases to more effectively combat organized crime including trafficking in persons.

31) Rome Statute of the International Criminal Court (1998):

"Art 7: (1) Crimes against humanity mean inter alia "enslavement, rape, sexual slavery, enforced prostitution, forced pregnancy, or any other form of sexual violence of comparable gravity.

(2) Enslavement" means the exercise of any or all the powers attaching to the right of ownership over a person and includes the exercise of such power while trafficking in persons, in particular women and children;"

"Article 8: (2) Grave breaches include inter alia "torture or inhuman treatment" and "willfully causing great suffering, or serious injury to body or health.""

32) Communication from the Commission to the Council and the European Parliament on Further Measures to Combat Trafficking in Women (1998):

As a follow-up to the 1996 Communication, this document urges the member states to make use of all instruments and to evaluate strategies and measures to combat trafficking. [151]

33) The Report of the International Office for Children's Rights (1999):

The most significant advancement made in this Report is the admission that even though the World Congress on Children was held in 1996, and public awareness was highlighted, it was tantamount that more work needed to be done at national levels before international levels could be implemented.

34) United Nations Convention on Transnational Organized Crime (1999):

This Convention targeted the smuggling of migrants and the trafficking of human beings.

35) International Crime Tribunal for Rwanda, Arusha, Tanzania, October 2, 1998:

Jean- Paul Akayesu was indicted, convicted, and sentenced to life imprisonment. He was sentenced specifically for "15 years for crimes against humanity, rape." This verdict is **HISTORICAL** in nature. This verdict demonstrates to the world those systematic acts of sexual exploitation of women and children, **RAPE,** and **GANG RAPES,** are not only intolerable, but also **CRIMES AGAINST HUMANITY.** [152]

36) Communication from the Commission to the Council and the European Parliament (2000):

This document focuses on combating trafficking in human beings and combating the sexual exploitation of children and child pornography.

37) International Crime Tribunal for Rwanda (2000):

Rwandan Court in Arusha, Tanzania, sentenced 8 defendants to death and 14 to prison for crimes against humanity during the 1994 Rwandan genocide.

38) International Crime Tribunal for Yugoslavia, February 23, 2001:

Three former Bosnian Serb commanders were found guilty of crimes against humanity at the United Nations War Crimes Court for raping, enslaving, and torturing Muslim women and girls in 1992. [153]

With all these mandates and treaties, why is human trafficking, and the exploitation of children increasing with such magnitude?

The late Mark Talisman, a leading international humanitarian, who was appointed Vice Chairman of the U.S. Holocaust Memorial Council by then-President Jimmy Carter-Chairman, had stated,

It [sexual exploitation of children] is the height of racism in the worst possible way. The feeling is they are expendable and done so with no consciousness. Simply, look at the way we treat our children in the United States. We do not cherish our children. It will take bully pulping or Presidential leadership to change it. **It will take another "We are the World" campaign.** It has to do with Children of Color, and it is the worst in Africa.[154]

Even though bureaucratic bodies cannot agree on definitions, they interestingly do find the time to agree on the difficulty of reaching a definition consensus.

There is no internationally accepted definition of the term "sexual exploitation." Delegates from all over the world who take part in the discussion and negotiations on the Trafficking Protocol to the new UN Convention Combating Organized Crimes are unable to agree on this term. Instead of "sexual exploitation," the use of terms as "forced labor, Representatives using propose servitude and slavery — a human rights approach while creating new international standards against trafficking in human beings. [155]

Bureaucratic bodies even formally acknowledge that.

Whereas the lack of **common agreed definition** of trafficking in human beings **is a major obstacle to coherent action and polices to fight this crime.**[156]

Another hurdle is that State laws differ on what constitutes the definitions of privacy, age of consent, prostitution, child prostitution, child pornography, and the distribution of child pornography. Consequently, these differences create enormous hurdles for law enforcement who tackle this issue, especially in those cases which cross country borders.

Finally, because this issue is transnational and transcriminal in scope, even the closely related lines of distinction between trafficking and smuggling must be drawn. [157]

As stated in part of the Report of the Secretary-General held in the General Assembly of the UN at its 50th Session in 1995,

The question must be asked, however, whether trafficking is the same as illegal migration. The two are related but different.... A distinction could be made in terms of the purpose for which borders are crossed and whether movement occurs through the instrumentality of another person. Under this distinction trafficking in women and girls would be defined in terms of the end goal of forcing women and girls and children into sexually or economically oppressive and exploitative situations and the fact that it is done "for the profit of recruiters, traffickers and crime syndicates."[158]

There are too many different definitions and too many State laws that differ. To eradicate the exploitation of children and to criminalize human trafficking, definitions need to be established uniformly immediately. This is a global crisis. And legislators and bureaucrats need to keep it simple. If someone is trafficked, they should be charged with kidnap. If they rape, they should be charged with rape. If they aid and abet with those who kidnap and rape, they should be charged with aiding and abetting criminals. Politicians and bureaucrats ought to be ashamed of themselves for not addressing this issue sooner. The numbers are just too staggering to be ignored and the numbers since I did this initial investigation have only grown.

There is no sane excuse for these numbers to have accumulated thus far no matter what the actual figures are. There should be major penalties for anyone who is involved with trafficking children both for sex and non-sex trade. It is a judicial travesty if it is anything short of a severe sentencing. Children deserve more respect than a slight sentence of one or two years. The traffickers deserve more severe penalties for trafficking children than if they were trafficking drugs.

State laws and their definitions need to be clear and simple, and only then with a huge increase of support to local law enforcement, and transcontinental coordination between State and local law enforcement, which includes training and staffing, will human trafficking and the exploitation of children and adults be eradicated. When international mandates, local and state laws differ so much from one country to the other, which is the status, the problem will persist, and continue to explode. It is irrelevant on the international bureaucratic level if treaties are signed, and state laws do not have a method by which to enforce them. As can be seen through history, definitions are necessary, and never have definitions and clear laws been more needed than *now* to protect children.

According to David Ould of the Anti-Slavery Organization in London, "This situation [legally] is a mess!"[159]

And, 25 years later since my first investigation, it is still a mess.

Definitions

Having read various definitions, the following are suggested definitions by the author.

CHILD: anyone younger than 18.

HUMAN TRAFFICKING: "all acts and attempted involved in the recruitment, transportation within or across borders, purchase, sale, transfer, receipt, or harboring of a person involving the use of deception, coercion (including the use or threat of force or the abuse of authority), or debt bondage for the purpose of placing or holding such person, whether for pay or not, in involuntary servitude (domestic, sexual, or reproductive), in forced or bonded labour, or in slavery-like conditions, in a community other than the one in which such person lived at the time of the original deception, coercion, or debt bondage."[160]

TRAFFICKER: The person or persons or organization who systematically organizes, transports, controls, and profits from transporting human beings.

SMUGGLING: the systematic, organized, and controlled movement of one or more individuals, or goods whether it be intra-country or inter-country for the purposes of delivering and profiting from the delivery of the human beings or goods.

CHILD SEXUAL ABUSE: Sexual engagement between a child and an adult (over 18) with physical penetration of the genitals and touching of the genitals. It includes sexual engagement between children for the pleasure of adults, as well as a child being encouraged or forced to view pornography or participating in the making of a pornographic film or photography.

COMMERCIAL EXPLOITATION OF CHILDREN: The financial gain or control of children for the non-sexual exploitation of a child as a domestic servant, agricultural worker, garment worker, slave, or soldier. Sometimes, the exchange is not for money, but for food, shelter, protection, drugs, or even tobacco.

CHILD PROSTITUTION/COMMERCIAL SEXUAL EXPLOITATION OF CHILDREN: The financial gain for the sexual pleasures of a child. Again, the exchange is not limited to money, but may include food, shelter, protection, drugs, and tobacco. *And, in 2024, people are arguing about "grooming?" Gifting is grooming.*

CHILD SEXUAL TRAFFICKING: The profitable business of transporting children for commercial sexual purposes. It can be across borders or within countries, across state lines, from city to city, or from rural to urban.

CHILD PORNOGRAPHY: Any visual or audio material, which uses children in sexual conduct. It consists of the "visual depiction of a child engaged in explicit sexual conduct, real or simulated, or the lewd exhibition of the genitals intended for the sexual gratification of the user, and involves the production, distribution, and or/use of such material." (United Nations) *This was the UN's definition 24 years ago. Makes you wonder — how did those child pornographic books get into the US school libraries? Exposure to pornography is a grooming tool for sexual predators.*

CHILD SEX TOURISM: The act of traveling from one country to another with the intent of having sex with children.

Law Enforcement

The fight against slavery is not a battle of one generation,
but a struggle that transcends time.

— Thomas Clarkson

In every industry, there is competition, and law enforcement is no different, but those who work this beat are vastly different. My experience is that that the normal competition is tossed aside when it comes to the children. These law enforcement officials do not care who gets the credit.

Every law enforcement official I interviewed over the last 24 years was interested in the safety of the children first. These people are true heroes. They confront the ugliest of society and look at the face of evil. And they need to be supported.

No US Congress, European Union, United Nations, or Parliament is going to stop the exploitation of children, or even add to the eradication of it unless they are all in agreement legally and stop normalizing the sexualization of children and stop normalizing the mutilation of children.

Any other political rhetoric is exactly what it is — professional palaverism — just chatter. The key to eradicating the exploitation of children falls on the shoulders of law enforcement. They are the closest to the issue.

The primary difficulty with law enforcement — and local NGOs that work with law enforcement- is that they are underpaid, understaffed, and not trained historically to deal with the ruthless traffickers and transcriminal networks, which controls this exploitation and any politician who advocates for the exploitation of children and adults might as well look in the mirror and admit they are traffickers and commodifiers.

There is a major law enforcement problem because international and the local laws are not uniform. In addition, there is not enough coordination across country

lines. Privacy laws, penalties for traffickers and child rapists, as well as laws regarding the distribution and production of child pornography films are different. Even,
the scope of an investigation is hampered because there are so many different laws.
In short, countries are not in compliance, and this is a fundamental problem for
the local law enforcement officials, who are desperately trying to eradicate the exploitation of children.

In some countries, traffickers of human beings receive lighter sentences than
drug dealers. In 2000, in Denmark, the maximum sentencing for drug dealers was
15 years. The maximum sentence for sex trade in 2000 was four years. Experts
then said then that there was more money garnered for sex trafficking than for
dealing drugs. [162]

There was an alarming increase in child pornography worldwide in 2000 when
I initially conducted this investigation. It has only grown since then even to the
point of normalizing it in schools almost a quarter of a century later with cartoon
pornography in children's books across America and legalizing the mutilation of
children.

If society does not get a grip on the depth of this depravity, we are raising
generations of paedophiles and going back in time commodifying our fellow human beings.

As a result, many state law enforcement agencies are finding a greater need for
countrywide co-ordination and inter- country co-ordination to combat this issue.[163] In 1999, the Dutch Police and public prosecutor's office launched The Joint
Platform against Child Pornography to tackle the production and distribution of
child pornography. [164]

An internationally coordinated effort is needed within the law enforcement
community to combat those who exploit children. Law Enforcement officials
wanted it over 20 years ago and they want it now. Law enforcement knows that
they are under-trained, understaffed, and that local law enforcement must communicate directly when dealing with the issue of exploited children.[165]

Jan Austad, a very astute and knowledgeable Interpol Agent, who specialized
in human trafficking in 2000 said, they do not even have any updated country by
country overview of laws. Part of the problem even if there was a database of laws,
is that "… laws seldom reflect law enforcement practices. European legal approach

in this field is for cultural and historic reasons vastly different from the American one."

Countries as Germany, Austria, The Netherlands, and Greece have rules regulating prostitution practices, while a country like Albania still prohibits it. Most other countries do not prohibit prostitution per se, but soliciting is usually illegal and they seek to punish those who exploit the prostitution of others. Laws can be difficult to untangle, in England, for instance, rules concerning prostitution are spread around in different laws, some concerning public safety matters, others concerning indecency. We [Interpol] are trying to assemble laws on trafficking women now, and it is very difficult, as many countries also in this area have spread the relevant laws all over the place." [166]

At an EU conference in Estonia in June 2000, delegates agreed that governments around the world must better enforce existing laws to effectively combat child prostitution.

"The laws are there, but they have to be enforced and, in some cases implemented," announced Margot Jyrkinen of Finland's National Research and Development Center for Welfare and Health.

Although most countries have laws banning sex with children, they do not have laws allowing them to prosecute those who travel abroad for sex with children. Delegates agreed that it was essential for law enforcement agencies to cooperate much more closely. [167]

Investigating trafficking of human beings is as difficult as investigating contraband smuggling. According to Armando Ramirez, it is hard because of the layers of legal camouflage. For instance, you may have a boat manufactured in Greece, registered by a US corporation in Delaware with an offshore account. The boat may be registered in Bolivia, which is a land-locked country, but operating between Montenegro and Italy. The big question is who is paying for it, who owns it, and who initially paid for it?[168]

Furthermore, international co-ordination does prove successful. In 2000, 12 nations were involved in the arrest of Ivan de le Vega, an international drug smuggling kingpin. Mr. de la Vega, a Colombia citizen, led the drug operation. It was based in Venezuela and Colombia. A US Navy ship stopped Suerte I, a Malteseflagged ship, off the coast of Grenada, after Venezuelan authorities intercepted smaller cocaine-filled boats, which were headed for the Suerte I.

In Europe, Greek officials arrested eight individuals with connections to the shipping companies, which were linked to the operation. Italian officials arrested an additional two others, and French officials arrested another. The arrests and seizures were the result of a two-year international investigation that resulted in 25 tons of cocaine. That is equal to a street value of $1 billion. Officials claim that this operation shipped approximately 68 tons of cocaine to the United States and Europe in the previous three years. [169]

Interpol was contacted after sweeping internet child pornography raids occurred in Russia and Italy in 2000 because these officials had no authority outside of their countries. Even Interpol was worried that it lacked the resources to broaden international tracking of criminals. That year, Interpol had only six individuals who worked part-time on information technology crimes. One of the major hurdles is that international law for cybercrime is not uniform. Even though efforts are being made in this direction, implementing, and enforcing it was an even longer off. [170] Even child pornography and child prostitution laws were not internationally standardized. [171]

In the United States, it is common among law enforcement to conduct a financial investigation simultaneous to a criminal investigation. That is not the case in other countries. Jan Austad and Agnes Fournier de Saint Maur, who was Head of the Branch of Trafficking in Human Beings at Interpol in Lyon, France, and Paul Holmes agreed that these simultaneous investigations should occur.

In France, once the court handed down a criminal conviction, there was no further investigation allowed into finances. And, in the United Kingdom there still is nothing akin to the United States RICO Statute.[172]

Child sex crimes are punished differently. In Denmark, the exploitation of children carried a maximum of four years in jail in 2000, compared to 10 years in other EU States. If there are loopholes in the law, the traffickers and pimps win the war.[173]

Even in Africa, the need for law enforcement coordination is needed. Ever since apartheid was outlawed, South Africa had become a mecca of international crime syndicates. Johannesburg was overridden with international gangsters. The country then had a population of 44 million and a police force of approximately 140,000, and some of the police were illiterate.

Botswana, one of its bordering countries to the north, had a stable economy and was one of the safest countries in all of Africa in 2000. Comparatively, Botswana had a population of 1.4 million and a police force of 6,500. In July 2000, The US State Department, under their Bureau of International Narcotics and Law Enforcement Affairs division, announced that they were setting up a regional academy in Botswana to train the police forces for the southern region in Africa. This academy was like the academies they had in Budapest, Hungary, and Bangkok, Thailand. South Africa was the original choice for the academy, but all three countries decided to place it in Botswana because crime is national, regional, and international.

In Italy, which is notorious for its tortuous judicial process, the prosecutors have the most arduous of tasks. Under Italian law, defendants are granted three trials before a conviction is final. But, according to Ramirez, part of the problem in Italy is that the "Italian police do not really care about crime. It is a cultural thing. None of the Italian police mix. There are no Spanish speaking or Spanish police officers in Italy. No cultural crossover like the French and the Arabs where many of the French police officers speak Arabic."[174]

One of the most different notions legally and judicially in Europe — as in most countries — is that there are no conspiracy laws like the American Racketeer Influenced Corrupt Organizations (RICO) Act. If there is no consummation, there is no crime. For this issue — the exploitation of children — this legally should be changed. [175]

Child Pornography
& the Internet

I have no ambitions in life anymore. I do not know how people will judge me in the future. I am very sad. I wonder often why people do such things to kids just to earn money.

I cannot erase it. It pricks like a pin.

— Two Sri Lanka teenagers lured on heroin to perform sex with foreigners
Usenet is used as an electronic resource to post, disseminate, and collect child pornography. It has been around for a long time and was one of the original methods for disseminating images.

Many of the individuals who are escalating child pornography website production are in the United States and it is incredibly simple to redirect any of these U.S. websites onto a server within another country. Experts have discovered U.S. websites 'redirected' onto servers with Japanese ('jp') or Russian ('ru') domains.

Although the internet operates on an international basis, the laws governing it operate territorially. Consequently, there is a genesis of legal arguments and subtexts, which cover this arena. Some of the material is worldwide, and other material is accessed locally. National laws vary, and again, because the laws differ, the existing system serves the profiteers, suppliers, and customers.

Some governments, such as Saudi Arabia, did not allow the internet in earlier years. The government perceived it as a threat to cultural and religious mores. Today, it is a cybercrime to publish any pornographic through social media.

In Iran, there was a strict off-line availability. Today, the Iranian government and the Islamic Revolutionary Guard Corps block social media such a Facebook, Twitter and Instagram and other media sites.

China allowed ISPs but maintained that the control must be through government agencies. Today, there is a war about TikTok apps being used to target U.S. children. Many Americans consider TikTok a national security issue in the U.S.

In India, almost a quarter of a century ago, the ISPs were responsible for objectionable content, but it was rarely monitored.

And, in Central and Eastern European countries, there were no controls over 20 years ago.

On the international level, important initiatives were openly discussed, but again, consensus was a difficult route. In March 2001, The Council of Europe held a hearing in Paris with internet industry representatives and attempted to negotiate a draft of the world's first treaty against cybercrime. Some bureaucrats only wanted to focus on sex on the internet. Some wanted to include racism and hate sites. In the end, everyone agreed that *something needed to be done.* The stand-off between the ISPs and the Council for Europe was on how to get the ISPs to cooperate with basic operating standards so that the criminals can be caught.

Regardless of how the child pornography was attained — WWW, Usenet, IRC, File Transfer Protocol, and the like, the illegality of child pornography was the same. The accepted definition among law enforcement was "what is illegal offline is illegal online."

Complexities arose at this stage because legal definitions and penalties in host countries and countries of origin were not the same. In countries where legislation was used to prosecute offenders, the legal tangles began because the offenders or suppliers in another country were in fact operating legally in their country of origin. There were serious implications and needed coordination among law enforcement, the courts, and the prosecutors.

There were serious investigation rules because of these differences. Evidence obtained in one country may not have been discoverable in another country because of privacy laws. In the Netherlands, for instance, investigations were hindered because privacy was held on such a high legal pedestal.[176] For instance, if a paedophile were arrested in The Netherlands in 2000 — hence, he is known — law enforcement was not allowed to post his picture publicly.

On the other hand, if the suspect was not identified and law enforcement was in possession of a picture, the agency was allowed to post the pervert's picture. In some instances, if a child pornographer had a website, and it was identified by law enforcement, a letter would be sent out to cease and desist. If the website was not taken down, a second letter would be sent out, and if it continued, only then, could law enforcement file charges. [177]

In France, once someone was convicted all the financial investigations automatically ceased. In most countries, there were not simultaneous criminal and financial investigations.

One of the major obstacles with international cases 24 years ago was jurisdiction. When a suspect resided in a different country than the one that was holding the logs for that user, it created a paperwork nightmare. It became an arduous process to serve subpoenas in other countries, which did not recognize the legal documents of the prosecuting party. As a result, this obstacle could potentially setback cases, and send them to the bottom of the pile. Many child pornography traders were aware of this and deliberately used foreign computer servers to frustrate law enforcement, so they investigate an "easier fish to fry."

If a resident of the U.S. downloaded child pornography in the United States, it was illegal. If that U.S. resident travelled to a country where downloading child pornography was not illegal, there was no prosecution, but if that U.S. resident downloaded child pornography onto his computer in the visiting country and then returned home with the computer, the U.S. resident could be prosecuted in the U.S. [178]

Prosecutions were further complicated because internet users — the child pornographers — could hide their tracks more easily than in the "real world." Investigators had to dig and track back through many stops on the internet. Cybercriminals are very clever. In fact, they are far more trained and equipped with more computer sophistication than most law enforcement agencies worldwide. They know how to use the internet. They know what the rules are and consequently, how to get around them.

International lawyers, on the other hand, try to protect their internet business clients and try to figure out how to maintain individual countries' scopes of law. For instance, in the United States, there is the First Amendment no matter how many want to shatter that in the last years. In Europe, courts have ordered companies, like the U.S.-based Yahoo, to take hate sites off the internet. So, what we had 24 years ago was globalization for the first time getting smaller and smaller and the countries' laws butting heads with industry lawyers trying to figure out how to produce compromises. The bureaucrats and international lawyers discussed the notion of a Cybercrime treaty for years. In the meantime, millions of children were being exploited while these bureaucrats and lawyers *tried to figure out* how to *compromise*. Obviously, everyone has failed to date.

ISPs wanted minimal restrictions. Governments wanted power to fight criminals.

Governments needed the ISPs' cooperation. They held the technology. Governments needed IPSs to store data on their systems for a period. ISPs said it may cost too much for them to do that for an extended period. Governments said it would take time to catch all the criminals. The truth was that the government's position was correct because law enforcement had to catch up with the technology, and they were not even there in 2000 if a cybercrime treaty was then signed.

There were understaffed police departments, which did not even have sufficient technology.

Paul Holmes' Vice Squad Unit had only 14 detectives in Central London. Their computers were not efficient enough to combat organized crime. In Third World countries, some police officials were not just computer illiterate, but illiterate.

The only way to beat the child pornography war was to create uniform laws against child pornography and give the utmost support to law enforcement. They needed to be trained so they had better skills, better technology, and more coordination than the criminals. Then everyone needed to launch a worldwide effort to go after the producers, the disseminators, and the participants in the world of child pornography. There should have been a no-holds bar for this campaign, including the enlistment of the media.

In 1998 in rural Greenfield, California, an eight-year-old girl named Allison, spent the night at her girlfriend's house. Ronald Riva, the friend's father, woke up Allison in the middle of the night, and raped Allison for the entertainment of about a dozen paedophiles logged onto the internet in four countries. Riva was sentenced to 100 years in jail. But the ordeal did not end there.

The investigation led to the world's largest internet pornography bust of a paedophile ring at that time, which called itself *Wonderland*. About 100 men were arrested. When the police seized Riva's computer, they found the name of a man named Ian Baldock from England. When his computer was seized, it revealed *Wonderland*. About 120,000 pornographic images were found of adults engaged in sexually raping victims as young as three months old. Most of the children involved were under 10 years of age. Two Americans created the club, and it was by invitation only. There was even a vetting process to join. Members rarely emailed images. Instead, they logged on to each other's libraries. There was also a status ranking among members. Those with the highest status were the ones who engaged in sex with the victims, filmed it, and made the images available to other members.

The most notorious and senior British member was the man I earlier mentioned – Gary Salt, who used to travel to members' home to exchange pictures. Salt was convicted on unrelated child sex offenses in 1999 and sentenced to 12 years in jail. This investigation led to sweeping arrests in Australia, Britain, the United States, and Europe in 1998.

In all, 750,000 images and 1,800 videos were confiscated. Approximately, 1,263 children were featured. Only 17 of them have ever been identified. Six of them were British. In 2001, seven other men were convicted, but they were given less time than Riva. [179] It cannot be overemphasized that Riva, Salt, and their colleagues were not isolated cases.

In September 2000, child pornography tapes and alleged *snuff* films were confiscated in Italy and Russia. Italian police served 600 subpoenas, arrested eight Italians, and charged them with possession or trading of child pornography. Although the trade emanated in Russia, only one of the two Russians arrested was held by the police. The second man was released because the distribution of child pornography in Russia was considered a minor infraction. The Italian police in this case claimed that the Russian crime syndicate kidnapped children from orphanages, circuses, and off the streets.

In this case, Italian broadcasters got carried away. They wanted to wake up the public. Excerpts from the tapes were aired during the dinner news hour. Stupidly the broadcasters showed a child laying on top of an adult male. Italians were horrified. The country rocked with anger. The Vatican weighed in with disgust for exposing innocent victims to this pornography on television. There was further disgust as the predators were identified. They ranged from businessmen to students. Within 24 hours, a few of the broadcast executives resigned.

In the aftermath, Russian officials claimed that in February 2000 — seven months earlier — they had arrested three members of this same syndicate, and as a result, discovered client lists in the United States, Britain, Germany, and Italy. One of the three men who was discovered having sex with a child on film was sentenced to 11 years in prison. The other two men were released again, because selling and distributing child pornography in Russia was not treated as a serious crime.

In October 2000, an Italian prosecutor charged 1,491 individuals for sending or receiving child pornography from a website.

In December 2000, Russian, British, and American officials arrested two men in Moscow and St. Petersburg for selling child pornography over the internet and through the mail in Europe and the United States. Police seized 588 videocassettes, 112 videodiscs, and more than 1,000 pornographic photographs, some involving children. [180]

In an interview during the summer of 2000, one Interpol official stressed that the increase in child pornography, due to the internet, was so alarming that First amendment rights and the like should be changed when it comes to child pornography on the web... because it is going into millions of homes.[181]

In the 1970s and 1980s, Holland and Denmark were the biggest producers of child pornography. The U.S. at the time was the biggest consumer according to some experts. At that time, in and around Amsterdam, there was a homosexual paedophile ring, which was flourishing in the production of child pornography.

By 2001, Romanians and Russians increasingly were involved in the production. Russian teenage boys were found on the borders of Holland and Germany in droves, where many of the films were produced. With the onset of digital cameras, all the downloading onto the internet was easier. In The Netherlands'

Pornographic Unit at The Hague, I viewed many photos believed to be of young eastern European boys. [182]

In January 2001, Swedish officials busted a paedophile internet ring, which Swedish Queen Silvia called "frightening." More than 50 suspects exchanged approximately 200 violent pornographic pictures of children, including again, toddlers and babies, some *only a few days old.* Much of the material seemed to be new.

As reported in the Associated Press by Lennart Simonsson, Detective Anders Persson of the National Police Child Abuse Unit was quoted,

"Some of the pictures depicted rape of children, some only a few days old." [183]

High level coordination between law enforcement had proved successful when used efficiently. In 1999, Melpunt, the Dutch Child Pornography Hotline, contacted the National Center for Missing & Exploited Children because they believed that a U.S. citizen was posting images onto a child pornography website. NCMEC's Exploited Child Unit (ECU) investigated and found the user's server was in Georgia. Local law enforcement subpoenaed the company's records, and found the user was living in Texas. Then ECU contacted the local sheriff's office in Bexar, Texas, which obtained a search warrant and seized the computer. The 16-year-old male was arrested for possession of child pornography. He had posted pictures of himself as well as photographs of other children. [184]

In April 2001, in the United Kingdom, a mother of three was jailed for 14 months for letting an internet chat room user have sex with a 15-year-old teenager in her home. Angela Sisson had cybersex with a man who later introduced her to a 30-year-old man named Andrew Mandefield, who was a father of three children. Mandefield traveled to Sisson's home and had sex with the teenager. Sisson knew the girl's mother. Mandefield was jailed for nine months and placed on the sexual offender's register for 10 years. [185]

In March 2001, British Home Office Secretary Jack Straw announced a task force to fight paedophiles who used the internet. The force included internet industry representatives, child welfare organizations, police, and government officials. This task force was a result of the report by the internet Crime Forum, which called upon the need for vigilance over the use of internet chatrooms.

"The government is committed to tackling child abuse in any form — paedophiles and child pornographers must not be able to use new technologies with impunity. What is illegal off-line is also illegal online. However, if changes in the law prove necessary to prosecute and deter specific forms of online child abuse, the government will act," said Straw. [186]

The media has a role to play in exposing predators today, as much as it had a role to play a quarter of a century ago, but they must be trained.

During the summer of 2000, some of the Italian and British press published names of alleged paedophiles. Experts estimated then that 250,000 paedophiles were in the UK.

According to Jim Reynolds, the renown paedophile expert who met with me early in this initial investigation, the UK recognized it had a huge problem with pedophilia. Italians admitted that they had a problem as well.

When the convicted paedophiles' names were published, chaos ensued. One UK man had the same name and lived in the same town as one of the convicted paedophiles and people mistook him as the convicted paedophile.

According to UK Detective Paul Holmes, they "almost stoned the poor chap!" [187]

In the late 1990s there was a report exposing that videos were being produced in Eastern European countries and distributed throughout Austria. [188]

The point is that law enforcement, BIG TECH and world leaders have known for decades about this filth and smut over the internet.

We have miserably failed to turn the tide on this Digital Age of internet Slavery.

Snuff Films

There was significant controversy concerning snuff films in 2000. There were two schools of thought. Technocrats defined snuff films as films where victims were beaten, tortured, raped, and killed on film, while the predator or intended user achieved a sexual release at the impact of murder, and then the film was sold for commercial value so the *new owner* could have the same sexual experience.[189]

The colloquial definition — the one referred to on the street and even within some law enforcement communities — focused on whether there was an actual murder. Sexual release was not an integral part of this definition.

These lines of demarcation are especially important for anyone investigating child pornography when claims are made that snuff films exist or are confiscated as was the initial claim in the fall of 2000 when tapes were confiscated in Russia and Italy

At the beginning of this investigation, I heard rumors — not anything solid — but some rumors that snuff films were on the rise. At that time, I was led to believe that snuff films were defined as the rape, torture, sexual abuse, and murder of the victim. I had yet to discover that there were those who held the belief that sexual motive was a *necessary* element to the definition of a snuff film.

I asked law enforcement officials everywhere about snuff films. The usual response was, "Have you ever seen one?" To which, I responded, "I have not seen *any*."

Jim Reynolds in London disputed the notion of snuff films, as did UK Detective Paul Holmes, as did other law enforcement on the European continent. I asked local law enforcement officers in Brussels, The Hague, Amsterdam, Italy, and even in Albania if they knew anything about snuff films. Everyone seemed to agree that films had been confiscated, but when analyzed, the trajectory of the bullets was wrong, and hence, they concluded that the films were fakes. Not being an expert on bullets or trajectory of bullets, I accepted the officials' conclusions, but nevertheless kept asking. Never once did anyone mention to me the distinction of sexual motives. It was only in April 2001 when John Rabun of the National Centre for Missing & Exploited Children informed me of that distinction. [190]

One night in Brussels after driving around the Red-Light district, I decided to return a few nights later. There is a section in the Red-Light where the transvestites walk the streets. Most of the transvestites claim to be from Latin America. During one of my walk-abouts, I asked two of them if they knew anything about snuff films. They claimed that snuff films existed and that they were produced in "Russia." I presumed that this was just a geographical term. They claimed that the tapes were distributed through Germany and Poland, and over the internet. Again, like the sex shop operator in London, these transvestites were horrified that anyone would rape a child. Many of them told me they were raped as children.

When the Italian and Russian bust happened in September 2000, reports filtered down that some of the films confiscated were in fact *snuff*.

Although the notion of snuff is alarming, it is important to understand its contemporary evolution.

In 1969 in the United States when Charles Manson and his gang brutally murdered Roman Polanski's pregnant wife, actress Sharon Tate and her friends, the rumors surrounding the murders included that the ordeal was videotaped. This later proved untrue, but the press labeled the rumors as the possibility of snuff movies. [191]

Then in 1974, Michael Findlay directed a horror film titled, *Snuff*. The film depicted a group of Charles Manson-like drugged characters who slaughtered people. The film was so horrific that it was banned in 32 countries. The last scene in which an actress was murdered was so ugly that some people really thought that a murder was committed, which caused a local prosecutor to demand that the actress appear before him. [192]

In the late 1970s, some feminists referred to snuff films when charging men with the exploitation of women. Then in the 1980s, the notion of snuff films shifted to gay films. In 1987, British police investigated a boy who was killed in a sadomasochistic game. More than 200 men were questioned. Videotapes were confiscated. Then rumors started flying that the police had dismantled a paedophile ring, which murdered boys on camera. In 1990, a court case began. In the end, there was no evidence of any boys being killed during the wild parties that these men attended in the 1980s. [193]

In the 1990s, rumors started again because children were thought to be involved in snuff films in satanic sects. Again, no evidence was found. [194]

Then, in 1991, British officials targeted known European sex offenders, traffickers, child pornography producers, and members of paedophilic networks. It was known as *Operation Framework*. The British officials worked in conjunction with the Dutch officials. In the end, the investigation went nowhere.

Although no charges were filed, what was discovered was a very wealthy rich Amsterdam paedophilic community and a British homosexual community involved in pedophilia in Amsterdam. In 1997, a sensational television documentary aired and referred to *Operation Framework*. As a result of that, law enforcement started another investigation. Houses were searched, individuals were put under surveillance, and even waters were dragged for children's bodies. Again, nothing surfaced although this second investigation put the public's fear to rest. [195]

Years later, during another investigation, I discovered that another journalist had tracked a snuff film produced in the Republic of Srpska in the Balkans. He tracked the film as it made its way to private showings in Los Angeles and even made it way to a wealthy estate in Connecticut, where men would show up in limos using only a first name and offered drinks before watching the film after paying a few thousand dollars.

Sex Tourism

Sex tourism is when one travels from one country to another to have sex with a minor. The definition differs from country to country because the age of consent differs from country to country. Although the Balkans is not a tourist stop per se because the strife and conflict lingered in 2000 even in regions where there were United Nations forces, sex tourism was a booming industry in other parts of the world.

Countries such as the Philippines, Thailand, Cambodia, Sri Lanka, India, Indonesia, Brazil, Costa Rica, the Dominican Republic, and Mexico are considered top sex tourism locations. Sex tourists — child rapists - are highly likely to come from Australia, Britain, Canada, Germany, Japan, and the United States.

Child-sex tourism was rampant in Thailand and the Philippines over 20 years ago, but a crackdown diverted the child sex tourism to Sri Lanka. Because of the political climate there, child-sex tourism then shifted to India. None of this meant that sex tourism no longer existed in these other countries. It just meant that the emphasis had shifted to India. Paedophiles were roaming the beaches of Goa, Kovalam, Puducherry (Puducherry), and Puri on the prowl for young children for sex.

Shiv Kumar, a social worker with Delhi-based Child Line, claimed that the reason that paedophilia had become so rampant was because some tourists believed that having sex with young Indian boys would reduce the risk of sexually transmitted diseases, especially AIDS and that having sex with children would make them more potent.[196]

According to the World Tourism Association (WTO) 24 years ago, 120 million trips were made annually for sex. Tour operators offered trips with the express sale of children. The operators did not necessarily use words offering sex with children. Instead, they displayed pictures of children in their vacation brochures. WTO claimed that paedophiles made 360,000 trips.

Kiario de Noticias, the Portuguese Daily Newspaper, quoted international organizations as stating that 12 million clients travelled for sex with children in Asia. The World Labor Organization claimed that approximately 800,000 Thai children were involved in sex tourism, followed by 100,000 in the Philippines, and 500,000 in India, and in the US, there were approximately 300,000. Outside of the U.S., the children involved seem to be motivated by poverty in many instances, whereas in the U.S., the motivation had to do with the breakdown of the family. The Spanish Minors Ministry claimed that eastern European children, as well as Portuguese, Dominican, Moroccan, were bought and sold into child prostitution rings in the Iberian Peninsula.[197] In Sri Lanka, 66,304 sexually exploited children had been cared for by the Salesians Order at the Don Bosco Negombo Center. [198]

Prosecuting these crimes was difficult because not every country had laws, which specifically addressed sex tourism. In the United States, if you travelled with the intention of having sex with a child and the intent could be proven, you could be prosecuted whereas in the UK, the crime had to be committed.[199] Intent was not enough.

Remember the story of the South African man in London that UK Detective Paul Holmes told me about in 2000. Retired undercover FBI Special Agent Bob Hamer's investigation of NAMBLA in the U.S. circa 2003 led to convictions of American men who intended to go overseas to rape boys.

Over 20 years ago, France passed a sex tourism law and prosecuted a predator who traveled to another country for sex with a minor.

Although many sex tourists are paedophiles, not all of them consider themselves paedophiles because they do not partake in these acts at home.

Some of my best local sources for this investigation in 2000 were in the hospitality and tourism industries outside of law enforcement and the traffickers and victims themselves. Many of the concierges, waiters, drivers, bartenders, maids, clerks know where the "action" was. It did not matter if one stayed in a five-star hotel or a three-star hotel. Taxi drivers knew a lot as well although there was always a catch before the revelations — "Not that I know first-hand…!" And, then they would start talking. Ninety percent of the time their stories checked out.

Conclusion

"I hope that you will not only listen but that you will act."

— Edwin Burung, a 16-year-old Filipino former street child addressing The World Congress Against the Sexual Exploitation of Children, 1996.

I don't expect those who read this book to make a lifetime commitment to saving children worldwide, albeit, the world would be a better place, but I do ask that those who read this book open their eyes and see beyond their own worlds and observe their own communities and their families and extended families who are more at risk today than ever — more so than even 24 years ago when I began this first investigation. We are spiraling out of control morally. The value of human life, which includes the quality of life, is too precious.

Children are the future, and if children are sacrificed, society is sacrificed. Having said that, I do believe that there is no sane reason anyone should be sitting on the sidelines of this issue. The exploitation of children is just too ugly an issue not to get involved with to support those who are on the frontlines of eradicating it.

A European politician stated to me in 2000 that the number one problem in Europe was *illegal immigration*. This demonstrated *profound ignorance*, and this type of ignorance was quite alarming then as it is today even after decades of migration since 2000 — the Mideast, the Arab Rising, the Sudanese conflicts, and the U.S. Southern border.

All migrations are fertile grounds for trafficking just as war zones are. Shame on American leaders for feeding the U.S. border trafficking operation. Shame on Joe Biden and all the other feckless politicians who have not shut down this fertile ground of abuse — republican and democrat.

Rape of a five-year-old or trafficking of an infant or toddler is *not* an immigration problem. It is a crime against humanity with lasting ramifications. It is sooner rather than later that politicians and legislators understand this and begin advocating moral outrage for allowing babies, infants, toddlers, youngsters, teenagers to be raped and sold like heads of lettuce. A quarter of a century since this first investigation, it is time to take on BIG TECH and get the smut off the internet.

Leaders, experts, politicians, legislators, local NGOs, local and state police must all think bigger than they have ever thought before. They should not just go to conferences, say wonderful things, and then go home. Lip service does not save children's lives. Something akin to a Marshall Plan should be developed with concrete steps of implementation and there should be a war declared on the mobsters, traffickers, and pimps who exploit children no matter whether it is for sex or non-sex trade.

Consequently, what I am recommending is something that is amazingly simple but has not been done universally. It is imperative that each country sanction a full and thorough commission into what the situation is in their country — the influx as well as the export of human beings and how their domestic and foreign policies contribute to the growth of this global shame.

You do not go to war unless you go to win, but you cannot win it unless you know who the enemy is. That is why the research on this issue is so important. It cannot be overemphasized that the research should not be turned into an endless stream of information. The research should be collected with one goal in mind — the eradication of slavery in the 21st century.

As previously stated, I commend the political bodies for their treatises, but they mean absolutely nothing if local law enforcement, who fights these crimes daily, are not trained, staffed, and supported technically, financially, and logistically.

Those who want to defund the police need to realize they are the first line of defense to protecting children outside of the home. Those who want to take away parental rights need to realize parents are the first line of dense inside the home. Any person, union, institution, or politician that pushes a policy that encourages a child to keep secrets from their parents is engaged in the same predatory behavior as a predator.

Finally — I had a conversation years ago with a reporter who was the Sarajevo Bureau Chief for a major American newspaper for three years. He admitted to me that he *heard* about the rapes in the Balkans in the 1990s.

"I never went into a brothel" he said.

In retrospect, I realized that he could not sell that story to his editors and chose not to pick that battle. That happens in journalism — both in broadcasting and print. I have first-hand experience in battling top management to break ground in covering new stories, and the battles can be frustrating and irrational at times, *but* this is a story worth fighting for and covering. What is at stake are children — everyone's children!

The night I took the train back to Amsterdam on June 27, 2000, after viewing the infant, toddler, pre-teen, and young teen picture at the Hague, I was so disgusted that I kept asking myself, "What kind of people commit these acts on children?"

The kind of people who commit these acts on children will continue to do so unless the public wakes up and makes it very clear that exploiting anyone, especially children, is indefensible and morally unacceptable human behavior.

If man does not take that position — and it is up to each of us and all of us collectively to show our moral outrage — the traffickers, pimps, and exploiters win. It is that simple.

For the younger generation of journalists, I will teach you how to cover corruption.

For the law enforcement who brought me inside, I am indebted to you for your patience with me.

For the colleagues, like Todd Woods, Founder of CDM.Press and our Histria publishing partner Kurt Brackob, I am sincerely appreciative. We know we have more to do, and I am forever thankful as we build teams of investigative journalists going forward with Investigative Journalists Lara Logan and Susan Katz Keating.

The Scourge of Child Abuse in Latvia

Authored by Memo Merlino

The origins of child abuse are distant in our past as humans, and the causes are multiple, but in the life of a child who has sustained it, the devastation is everlasting and the cycle, often, repeats itself when the child becomes an adult.

Children are the most defenseless and most vulnerable members of society. By nature, they trust adults, to whom they look up to as role models. They accept discipline and adult authority, but when they are subjected to verbal, physical, and sexual abuse, children know instinctively that they are being trapped into a nightmare of pain, degradation, and despair.

Children live a life of virtual reality, as they fantasize about themselves, and a world full of innocence, especially at an early age. They tend to pretend that abuse is not happening to them, as a defense mechanism. But the trauma, while buried in the unconscious memory, never, ever leaves them.

Child abuse is a family secret, an institution's quashed evidence, be it one of an educational organization, government agency, or worst of all the aftermath of an occupying army in a conflict, when children are brutalized, raped, and murdered. We have seen that recently in Sierra Leone, in Chechnya, and in Kosovo.

While in Latvia most people are unaware that child abuse goes on, it does. The danger is in the fact that it is not recognized as such, because it is easier to dismiss as a child's fantasy. Males, who are usually the perpetrators of such appalling crimes against children, do not regard it as a crime, because the punishment, if caught, is incommensurate with the offense.

In Latvia, the government itself perpetrates child abuse, through its inept legal system. Minors are arbitrarily kept in juvenile jails and sometimes in adult prisons without due process of the law. Most of these youngsters have committed petty crimes, and not violent crimes. In most cases they have served more time than the actual sentence would bring. It is time to have a general amnesty for these children.

In Riga and Jurmala children still beg on sidewalks and at McDonald's restaurants or other restaurants. It is time to take care of these children. In countless homes adult males and to a lesser degree females abuse alcohol, which begets child abuse in many forms that span from a meager diet for the children to actual violence and sexual abuse. It is time to have a national campaign to protect children from the abuses of their parents.

Child prostitution and child pornography also exists in Latvia. It is time to enforce the law.

To be truthful, most children in Latvia are well cared for. But we do not know the extent of child abuse in Latvia, as it is not known in many other countries as well. We are seeing the tip of the iceberg, because most of it is not reported.

We need for school administrators and teachers to be aware of child abuse. If child abuses go on in an educational institution, children need to be listened to and not dismissed by teachers out of fear or other reason.

Let us make Latvia a model country and a beacon for the world in this fight against crimes perpetrated on children. This is worth more than joining NATO or the EU. In fact, Latvia would be welcomed by both if the country demonstrated that fighting children abuse, as the ultimate human rights imperative, is the number one priority.

Published in *Baltic Times*, December 21, 2000

Addendum
The Media 2000-2001

In the course of history, the media's role is never more important than when exposing inhumane and criminal acts or government and institutional corruption. Exposing the exploitation of children and marginalized populations should be at the top of the media's list.

The media had reported hundreds of stories covering the exploitation of children by 2000 and 2001, but unfortunately, the magnitude of the story had missed its mark of impact because the stories were locally driven.

The following media stories and excerpts from non-governmental and governmental reports by regions in 2000/2001 are grouped below. It is important that the public understands that we knew of this topic in that era and today, it has only become worse because of the implosion of the internet and the expanded commodification of humanity by thugs, traffickers, institutions, and governments, and keep in mind, trafficking has now been further commodified in 2024 by the globalists in conjunction with governments and international bodies.

All these stories are from that earlier era to made it transparent to readers, we knew what was going on then and the model used since then to fight this scourge is bankrupt because the numbers have only increased.

EUROPE

AUSTRIA is a Country of Transit and Destination.

Many African and Eastern European girls are trafficked to Austria. [200]

BELGIUM is a Country of Transit and Destination.

In Belgium, a Royal Decree (KB16.06.95) makes it possible for NGOs to take court action on behalf of trafficked victims. Victims who lodged a formal complaint against a trafficker could receive a residence permit until the trial was completed. Belgium was host to some 36,000 asylum seekers, a large majority of whom were Kosovars and Algerians. Other nationalities of note were from Nigeria and Macedonia. [201]

In 1992, Marc Dutroux, Belgian's most notorious child killer, was released from prison after serving 3 of a 13-year sentence for multiple child rapes. In 1996, Dutroux was arrested again for abducting, raping, torturing six girls, and for murdering four of them. Two abducted girls found alive were 12 and 14 years of age. The murdered girls were 8 — 19 years of age. In 1998, while at a courthouse, Dutroux overpowered the police, stole a car, and escaped. Three hours later, he was captured and arrested. He was later sentenced to five years in prison and fined. [202] Dutroux is due to go on trial in 2002 for the four murders and six abductions.[203]

According to Jean-Marie Dedecker, a Belgian Senator, for the past 15 years, Brazilian and African children have been recruited to Europe to train as soccer players. They arrive with a three-month visa, and if they fail to meet the high standards, they are let loose on the streets without a ticket home and lacking proper papers. [204]

FRANCE is a Country of Transit and Destination.

Over 300 children under the age of 10 out of hundreds of illegal immigrants were discovered crammed in deplorable conditions in the hold of a Cambodian-registered cargo ship, which was run aground on the French Riviera coast 40 kilometers from Cannes. The ship, filled with mostly Kurds, set out from Greece, with a stopover in Türkiye. The occupants paid $200 to get on the ship, then another $2,000 once on board.[205]

The French government decided to remove border police from small Normandy ports.

The posts at Dieppe and Ouistreham, near Caen, were to be dismantled in June 2001. British authorities believed that the dismantling will only forge a new route for the smugglers.[206]

Over 300 children illegally cross the borders into France annually seeking political asylum. More than 80 percent are boys. French authorities could not legally send them home. The French government was required to take care of them. Sometimes they were placed in hostels where there are no visiting rights. [207]

Three Frenchmen were charged with paedophilia crimes stemming from 1987-1996 involving purchasing sex with children on the French version of the internet, Minitel. If convicted, all three could face 20 years in prison.[208]

When Swiss police searched a suspected Swiss criminal's apartment, they discovered an old video of Amnon Chemouil, a French citizen, having sex with an 11-year-old girl in Thailand in 1994. Having sex with a minor — even outside of France — violates France's penal code even if the sexual act occurs in a country where sex with a minor is legal. This is the first case tried under the 1998 sex tourism law. Chemouil pled guilty and was sentenced to seven years. The girl was tracked down in Thailand and brought to France to testify. [209]

In Paris, Colombian children were used in child pornography videos.[210]

GERMANY is a Country of Transit and Destination.

Prostitution is not illegal in Germany, if it is confined to designated urban areas.

Trafficking in women and children is illegal, as is working as a prostitute with a tourist visa. The Russian and Ukrainian Mafias mix with the German Mafia.[211]

Sex tourism has become a major problem in countries east of Germany for some time. In June 2000, the German police, in conjunction with Czech officials, began a public awareness campaign discouraging Germans from having sex with Czech minors. At eight border crossings, Germans were handed leaflets explaining the problem. Child prostitution is exploding along the Czech border near the German federal state of Saxony. It is less of a problem near Bavaria or on the Czech/Austrian border. The legal age of consent in the Czech Republic is 15. Nine children under the age of 15 were abused in 1999. Along with that, 89 youths between the ages of 15-18 were sexually abused. One official claimed that these figures are incomplete because "child prostitution is extremely hidden." In Germany, approximately 200,000 children are sexually abused every year. Under German law, those found guilty face a minimum of only one-year in prison. [212]

In August 2000, German and Czech officials agreed to exchange information more quickly to combat sex tourism. As a result, in December 2000, a German man was arrested after he crossed the Czech border between Bohemia and Saxon to have sex with a minor boy. Since 1992, approximately 60 children in the Czech Republic have been victimized by German paedophiles. The youngest was six years old. [213]

Since 1993, more than 1.5 million immigrants have arrived in Germany seeking asylum.

With unemployment at a staggering 21.4 percent in places in the Dessau-Bitterfel region, foreigners are not welcome. Foreigners want employment and Germans cannot find work, and what has evolved is a low tolerance for foreigners. Anti-immigration feelings range from verbal abuse to murders. Asylum seekers are housed in homes, but not allowed to work or travel outside of their district, while they await the final decision on their immigration status. And even if they wanted to travel, in some incidences, land mines still cover German fields. Foreigners receive $190 a month, plus housing and health care. [214]

Germany has more than seven million immigrants. Many are Turkish. Since the fall of Communism, violence has become an unpleasant fact in Germany with little to no tolerance for foreigners, which is coupled with high youth unemployment. [215]

Busloads of Germans travel to Czech Republic for child prostitution. Police co-operation between German and Czech is needed desperately. [216]

Reports of German police units in Macedonia regularly visiting under-age brothels for prostitution. In a documentary released in December 2000, a German soldier claimed that soldiers visit brothels in Tetovo, Macedonia, where they slept with 16-year-olds and younger. A soldier claimed that their superiors were aware. A brothel owner interviewed claimed that since the arrival of the troops in 1998, the number of brothels had increased. A 16-year-old Bulgarian prostitute claimed that she slept with hundreds of German soldiers. [217]

In April 2001, German and Czech Justice Ministers agreed to cooperate along their shared borders to combat child prostitution. Teams of state attorneys in each country will cooperate to stop the sexual exploitation of children. [218]

IRELAND is a Country of Destination.

Ireland is currently considering measures to allow trafficked victims to stay for a period to allow them to testify against their pimps and/or traffickers. [219]

There is a substantial rise in asylum seekers and illegal immigrants from Nigeria, Romania, and Democratic Republic of Congo, Libya, Algeria, and Kosovar Albanians. As a result, racism and xenophobia has increased. [220]

ITALY is a Country of Transit and Destination.

A generation ago, Italy exported immigrants. Today, it has become one of the key entry points to western Europe for refugees from Albania, Türkiye, Eastern Europe, Africa, and Asia.

There are approximately one million registered foreigners, although that number is far smaller than the number in Britain, Germany, and France. Italy had an extremely high rate of unemployment — anywhere from 10-25%. It is higher in the southern region. The Italian birthrate is also exceptionally low. Today, most Italians have one or no children. It is just too expensive. It is quite different from 40 years ago. Most of the households are two-income families because of finances. The mothers are still the primary caretakers. Consequently, they can handle one child, but two makes it very difficult. Although there is a higher rate in population in Italy, it is not due to Italians. Immigrants have more children than Italians. Italians work in the service-oriented industry, such as restaurants and bars. Immigrants are either domestic servants or on the streets. Naples is 50 percent Albanian. Because Italy is a socialist country, the children stay in school much longer, and many times one will find someone with a master's degree working in an unskilled labor job. A two-bedroom apartment in Rome costs about $2,000 monthly. Italians live in small apartments with no air-conditioning or heat. Electricity is extremely expensive.[221]

Victims who lodge formal complaints against traffickers receive a residence permit until the trial is completed.

In March 1999, Italians set up refugee camps near Bari and Brindisi, which could accommodate 40,000 Kosovo Albanians.[222]

In May 1999, five people were killed when an Italian Coast Guard collided with a dinghy filled with Kosovo Albanian refugees. The accident took place halfway between Albania and Italian coasts on the Adriatic Sea. A mother and her two small children were killed. Most of the 34 refugees were thrown overboard. Refugees from Kosovo were automatically given asylum in Italy because of the war in Kosovo.[223]

In October 2000, a 15-year-old Slovenian model, represented by an Italian agency, was drugged and gang-raped by three men in Milano in the bathroom of a nightclub.[224]

In November 2000, Russian and Italian officials agreed to join forces to fight against sexual exploitation of children and child pornography over the internet.

In late October 2000, Naples officials sought warrants for 830 Italians and 760 people in Europe, the Americas, and Asia after law enforcement discovered a child pornography website. Italian officials and Microsoft set up a fake porn website as a sting. The site was called amantideibambini, or child lovers. Some of the exchanged images included murdered children. The material costs for videos and images ranged from $600-$4,000. SNIPE was the code word for videos of nude children.

CP was the code for ordering images from a paedophiles' private collection. The most gruesome was called Necros Pedo. These images depicted children who had been tortured, raped, and killed. [225]

LIECHTENSTEIN is a Country of Transit.

For years, Liechtenstein has been a wealthy principality of only 32,000 citizens housing millions of dollars in its 300 banks. Accusations of harboring monies begotten by the Colombia drug Cartels, Italian Mafia, Russian crime syndicates instigated an internal examination of Liechtenstein's banking and prosecutorial procedures for money laundering. Liechtenstein officials claim that their banking system is not any different than other countries' financial systems. In July 2000, under pressure from the United States and European countries, Liechtenstein declared that bank accounts are no longer anonymous.[226]

MALTA is a Country of Origin.

Malta girls are trafficked to Britain.[227]

THE NETHERLANDS is a Country of Transit and Destination.

The women in the windows in the Red-Light District charge between $25-$50 for 15 minutes; the feed is paid in advance. They pay $90 a day for rent. Neither minor nor trafficked adults are allowed to work in the windows in the Red-Light District. Prostitutes work between 12-17 hours a day, receiving 10-24 clients daily. All the women — and in some cases, transvestites — have alarm buttons if anything gets out of hand. Eighty percent of prostitutes are foreigners. Seventy percent have no immigration papers, suggesting that they were trafficked.

Thirty-three percent of prostitutes come from outside of the EU. This is higher in larger cities. Since 1990, the number of trafficked women is from Central and Eastern European Union. In 1994, many trafficked victims from underdeveloped countries had children in their homelands. In 1994, many traveled by car to The Netherlands. The primary legal component to being a prostitute in The Netherlands is whether the prostitute was coerced or forced. It does not matter whether it is a child or adult. Smuggling immigrants has a lesser fine than trafficking adults and the severest fine is for trafficking children, and even more so if violence is involved. Excluding pornography, the Dutch sex trade generated $500 million annually as of 1997. [228]

In November 2000, police raided 19 addresses across 12 police regions looking for child pornography. In the end, they confiscated computers, CDs, discs, and videotapes. Three arrests were made. Much of the footage was old. Ownership of child pornography carries a fine of up to four years in prison. [229]

Prostitution is not against the law in The Netherlands, but you must be over 17 and work voluntarily. As of late 2000, brothels are once again legal in The Netherlands. It is against the law to force another to engage in prostitution, induce a minor to engage in prostitution, recruit, abduct or take a person to engage in prostitution in another country, receive income from prostitution involving a minor or a person forced into prostitution, force another to surrender income from prostitution, and traffick human beings. All these penalties carry a maximum of 6-8 years in prison. Nationals outside of the EU, who do not have resident permits, or have tourist permits, or are in The Netherlands legally but without a visa, are not allowed to work as prostitutes.

Foreigners who are self-employed prostitutes are not allowed to work in The Netherlands because they do not add to the interest of the country, but EU Nationals who settle in The Netherlands are allowed to work in the sex trade if their primary income is in another industry. If a trafficked prostituted victim is illegally in The Netherlands, and is found, that victim is entitled to government assistance. If they work with police and charge the trafficker, they are granted a temporary residence permit pending outcome of the trial and may be eligible for a permanent residence permit depending upon humanitarian or personal reasons. Each case is handled individually. Once a victim is discovered, she is given three months to decide how she wants to cooperate. The victim is allowed to stay in the country, and may use public facilities and services, such as counseling, medical, and financial and legal services, but if the victim has a temporary residence permit, the victim is not allowed to work during this time. [230]

In July 1998, an international paedophile group was exposed. The ring stemmed from The Netherlands, Germany, the U.S., Israel, and Russia. Approximately 9,000 images were found in an apartment in The Netherlands. The cruelty and ages of the victims stunned law enforcement officials. Some appeared to be no more than 12-15 months old. Some men were raping 5 and 8-year-old girls. [231]

PORTUGAL is a Country of Destination.

There are Brazilian, Colombian, and Eastern European prostitutes in Portugal.

SPAIN is a Country of Transit and Destination.

There are increasing raids on roadside brothels, where police find Latin American prostitutes who claim that they were lured abroad with the promise of legitimate jobs. [232]

Many West African girls are trafficked into Spain by boat and fanned out across Europe.[233]

SWITZERLAND is a Country of Transit and Destination.

The Swiss Federal Police launched a campaign to step up the fight against organized crime and financial crimes. The Money Laundering Reporting Office has reported that Swiss banks blocked one billion dollars in accounts, which may have been used in money laundering activities. [234]

THE UNITED KINGDOM is a Country of Transit and Destination.

Seventy percent of prostitutes in London's Soho District are Eastern European. There is a major off-street trafficking in Glasgow. [235]

In June 2000, 58 Chinese smuggled immigrants were found dead in a truck in Dover, England. All suffocated except for two immigrants. In all, nine defendants were charged in England and in The Netherlands. Six Dutch and three Turkish defendants were charged with manslaughter. The gang can be traced back to 1997 when it smuggled another group from The Netherlands to Belgium and across the English Channel to England. Then in April 2000, they repeated another transport of illegal immigrants. In all, 130 were smuggled. The driver of the truck was charged in England. Additional charges of forgery, trafficking, and operating in a criminal gang will be added. [236] Perry Wacker, the Dutch driver, was found guilty of manslaughter in the deaths of the 58 Chinese and sentenced to 14 years in jail. The Court record shows that the victims each paid approximately $20,000, and were flown from Beijing to Belgrade, and then by car and van, and moved through Hungary, Austria, Germany, France and into The Netherlands. They departed from Zeebrugge in Belgium for a six-hour ferry ride for Dover, England, where they perished on a 91-degree day. [237]

Hundreds of women and girls are trafficked into the UK for prostitution. Many of them are from Eastern European countries and live like slaves in debt bondage. [238]

Some girls — as young as 12 years old — are brought from Africa to the UK as asylum seekers. They believe that they will be employed in legitimate work, and later find themselves in brothels. Gatwick Airport in West Sussex has traditionally been the primary entry point. When the girls arrive, they are then put in the care of social services and placed in a home. The girls then sometimes disappear after being released to so-called sponsors or relatives who have false documentation. Many of the girls are controlled by voodoo practices in their homelands. [239]

NORDIC COUNTRIES

In August 2000, a joint action plan was drawn up by Nordic countries to seek an end to the trafficking of Baltic women to Nordic countries.

DENMARK is a Country of Destination.

Possession of child pornography involving those under 15 years-of-age is only punishable by fines. The maximum sentence for producing or commercially distributing such photos is two years in prison. Police detained 37 men and fined them for distributing the pornographic material. The material was exchanged via email and in internet chatrooms where pictures were electronically dispersed.[240]

FINLAND is a Country of Destination.

Finland reported an increase of AIDS. The government claimed that it was due to the UN peacekeeping forces sent abroad who had returned home. [241]

Many Finnish johns take the ferry to Estonia to go to the brothels. [242]

LUXEMBOURG is a Country of Transit.

The government demonstrates a strong commitment to children's rights and welfare through its well-funded systems of public education and medical care. The law mandates school attendance from the ages of 4-16. Schooling is free through the secondary level, and the Government provides financial assistance for postsecondary education.

There is no societal pattern of child abuse. A physicians' organization estimates that 200 cases of child abuse are treated in hospitals annually that results in legal proceedings. This group is working to reform judicial procedures to permit videotaped testimony in court proceedings and the testimony of child psychiatrists, as well as the coordination of hospital records in child abuse cases. In May 2000, the government set up a hot line for young people in distress; by the end of the year, it had received 183 calls.

In May 2000, the government passed a comprehensive new law dealing with the sexual exploitation of children. The law increased penalties for adults who traffick in children, facilitate child prostitution, or exploit children through pornography. The law also extended the country's criminal jurisdiction over citizens and residents who engage in such activities abroad. No such trafficking was reported during the year.

NORWAY is a Country of Destination.

In Norway's northernmost county, trafficking and prostitution was on the rise.[243]

SWEDEN is a Country of Destination.

The Swedish newspaper, *Svenska Dagbladet* reported, "All around the Baltic Sea, brutal sexual exploitation of children is taking place, maintained by Swedish males and the internet... . Measures must be taken against Swedish men, who never would dare to have sexual intercourse with 14-year-old teenagers in Sweden, who believe that they may legally utilize young girls in Tallinnor or Riga [Latvia]" Child sex trade has increased due to the low risk compared to drug trafficking. [244]

In 1999, new legislation was introduced in Sweden, which criminalized men — the clients who buy the services of prostitutes. Paying for sex is now illegal and punishable by fine or prison sentence. [245]

EASTERN EUROPEAN COUNTRIES

CZECH is a Country of Origin, Transit, and Destination.

There are many Slovakia gypsies who have remained in the Czech Republic, and many encourage their children to go into prostitution, but the children are not necessarily protected because many of the Romani people do not have citizenship. Prostitution is legal. Children under 15 are considered a child. Children between 15-18 are considered minors, and minors are not protected under the Czech Penal Code regarding prostitution. Prostitution is linked to Organized Crime.

Most prostitutes come from Slovakia, Ukraine, Bulgaria, and Thailand. There is a new law considered outlawing prostitution of those younger than 18. The Czech Republic is a country of transit, origin, and destination. Laws must protect Czech residents as well as foreigners. [216]

There is hardly any relevant information about child prostitution. In 1998, the police found 1,000 cases of sex abuse outside of families. In commercially sexual cases, 1,150 cases were discovered in 1999. Foreigners were the culprits in many of those cases.[247]

The European Parliament passed a resolution calling upon the Germany and Czech governments to "pay urgent attention" to sex tourism, child pornography, child prostitution, and trafficking of women at their borders. Prostitutes are on the streets and found in erotic clubs. [248]

There is an increased co-ordination between local law enforcement and two NGOs; La Strada and the International Organization for Immigration. While police cannot afford to take care of the prostitutes who want to get out of prostitution, these NGOs are able to help. Police detained 10 individuals suspected of procuring after raiding seven erotic clubs. Thirty-five prostitutes were detained as well. In addition, three members of an international gang, which imported girls from Ukraine, Moldova, and Slovakia, were also detained. [249]

Dubi forms a five-mile sex strip lined with bars named, "Libido," "Kiss," or "Alibi." Young women stand on every corner. About 70 percent are foreigners from Bulgaria, Belarus, Ukraine, and Russia. Several hundred cater to sex tourism for German clients. In nearby Teplice, orphanages house prostituted babies, and there is even a market for pregnant prostitutes. Nine pimps were being prosecuted in 3 cases involving 12 children. The youngest was nine years old.

The average rate on the street for sex is $35 for 30 minutes. In a brothel, it is $75 for 30 minutes.[250]

HUNGARY is a Country of Origin, Transit, and Destination.

Hungary is a county of transit and destination for prostitutes from Ukraine, Russian, and Romania. Women are more affected by unemployment. There is a rise in prostitution. There are high-class call girls in the cities, and brothels on the outskirts filled with trafficked prostitutes who are beaten and raped. In 1999, the Hungarian Penal Code incorporated laws against trafficking of human beings. [251]

Two 17 years-old girls arrived in Bucharest from Moldova to train with the ballet institute. They were kidnapped getting off their train. Eight months later, one was discovered in a brothel in Serbia after being sold and forced into prostitution. The second is missing. [252]

POLAND is a Country of Origin, Transit, and Destination.

Polish police busted a transnational organized network running dens, sex slavery, and coercing women into prostitution. Twenty nationals from Ukraine, Bulgaria, Romania, Moldova were detained. Detained victims had been beaten, raped, and forced into prostitution. Fraudulent Polish visas, and Polish and Czech border guard seals were confiscated. [253]

Underground tunnels had been discovered under the Belarussian/Poland border. Afghan and Vietnamese illegal immigrants were captured. 254

Poland has been pressured to clean up the corruption on its borders as part of its preparation in the European Union, which means that the Schengen Agreement will be adopted by 2005.

Smugglers and traffickers changed part of the routes. In the past, the Poland-Lithuania border was remarkably busy. Traffickers now use Slovakia, the Czech Republic, and Austrian borders. Even the border between Ukraine and Poland is tightening. Gangs charge as much as $20,000 per person. In 1999, 6,000 were caught trying to smuggle into Poland.[255]

TURKEY/GREECE

TURKEY is a Country of Origin, Transit, and Destination.

A smuggling boat, carrying illegal immigrants crashed on rocks off the coast of Türkiye. Fifty people were missing at sea. Another 32 were saved. The boat was registered in the Russian Republic of Georgia. A Greek captained it, and the 10-man crew was comprised of Greeks, Georgians, and Albanians. Pakistani, Iranian, and Bangladeshi immigrants were on board. The 399-ton vessel made its way from Israeli port of Ashod to the Turkish city of Antalya. The ship was attempting to return to Piraeus, Greece. [256] Istanbul is the hub to trafficking in Türkiye. Girls from Ukraine, Moldova, and Russia are trafficked to Türkiye. [257]

Street children, as young as 6-years-old, are the most visible part of the population in Türkiye. They stand out begging for gum or just a few coins. The street children's population has grown dramatically in the last few years. About a thousand people a day leave the rural areas for the city to better their lives. The World Bank gave a grant to Hope for Children Association, which offers job training and education classes. [258]

GREECE is a Country of Origin, Transit, and Destination.

Prostitution is legal in Greece. [259] Hundreds of thousands of Eastern Europeans have flooded into Greece. Immigration laws are inadequate, which resulted in chaos and a rise in crime. It is a country of destination for Eastern European and Asian girls, as well as a country of transit for Kurds. Prostitution is rampant. Greece is a member of the EU and NATO, and has forged business ties with Balkan countries, although there have been some serious disputes with Albania and Macedonia.[260]

Sixty-three Kurds were detained in Mykonos and three men were arrested for smuggling them in after traveling from the Turkish coast. [261]

AFRICA

There are close to ten million orphans in Africa. They have been orphaned because of AIDS, starvation, genocide, war, conflict, crime, or disease. It is fair to state that the African children are at an all-time elevated risk of being preyed upon by predators. There are six million refugees and 17 million displaced persons in Africa. More than 80 million children have no access to elementary school. The unemployment rate has doubled between 1975 and 1995, from 10 to 20- 22 percent in African cities. Landmines threaten people in Angola, Mozambique, Eritrea,

Somalia, Sudan, Congo, Rwanda, and other countries. Of the 1.9 million victims of conflicts in sub-Saharan Africa during the 1990s, 63 percent were women and children. Although African countries have internet access in capital cities, many Africans have no access to computers and little understanding of the internet.

ANGOLA is a Country of Origin.

This country is not only enmeshed in the Congo Conflicts, taking sides with the Congolese Army, but it has been engaged in its own civil war for over 26 years. Ten of thousands of refugee children roam the streets because of war, displacement, disease, and poverty. In towns, they live in sewers and rubbish dumps.[262]

BENIN is a Country of Origin and Destination.

There are growing signs that economic pressures and persistent poverty are leading to a resurgence of the traffic in child slaves in Western Africa. Children are for sale as both domestic and commercial laborer — and for sexual exploitation.

Until recently this trade had been seen as a phenomenon of war-ravaged societies such as Angola, Sudan, Somalia, or Chad — where girls as young as 10 years old were servants and concubines at rebel military bases. But now, even in peaceful areas, the traffic has grown.

Countries in the front line of this trade include **Benin, Burkina Faso, Cameroon, Cote d'Ivoire, Gabon, Nigeria, and Togo.**

Brokers scout for children among poor families in rural areas in Benin and Togo. Some of these traffickers kidnap children, others persuade parents that their children will receive professional training, or a good education with a wealthy family — most parents are corrupted by receiving a little cash.

Once the children are delivered to their host family they receive no money — they are 'bonded' to the traffickers or to the person to whom they are sold. A considerable number run away and are unable to find alternative employment, so they resort to prostitution.

Traders say that girls from Benin and Togo are particularly in demand by wealthy families in Lagos, Nigeria, or Gabon. In one instance, the Benin authorities found 400 children aboard a boat anchored in Contonou harbor. In July 1997, Benin police arrested five men preparing to ship the children to Gabon. The children, some only 8, were brought from their families for as little as $30.

A children's market was tracked down in Lagos in 1996, where malnourished children from 7-17 years old were waiting for buyers. A special child slave market has long been common in Abidjan in Cote d'Ivoire, where wealthy local women come to buy their 'helpers.' Parents may be paid as little as $15 to 'lease' their children to Arab Gulf States, Lebanon, and Europe. [263]

It was believed that approximately 180 children were onboard a Nigerian-registered vessel, which initially set sail from Douala in Cameroon and then entered the Benin harbor of Cotonnou and set sail from there in mid-April 2001. The children were believed to be trafficked victims. For weeks, the boat could not be found at sea. The boat was expected to go to Gabon.

West African port authorities were put on full alert while the boat was out to sea. When it finally came into port, those on the vessel included 139 passengers, and only seven children accompanied by their mothers. [264]

BURUNDI is a Country of Origin.

In 1998, there were reports of sex trade of 11-12-year-old girls from Burundi to Belgium. [265]

BOTSWANA is a Country of Origin.

The laws do not prohibit the trafficking of persons. There are occasional reports of law enforcement committing human right abuses. About two-thirds of the country's export industry is based on diamonds. Violence against women is a fundamental problem. Sexual exploitation and criminal sexual assault are increasing. Rape is a grave national problem, and the government acknowledged that given the high incidence of HIV/AIDS, sexual assault has become an even more serious offense.

In 1998, Parliament enacted legislation that increased all penalties for rape, incest, and other forms of sexual assault by imposing minimum sentencing requirements where none existed before. The minimum sentence for rape is 10 years, with the minimum increasing to 15 years of corporal punishment if the offender is HIV positive and to 20 years with corporal punishment if the offender knew of his or her HIV status. Sexual harassment is a problem. Sexual harassment by teachers is a national concern. There are 26,000 registered orphans. UNICEF estimates that there are an additional 40,000 unregistered orphans. There is an increase of orphaned children on the streets, begging, and engaging in prostitution. Only an immediate family member may employ a child under 13. No child under 15 may be employed by an industry. No child, under 16 years old, is allowed to be employed by anyone under hazardous conditions, including mining. Child labor laws were limited because there was limited research so it would have been difficult to say whether the laws were even enforced. [266]

BURKINA FASO is a Country of Origin.

See note for **Benin**, which refers to **Burkina Faso**.

There is a visible increase in child sexual exploitation as of 1996. Children are trafficked from Togo to Burkina Faso for prostitution. [267]

CAMEROON is a Country of Origin.

Because of the prominent level of illiteracy, the involvement of children in peer education is seen by NGOs as important for the combating of commercial sexual exploitation.[268]

Child trafficking and trade has reached alarming levels in Cameroon. It is now considered a major supplier across West Africa. The northwest, southwest, extreme-north, and western provinces and the major cities of Douala and Yaoounde are considered major suppliers of the children.

Middlemen travel to rural areas and the parents willingly give up their children not knowing that they will be subjected to exploitation. Parents agree to adoptions for a better life for their child or agree to allow their child to work as a maid. Cameroon social affairs ministry claim that 4-10 children are kidnapped monthly. Children are taken across national borders for pedophilia gangs and are also exploited as drug dealers. Middlemen are paid about $135US for a child. [269]

CENTRAL AFRICAN REPUBLIC is a Country of Origin.

Democracy is not safeguarded. The country has been destitute for years. Children here are the first victims. There is a special unit established to protect children from sexual exploitation, but there are not enough funds to guarantee its success.[270]

The presence of international peacekeeping forces in the capital has aggravated the problem of teenage prostitution. [271]

CHAD is a Country of Origin, Destination, and Transit.

Laws prohibit trafficking of persons. Violence against women is a problem, especially in domestic circumstances. Child forced labor is a problem. Thousands of refugees from Sudan live in Chad. Most Chadian refugees live in the Central African Republic, Niger, Libya, Sudan, Nigeria, and Cameroon. There is little commitment to children's rights. Laws prohibit sex with a child under 14, even if married, but this is rarely enforced. Families arrange marriages for girls as young as 11 or 12, sometimes forcibly, for dowry. Female Genital Mutilation (FGM), introduced by Sudanese, is widespread — 60 percent, even though it is outlawed, and laws allow prosecution. FGM is advocated by women and performed by women.[272]

COTE d'Ivoire is a Country of Origin, Destination, and Transit.

Côte d'Ivoire girls are trafficked to the United Kingdom and Belgium.[273] Young girls, aged 4-8, are employed as domestic maids. They are overworked, denied medical attention, prevented from watching television, raped, and treated as slaves. Many of the girls are from poor rural areas. Some "false" parents sell girls to women agents who give them to households for monthly stipends of US$1. The money is paid to the agents. The girls get nothing. [274]

CONGO is a Country of Origin.

Fighting in the Congo began in 1998. Since that time, over 2 million people have been internally displaced and 300,000 have taken refuge in other countries. Approximately, 1.7 million are dead from the fighting, famine, and disease. Approximately 16 million people in the Congo are facing human rights violations, poverty, and food shortages. Of the 16 million affected by the war in Congo, only 50 percent receive humanitarian assistance. [275]

The Ugandan government handed over 163 Congolese children aged 9-17 to the UNICEF- led team. The children were from the northeast section of Congo in the town of Bunia. They were flown into Uganda by the UPDF (Ugandan rebels) for military training in August 2000.

UNICEF estimates that there are 20,000 child soldiers in the Great Lakes region. Among the 163 children were three girls. [276]

The Congolese government has shown an indifference to the plight of the street children in Kinshasa, where children as young as six years old are begging for food and engaging in prostitution just to eat. [277]

DJIBOUTI is a Country of Origin.

Prostitution is prohibited, but government officials say it does exist. By prohibiting it, the government has driven it underground, and it is believed to have increased it. Young children are involved.[278]

EQUATORIAL GUINEA is a Country of Origin.

Child labor is a problem. "No provisions for the welfare of children are legislated. The government devotes little attention to children's rights or their welfare and has no set policy in this area. Education is compulsory up to age of 18, but the law is not enforced. Girls receive one-fifth the education of boys' education. The minimum age of child labor is 18 years old, but the Minister of Labor does not enforce this. Underage youth perform both family farm work and street vending. Minimum monthly wages are approximately $41US. There is no law known to prohibit trafficking in persons; however, there were no known or reports of persons trafficked into or from Equatorial Guinea. [279]

ETHIOPIA is a Country of Origin.

More than half of the 100,000 prostitutes in Addis Ababa are under 18. [280] It is not unusual to see child prostitutes as young as 13 standing in the slum doorways of Kera, Merkato, or Arat Kilo. Most of the money earned goes to the owners or renters of these slum houses. The children are abused and neglected. If the children become pregnant, many times they are just turned out on the street.[281]

ERITREA is Country of Origin.

Because of the protracted war between Ethiopia and Eritrea, many soldiers were children.

GABON is a Country of Origin.

See note for **Benin**, which refers to **Gabon**.

GAMBIA is a Country of Origin and Destination.

Sociologist Halifa Sallah says that the Gambian child is treated as a possession and that the Gambian child's status is going through a transition as the country is going through a transition. [282]

GHANA is a Country of Origin.

In Accra alone, there are 125 brothels where young girls are forced into prostitution. After prostitution, girls pose naked for pictures, and are given US$300. In the Trokosi tribal tradition, thousands of virgins are given to priests to appease the gods for crimes committed by relatives of the family. After the initiation, the girl becomes the property of the gods and is the property of priests for 3-5 years. If the girl tires or dies, the families are required to replace her. For serious crimes, families enslave girls to the priests for prostitution for generations. If the priest dies, the girl is entrusted to his successor. Trokosi practice violates Ghanian law even though the tradition thrives. In 1998, a bill was passed which punishes anyone, including Trokosi priests, for enslavement. Punishment is for not less than three years. As a result of a 7-year campaign to overturn this Trokosi tradition, 436 women and girls have been freed from Trokosi slavery. [283]

Police arrested several individuals in northern Ghana suspected of child trafficking. A man and woman were arrested by Burkina Faso authorities in late March 2001 with 14 children aged 10-18 years old. The group was enroute to Gambia, where the children were to work for a fisherman. Another man was held in Burkina Faso because he had false papers. Another man was arrested in central Ghana after being stopped by police. He had six children with him and claimed to be taking them to his farm to work and claimed that their parents in the Upper West region had given him their permission. The arrested were taken to Bolgatanga in the north and the police had to use teargas to disperse the hundreds of people who showed up to protest the arrests. [284]

Dr. A. Afrifa, who is with the Department of Psychology at the University of Ghana Legon, wrote an Opinion in the local newspaper addressing the issue of child rapists and child molestation, which he calls frighteningly increasing in Ghana. He cites five cases:

1. A 63-year-old man pled guilty to sex with an 8-year-old.

2. A pastor had sex with a 9-year-old girl.

3. A 58-year-old head teacher had sex with two girls, aged 6 and 8.

4. Four men had sex with a 12-year-old girl.

5. A policeman raped a 16-year-old girl who was sent to the police station for protection.[285]

GUINEA is a Country of Origin, Transit, and Destination.

For the past decade, Guinea has been home to 500,000 refugees from its neighboring Sierra Leone and Liberia because of the conflicts in those two countries, even though Liberia's conflict technically ended in 1996. Guinea, one of the world's poorest countries, has more refugees than any other country in West Africa, and the situation is turning into a humanitarian nightmare. In 2000, International Relief agencies abandoned thousands of refugees in Sierra Leone. When conflicts broke out, the refugees spanned the countryside. Hundreds of thousands fled into jungles and further into Guinea. Thousands have been killed and others have died of starvation and hardship. Since 2000, at least six different rebel groups in Guinea, Sierra Leone, and Liberia turned the area into a war zone. From February-April of 1998, the rebel Revolutionary United Front's "Operation No Living Things," burned villages, raped women, kidnapped children to serve as soldiers. Hacking off limbs of young children and adults was the weapon of choice.[286]

KENYA is a Country of Origin and Destination.

A polygamous man killed his second wife to sell their 12-day-old baby to a Nairobi cartel for about US$2,500. The child was grabbed from her mother's arms as the mother was hacked to death. [287]

David Ould of the Anti-Slavery Organization in London claims that white women travel to Kenya for sex tourism. [289]

African women attended a seminar at the Center for Population Development Assistance in Washington, DC. Women have seen an increase in prostitution in their countries. They claim that the families of these girls do not realize what is going on. They told of a Kenyan girl who went abroad to find a legitimate job. She found herself in Pakistan and was forced into prostitution where she was beaten and raped. Somehow, she was able to write her family and begged them to get her. She warned them not to contact her directly before rescuing her. She insisted that they get her because there was no way to escape, and warned them that if they contacted her, she would be killed. She also expressed fear that the other girls would be harmed as well, and possibly even her own family. These African women claimed that African families indeed acquiesce to the girls going away and if the girls fall into prostitution, the families do not want to know about it. The families look the other way. African families have seen other families send their daughters away and send money home, and sometimes these families are able to buy a new home. This is the primary reason the families look the other way. The difference now is that there is a new level of violence, which is dramatically different from the past. The girls are transported every two weeks to eliminate a possibility of bonding between the girls, the clients, and the locals. [290]

LESOTHO is a Country of Origin and Transit.

Child labor is a problem in Lesotho. Children are employed in the garment and textile industries. Lesotho is a transit point for trafficking. Twenty percent of prisoners are juveniles. Girls under 15 years of age are often hired as domestic workers. Work can start as early as 5am. and continue until extremely late at night. The girls have extraordinarily little time to rest and sleep and are without decent bedding. Child domestic workers are lonely and depressed due to their working conditions, and they are exploited in terms of earnings. There is no legislation protecting their rights in Lesotho. Simultaneously, 10.3 percent of boys, 6-15 years, are full-time herd boys and a third of these are under 10 years of age. These children do not attend school.[291]

LIBERIA is A Country of Origin.

"At the center of the region's instability, say Western diplomats and United Nations officials, stands one man, President Charles Taylor of Liberia, who has been accused of stoking the conflicts to satisfy a rapacious appetite for the substance that has fueled other wars around Africa: diamonds. A recent United Nations Report charges that Liberia has used its place as the center for arms and diamond trafficking in the region to stir up the war in Sierra Leone. The Report states, "President Charles Taylor is actively involved in fueling the violence in Sierra Leone." [292]

MADAGASCAR is a Country of Origin.

The law prohibits trafficking. However, there are reports that young girls were trafficked to the nearby island of Reunion and to Mauritius for prostitution. The UN Committee on the Rights of the Child expressed concern over insufficient measures to protect the street children.[293]

MALAWI is a Country of Origin.

Malawi's AIDs crisis has reached dangerous numbers — 80 percent.[294]

MALI is a Country of Origin, Transit, and Destination.

Child labor is a huge issue in Mali. Children work in the rural areas in the agricultural industry as well as street vendors in the cities. Mauritania's Haretine (Black Africans) are slaves to the Beidanes (white Arab-Berber nomads). Beidanes often roam with their slaves into the Mali desert. Mali children are trafficked and sold into Côte d'Ivoire plantations. Debt-bondage was common in salt mining communities north of Timbuktu in the mid-nineties. [295]

MAURITANIA is a Country of Origin and Destination.

There are reports of foreign paedophiles using young boys for sex.[296]

MAURITIUS is a Country of Origin.

The government released their 1998 report on child prostitution. Girls 11-13 years old were forced into prostitution, even on the island of Rodriques, which is a Mauritius dependency.

The prostitution network was organized. The networks are disguised as institutions which take care of the girls. Families hand over their children to the institutions. Older prostitutes ask for trips to other islands and sometimes clothes and shoes. The clients are men over 40 who range from politicians, lawyers, and ministers.[297]

MOZAMBIQUE is a Country of Origin.

Children are trafficked by truck and on foot from Mozambique into South Africa near the Kruger National Park. Traffickers are Mozambican and South African. Children are between the ages of 8-17. Most are illegally in South Africa. Trafficking is informal compared with the European and Asian syndicates. Children are sold for $30-$60. When they are discovered in South Africa, the children are escorted to the border and sometimes left on their own or put on the train back to Mozambique. Occasionally, embassies are involved with returning the children, but no records are kept on the children.[298]

NAMIBIA is a Country of Transit.

Reports confirm sexual exploitation of children for commercial prostitution.

NIGER is a Country of Origin.

There are reports of extensive child labor in Niger in mining and quarrying and in the chemical industry, specifically, with the production of torn-hydrated sodium carbonate. There are about 500,000 children working in Niger. [299]

NIGERIA is a Country of Origin and Destination.

Her Excellency, Chief Mrs. Amina Titi Abubakar, wife of the Nigerian Vice-President, is a leader fighting the exploitation of women and children. She is the founder of Women Trafficking and Child Labour Eradication Foundation (WOTCLEF). At least 454 Nigerians, mostly women and children, were brought back to Nigeria after being trafficked abroad to five foreign countries. They were returned between last year and July 2000. They were deported from the United States, Italy, Germany, Saudi Arabia, and The Netherlands. Italy had the highest number of victims at this time. Netherlands came in second. [300]

According to Amina Titi Abubakar, the international sexual slavery malaise, especially in Nigeria, is very alarming and requires urgent attention. In the past, the Gabonese Ambassador to Nigerian wanted to repatriate about 25 Nigerian children a month. She claims that most Nigerians do not know the extent of the problem for the Nigerian children. She does not believe the issue is necessarily based on poverty, but on a moral decline and says, "people want to be like the Joneses." She believes that the victims should not be prosecuted; the traffickers should be punished.[301]

A Muslim girl was flogged after being forced by her father to have sex with three men.

The initial flogging was delayed because she was pregnant.[302]

Of the 1,880 — 2,500 minors who work on the street as prostitutes in Italy, 1,500 — 2,300 have been trafficked from Albania and Nigeria[303]

RWANDA is a Country of Origin.

In 1994, the Rwandan Genocide shocked the world, but the aftermath to that conflict still lingers. Approximately, 800,000 were murdered and hacked to death. About 106 non- governmental organizations swooped down into Central Africa to assist in this horror. Seven years later, hundreds of children, who were separated from their families in refugee camps in the nineties, are still living abroad. They were taken by NGOs at the time and transported to Europe and placed in French, Belgian, Tanzanian, and Italian homes. Today, the Rwanda government is trying to get those children returned to their families, and in instances, European governments, such as Italy, will not co-operate with the children's families.[304]

"As Rwandans commemorate the 1994 genocide, there are reports that foster families are exhibiting "unbearable depths of exploitation, discrimination, torture, and tormenting acts" against the recently adopted orphans, the Rwanda News Agency (RNA) said. It said the assessment is drawn from interviews and seminars carried out in Kigali ville, Kigali Butare, Ruhengeri, Kibuye and Umutara prefectures by various government departments and NGOs "attest to this fact." [305]

SENEGAL is a Country of Origin and Transit.

A West African Regional Conference on Sexual Abuses and Exploitation of Children was held in Dakar. Representatives from Benin, Burkina Faso, Cameroon, Morocco, Niger, Rwanda, Senegal, and Togo attended meeting. [306]

Girls from Senegal are trafficked to Europe. [307]

SIERRA LEONE is a Country of Origin.

The Kamajor — the pro-government militia — has admitted to recruiting thousands of children to fight the ousted military junta. Three thousand children are in the eastern section of the country. Children as young as 10-1 4 years old are in battle. In the north, children are recruited. UNICEF and Sierra Leone national radio and television began a campaign to demobilize and rehabilitate the children.[308]

In 2000, 200 women and children, who were held as sex slaves were released following the end of a UN peacekeeping hostage crises. Women and children were traumatized by rebels who gangraped them, burned others alive, and mutilated with machetes. UN officials believe they released them because they became a burden to rebels because they were malnourished. The boys were trained as soldiers. The girls were sex slaves. The UN believes that the rebels have abducted 20,000 children.[309]

SOMALIA is a Country of Origin.

Thousands of refugees live abroad in Ethiopia, the United States, Scandinavia, and Arab countries due to the continued war. Approximately 20,000 shooters are in Mogadishu. [310]

SOUTH AFRICA is a Country of Origin, Transit, and Destination.

Visas are not needed to enter South Africa from Thailand. This has resulted in the ease to which Thais are trafficked to South Africa and forced into the sex industry against their will. There are three times the number of Thais in South Africa today than three years ago. [311]

Parallel to the author's investigation, ICMEC commissioned Howard Davidson, the Director of the American Bar Association's Center on Children and the Law in Washington, DC, to attend the 13th International Congress on Child Abuse and Neglect in Durban, South Africa, in September 2000. This was the first major child abuse conference held on the African continent. There were over 1,000 attendees from 63 nations. Of those nations represented, only 19 were from African countries. In his report, Mr. Davidson wrote, "One of the strongest messages communicated by presenters was the concern for the absence of strong criminal laws against those trafficking children for sexual purposes, both within countries and across borders."[312]

The child sex trade is growing due to legal loopholes that allow child exploitation to go unpunished. Economically desperate and violent parents are selling children, as young as four, to local and foreign and crime syndicates. Demand is also increasing. Some report that there are 38,000 child prostitutes in South Africa. Poverty is a key factor. Of the 2,000 child prostitutes arrested in Cape Town, 25 percent were children. Angolan, Zimbabwe, and southeast Asian children are trafficked into South Africa. Children from Mozambique are trucked through South Africa's Kruger National Park. [313]

More than 70,000 babies are born with HIV-positive annually. [314]

Cape Town is a sex tourism mecca. Prosecutions for pedophilia are rare in South Africa. [315]

A child molester who works with disabled children was sentenced to 10 years in jail for assaulting a 16-year-old girl with Down's Syndrome. The Medical Research Council released results, which claim that most rapes are perpetrated on girls under 15 and that in 33 percent of these cases, the teacher was the culprit. It is believed that disabled children are at a higher risk.[316]

William Bantom, the Mayor of Cape Town from 1995—2000 and a Minister in the Church of the Nazarene since 1968, was caught downloading child and adult pornography. He resigned as Mayor and was expelled from the New National Party, the former ruling party during apartheid. Bantom was the first Black Mayor of Cape Town. He is a 54-year-old father of two.[317]

Studies show that orphans with AIDS end up in the sex trade. Even eight-year-olds are sold for food. One Mozambican mother was arrested in South Africa for pimping her daughters, age 7 and 10, for sex for $26 a week on a Johannesburg Road. [318]

In the Gauten and Western Cape area of South Africa, children between 4-17 years old are most vulnerable to being sold into international syndicates. They are abducted and thrown into debt bondage or sold by their parents. Nigerian criminal syndicates operating in South Africa are domestic child traffickers. At present there are no services for trafficked or sexually exploited children in South Africa. Children found in prostitution are ignored, sent to places of safety, imprisoned, or returned home to their parents. South African police are involved in the sex trafficking industry. This makes it even more difficult for children to report crimes. [319]

The South African system for collecting crime statistics is flawed and unreliable.[320] Half of South Africa's population is comprised of children. Sixty percent of them are under 16. Seventy percent of them live in poverty. There is a 400 percent increase in orphans with AIDS. It is estimated that by 2010 there will be an estimated 3.6 — 4.8 million children orphaned by AIDS. They are girls, from 4 -17, from rural and urban areas in search of work for survival, or children who have left home, having been sexually abused, or run away from places for safety to live on the streets. Exploiters are from all occupations. There are no "specific" social services for trafficked or sexually exploited children. **There is no anti- trafficking legislation in South Africa.** Children are trafficked INTO South Africa from Mozambique, Angola, Lesotho, Zimbabwe, Swaziland, Nigeria, Thailand, and Eastern European countries. Transit African countries include Swaziland, Namibia, South Africa, Kenya, Zimbabwe, Singapore, and Eastern European countries. Crime syndicates involved in South Africa include Nigerian Drug Lords, Chinese Triads, Israeli Mafia, Russian Mafia, and Eastern European Syndicates that are comprised of former military personnel. Those in South Africa who are linked with crime syndicates include South African and foreign nationals, brothel owners, former sex workers and victims, government officials — local and international — border police and police agents, pimps, former military and police personnel, and local gangs. In South Africa, there are no services for foreign children who are trafficked in South Africa. Children are treated as illegal aliens and returned to their countries of origin. There is no repatriation process. Children are escorted to the border and left or put on a train or plane to their country of origin. Sometimes embassies of a specific country are located, but not always.[321]

Thousands of young schoolgirls are victims of sexual violence and harassment while attending school. The perpetrators are rarely reprimanded. Many students leave school, and some have contracted AIDs. Girls fall victims to fellow students and more often to teachers and employees. [322]

The Greater Nelspruit Rape Intervention Project (GRIP) is a controversial anti-rape volunteer organization in Nelspruit, Mpumalanga, South Africa. Two provincial hospitals want to evict GRIP because they provide free anti-Aids drugs to rape victims. According to GRIP, 70 percent of the rape victims are under 18 years of age. In October 2000, GRIP was initially evicted. The stated reason was because GRIP differs with the ANC's policy, which prevents the distribution of anti-AIDs drugs in provincial hospitals. To assist GRIP in its recent predicament, the Nelson Mandela Children's Fund provided funding for one year with the caveat that none of these monies would be expended upon the anti-AIDs drugs.[323] One in nine have AIDs in South Africa. [324]

SWAZILAND is a Country of Origin.

Swaziland has an extremely high HIV/AIDS rate. Experts claim it to be 65 percent. [325]

Swaziland children are trafficked into South Africa for sex trade.[326]

SUDAN is a Country of Origin.

Black children in the South were rounded up by the government and forced to become soldiers and fight against their own people. The children are used as slaves. [327]

An estimated 2 million people have died in 17 years of fighting and famine.

Approximately 4.4 million have been displaced from their homes. [328]

In 1997, UNICEF criticized Sudan, Uganda, and Algeria for brutalizing their children in political and military conflicts. Children are being abducted, sold into slavery and in some cases, resold to their own parents. [329]

TANZANIA is a Country of Origin.

In 1998, the Tanzania Media Women Association found that poverty and sexual abuse in the home are among the factors underlying the increasing number of children in the sex trade.

TOGO is a Country of Origin.

See **Benin** Note, which refers to **Togo**.

Thai girls are found to be working as prostitutes in Western African. Prostitutes are commonly referred to as "Natashas" because some come from Russia.[330]

Child trafficking is a genuine problem. In 1997, close to 700 children were recaptured on the Benin, Nigeria, border with Togo. In January 1998, 199 Togolese children were returned to their families. [331]

UGANDA is a Country of Origin and Destination.

Up to 8,000 children were abducted and forced through brutal methods to become child soldiers in the northern region. Children as young as 11 have been recruited. Those who try to escape are tortured and killed. Children are forced to kill other children. Over 200,000 are displaced in North. In 1994, the Lore Resistance Army (LRA) abducted children from schools. Experts say it is estimated that 90 percent of LRA are abducted children. Sudanese government supports the LRA.[332]

There is a substantial increase in street children in Kampala. They beg for money and engage in prostitution. [333] In 1997, UNICEF criticized Sudan, Uganda, and Algeria for brutalizing their children in political and military conflicts. Since 1999, there are over 1,500 street children in Kampala, Uganda — the nation's capital.[334]

ZAMBIA is a Country of Origin.

This country, considered one the worst African countries for sexual exploitation of minors and has one of the highest levels of AIDS in Africa.[335]

ZIMBABWE is a Country of Origin and Transit.

Reports confirm the sexual exploitation of children for prostitution. Malnutrition is linked to 27 percent of children's death.

EAST ASIA AND THE PACIFIC

ASIA: UN Report (September 2000): "Sexual abuse of children is often one of the most hidden and underreported forms of sexual violence in Asia. Child victims of rape, incest, trafficking, prostitution, and pornography face grave physical and psychological health conditions."

AUSTRALIA is a Country of Origin and Destination.

A new law allows prosecution under conspiracy and incitement laws that carry life sentences for conspiracy to commit rape, and up to 7 years for intercourse with a female under 13. [336]

Stiff jail time for sex exploitation passes the Senate with a maximum of 25 years for sexual exploitation. There is a penalty of 15 years or 19 years if the victim is under 18, if activity falls short of sex slavery, but involves a victim working in conditions of sexual servitude.

Deceptive recruiting will attract a maximum penalty of 7 years, and 9 years if the victim is under 18. Australians can be prosecuted in Australia if they commit sex tourism abroad. [337]

The first Australian (70 years old) is charged with sex tourism abroad in Thailand.[338] There are more Australians prosecuted overseas for child sexual abuse than any other nationals.[339]

A serial Australian child abuser admitted to 130 child sex offenses against 11 girls, aged 4 and 5 and filming them as well. The police confiscated a tape. He committed the acts over 5 years from 1995-2000. He pled guilty to 9 counts of penetration of a child under 13, 20 counts of indecent dealing with a child under 13, 76 counts of making an indecent recording of a child under 13, 18 counts of procuring a child under 13 to perform indecent acts, 6 counts of possessing child pornography and 1 count of showing offensive material to a child under 16. According to police, the perpetrator has an "enormous sexual appetite." The police found a 'distressing" 25- minute video of the perpetrator raping one girl.[340]

MYANMAR: (FORMERLY BURMA) is a Country of Origin and Transit.

Most citizens live on less than one dollar a day. Four out of ten children are malnourished.

The dictatorial Generals oversee a society infested with drug smuggling (heroin and amphetamine), drug-money laundering, and sexual exploitation of young women. Among prostitutes, there is an epidemic of AIDS proportional to that in Africa. [341]

There are 20,000-30,000 women and girls from Myanmar trafficked to Thailand brothels. According to Asia Watch, approximately 10,000 recruits are added annually. According to UNIFEM, the total numbers are assumed to be higher since the majority of the 917,000 immigrants to Thailand are from Myanmar.

CAMBODIA is a Country of Origin, Transit, and Destination.

There is a great interest in Cambodia as a destination for sex tourism. The average income of a Cambodian adult is US$300 annually. One-third of all sex workers is estimated to be children who are 12-17 years old. More than 70 percent of children surveyed near Angkor Wat and nearby villages said that tourists approached them for sex.[342]

Due to the rise in sex tourism, children as young as 8 are vulnerable due to the rise in tourism overall.[343] A man who lured 2 8-year-old girls to a park for pornographic photography was given a sentence of 3 years, although Cambodia law calls for 10-12 years for debauchery with a minor. A Judge justified his decree by stating that the girls were not raped.[344]

A man from the United States was charged with rape and indecent assault of a 15-year- old girl. They were found naked in a hotel bed. If found guilty, he faces up to 10 years in prison. [345]

A British man, who was the Director of an English-speaking school in Phnom Penh, goes on trial for bribing girls, 8-10 years old, and coaxing them into pulling up their skirts and touching themselves while he videotaped them. He could face up to 10-20 years if convicted. [346]

According to a 1996/97 Human Rights Commission Report 14,725 women were found in brothels. Of those found, 81 percent were Khmer, 18 percent were Vietnamese, and 1 percent were from other countries.

CHINA is a Country of Origin and Destination.

GREATER MEKONG SUBREGION is a region of Origin.

Most female victims were 6-12 years old.

CHINA'S SOUTHERN YUNNAN PROVINCE is a region of Origin.

According to Chinese government statistics, approximately five hundred women and girls were trafficked from Yunnan Province alone.

EASTERN CHINA is a region of Origin.

Four gang leaders were sentenced to death for raping and selling poor rural women as brides. Women were sold for US$2-6. Over 123,000 women (approximately 110,000) and children (approximately13,000) were freed as result of a trafficking crackdown. [347]

The cost of smuggling human beings into the United States from China is approximately $60,000. The Bank of China in New York City was a primary institution for bank transfers for traffickers for years. Cheng Chui-ping is known as the "Mother of All Snakeheads." Snakehead is the jargon used for the leader of those who guide illegal immigrants across borders. Cheng was arrested in Hong Kong in April 2000. She is in prison, while waiting for extradition to the United States. She allegedly ran a $40 million illegal immigration business out of New York City and China. [348]

Chinese gangs have switched their focus from United States to Europe. China does not share the old Soviet Union rules of barring its citizens from leaving the country. Many Chinese immigrants come from southeast coastal areas, such as the province of Zhejiang, which is known for the illicit trade of goods and human beings. Under Milosevic's regime, visas were granted to China from Belgrade. Weekly, two DC-10s arrived from China into Belgrade. A ticket costs $500-$900. Belgrade had its own corruption for smuggled consumer goods coming from China. The Chinese are also allowed to buy resident permits in Serbia for a few thousand dollars. [349]

To go from China to England can cost as high as $45,000. If trafficked to Japan or Hungary, the cost is approximately $12,000.[350]

HONG KONG is a City of Destination.

Trafficked children's numbers are increasing.

TAIWAN is a Country of Destination.

Trafficked children's numbers are increasing.

INDONESIA is a Country of Origin and Destination.

Girls were systematically kidnapped, raped, and forced into slavery in Timor. Girls were taken from Timor-Leste to West Timor. High military and rebel officials rape younger girls. Older girls were used by the lower ranks. [351]

Research conducted in September 2000 by Irwanto Ph.D., a consultant to the International Labour Organization (ILO) found that foreign businessmen are drawn to Indonesia not just for the country's economic potential but also for the proliferation of child prostitution. Research found that Korean and Singaporean businessmen were being sexually serviced by young girls from the islands of Java and Sumatra. Irwanto conducted his research in Batam Island, Jakarta, Medan, and Bali. Child slavery is a problem as well. In Jakarta, young girls are recruited from villages in Java, Sumatra, and the Sulawesi islands. Jakarta also served as a transit point for the girls who were then sent onto Brunei, Hong Kong, South Korea, Singapore, Taiwan, and Saudi Arabia. Irwanto's two primary findings revealed that children were employed as drug traffickers and that young village girls were sent abroad as housemaids and ended up as sex slaves. [352]

JAPAN is a Country of Origin and Destination.

A Japanese national was arrested in Hawaii for smuggling Japanese women into the U.S. to work as nude models on the internet. Another Japanese national was arrested earlier in California.[353]

Crimes against children and women are on the rise in Japan. In late 1999, Japan passed laws prohibiting sex with 17-year-olds or younger, and banned the sale, production, and distribution of child pornography. Japan is a large market for domestically produced child pornography. Activists claim that 80 percent of the world's child pornography is produced in Japan. Sex tourism to other Asian countries by Japanese men has increased. Most arrests in Japan are for posting on the web.[354]

Japan is a market for Russian and Eastern Europeans.

KOREAN is a Country of Origin.

South Korean officials uncovered a website called, "Lolita," which features sex between adult males and female children. It is believed to be Korean based because the local bank accounts and domestic delivery service company used, which delivered CD-ROMs and tapes of the website scenes, were Korean. Although it was a newly created website, it had 320,000 "hits" on the site.

LAOS is a Country of Origin.

The government estimates that over 15,000 youths in Savannakhet province sought work in Thailand.

MALAYSIA is a Country of Destination.

Pornography is increasing to Malaysia. An all-women syndicate comprised of 6 Indonesian women ranging from 19-25, and a 41-year-old, were arrested for operating an illegal video library stocked with pornography. About 13,800 CDs, DVDs, and videotapes worth about $100,000 were seized. Singapore typically bans and censors publications and film that has excessive amounts of sex and violence. The library operated like a club with about 1,800 members. The women face fines from $20,000-$40,000, and a possible 2-year jail term. [355]

MONGOLIA is a Country of Origin.

Child prostitution, especially procuring and offering of child prostitution, is rampant. The law does not specifically prohibit trafficking in persons, and there is evidence that Mongolian women and teenagers are working in the sex trade in Asian and Eastern Europe. [356]

NEW ZEALAND is a Country of Origin and Destination.

Otahuhu has a large sex trade including girls as young as 12 years old. Thai girls as young as 18 years old were forced to work in brothels in Auckland. There are an estimated 6,000- 8,000 prostituted women in New Zealand. In Auckland, of 4,000 prostitutes, eight hundred are Thai, and 400 are other Asian women. [357]

CD-ROM games are a focus of child pornography. In December 2000, an 8-year-old received a CD-ROM for Christmas. He was expecting to play computer games but found instead direct links to hard-core Russian pornographic sites. In New Zealand, if one knowingly distributes or supplies objectionable pornographic material on pirated CD-ROMs, the fine is $20,000 an image or one year in prison. Unwittingly distributing such material carries a fine of $5,000 an image.[358]

THE PHILIPPINES is a Country of Origin, Transit, and Destination.

The Philippines is considered one of the meccas for sex tourism and a paedophile playground. The numbers of children trafficked for sex fluctuate, but overall are alarming. Half of the women trafficked in China are from the Philippines. A recent study demonstrates that there are 75,000 children forced into prostitution and blame it on poverty. Anywhere from 60,000-600,000 children are prostituted. One fourth of the sex trade is Filipino children who are shipped overseas. The Philippines is the fourth among 9 nations with the most children in prostitution. Most of the children involved in prostitution are victims of incest and sexual abuse and come from semi-rural areas. In 1996, 492, of 3,776 reported cases of child abuse involved pornography, prostitution, paedophilia, and trafficking. ECPAT reports that children as young as 6 are trafficked. The numbers of children trafficked are increasing, and the ages of those children are decreasing. [359]

SINGAPORE is a Country of Origin and Destination.

Thousands of girls from China's southern part are trafficked into Thailand's sex industry; and go on to Malaysia or Singapore. [360]

THAILAND is a Country of Origin, Transit, and Destination.

Child sex abuse cases are on the rise. The resort area of Pattaya, Thailand, is a sex tourism haven. Here you can pay $3 for sex with a child. UNICEF says that pimps and mafia trafficked approximately 400,000 Thai children.

Approximately 6,000 Thais living abroad were rescued between 1999-2000. Victims were lured with promises of legitimate jobs and forced to work in sweatshops or into prostitution. Approximately 150,000 Thais immigrate to Taiwan. There are a considerable number of Thais working in Singapore and Malaysia.[361]

Chalerm Promlert, a 64-year-old Thai Senator, was accused of having group sex with four young girls between 14 and 15 years of age. A 17-year-old arranged the meetings. The Senator allegedly paid each of the girls US$23.30. If found guilty, he could face up to 20 years in jail. [362]

According to Coalition Against Trafficking in Women, in 1996, 1 million women and girls of various nationalities have been trafficked into Thailand for sex.

More than two million women and children have been sold into slavery. Experts claim that 35 percent are children under the age of eighteen. [363]

VIETNAM is a Country of Origin.

UNIFEM estimates that, 6,000 women and girls have been sold to China as of May 1996.

When Swiss police searched a suspected Swiss criminal's apartment, they discovered an old video of Amnon Chemouil, a French citizen, having sex with an 11-year-old girl in Thailand in 1994. Having sex with a minor — even outside of France — violates France's penal code even if the sexual act occurs in a country where sex with a minor is legal. This is the first case tried under the 1998 sex tourism law. He pled guilty and was sentenced to seven years. The girl was tracked down in Thailand and brought to France to testify.[364]

BALTIC/NEW INDEPENDENT STATES/CENTRAL ASIA

ARMENIA is a Country of Origin.

In Greece, more than 40 percent of minors in prostitution are from neighboring regions and countries, including Uzbekistan, Kazakhstan, Armenia, Albania, and Iraq. Armenian women work as prostitutes in the Middle East, and there have been reports of trafficking in women and girls in the past. [365]

AZERBAIJAN is a Country of Origin.

Prostitution has risen due to an influx of refugees. [366]

BELARUS is a Country of Origin and Transit.

There is an increasing number of children reported in prostitution. There is an increasing concern because of the social problems emerging due to this increase. [367]

ESTONIA is a Country of Origin, Transit, and Destination.

Approximately 1,200 children are engaged in prostitution. Of the 2,000 prostitutes reported in Estonia, 30 percent are children. Other experts claim that the children encompass 50 percent. [368]

Estonia is about the size of The Netherlands, but with the tenth of the population. Its per capita use of mobile phones, internet banking, and other technology is higher than France's or Italy's. [369]

KAZAKHSTAN is a Country of Origin.

Television Commercials dealing with sex trade are being aired in Kazakhstan — "Girls as young as 15 are dragged into this [sex trade] business... ." The television commercial ends with a disclaimer stating that "Kazakhstan courts are not effective and law enforcement agencies do not have sufficient power to prevent this illicit trade" [370]

KYRGYZSTAN is a Country of Origin.

Prostitution has flourished through the former Soviet Union because of poverty and increased organized crime. The International Organization for Migration released a report claiming that thousands of women and girls were tricked into working abroad as prostitutes and forced against their will. They were promised jobs as dancers or restaurant jobs. The study was based on interviews with one hundred girls and women, who were forced to work without pay and physically abused. Sixty-two of those interviewed were forced to work without pay. Thirteen Kyrgyzstan travel agencies were used to supply false documentation.[371]

LITHUANIA is a Country of Origin.

There are an estimated 450 child prostitutes in Vilnius.[372]

LATVIA is a Country of Origin.

"A district court… sentenced the former director of a Latvian beauty pageant to two-and- one-half years in prison for sexually abusing… four underage boys… ."[373]

There is a lack of funding for trafficking investigations and even less interest by the police.[374]

MOLDOVA is a Country Origin and Transit.

Police crack a network that was smuggling prostitutes from Russia, Moldova, Ukraine, and Romania via Albania to Italy.[375]

RUSSIA is a Country of Origin, Transit and Destination.

Kyiv and China are the major hubs of trafficking Chinese. Russian girls were trafficked throughout the world. Slave trading in Chechnya is a huge business. Wahhabi fundamentalists from Urus-Martan are the hostage and trafficking experts. Urus-Martan was the center of slave trade. Notorious gangs of Ramzan Akhmadov of Urus-Martan kept slaves in cellars. [376]

Winrock Foundation runs two anti-trafficking projects.[377]

In December 2000, Eduard Lapatik, head of Moscow's Criminal Search Unit, and the Russian police searched Vsevolod Solntsev-Elbe's apartment in Moscow and found child pornography camouflaged in shrink-wrapped National Geographic labeled nature film boxes. In addition, they found his mailing list.

One of the names on the list was Glenn Martikean, a 44-year-old man from Indiana in the United States. E-mails on the computer showed that Martikean was coming to Moscow. In late March 2001, four people in the United States were arrested for their involvement in an international child-porno ring called Blue Orchid. Martikean showed up in Moscow, where a policeman met him while posing as a pimp. Martikean represented that he wanted to have a sex with a young boy, so when the boy was sent to meet him, the police were listening and burst through the doors after Martikean asked the boy to undress.

While in Moscow, Martikean's Indiana home was searched. The police found 280 printed-out images of pre-pubescent boys, ranging in age from 8-12 and engaged in sexual activity with one another.

Under Russian law, Martikean committed no crime in Moscow. There is no law against the possession or procurement of child pornography. It is considered a minor offense and victimless crime, and punishable by a maximum sentence of two years, and in most cases is never prosecuted at all in Russia. The age of consent was lowered in Russia in 1996 from 16-14.

Martikean was indicted in the U.S. for trading in child pornography and travelling with the intent to have sex with a minor. U.S. Agents believe that Martikean has been an active paedophile for years and have identified allegedly five victims in the U.S. [378]

SLOVAKIA is a Country of Origin, Transition, and Destination.

A Czech photographer was sentenced to five and a half years in prison for videotaping child pornography. He sold two photographs and abused four boys. He is due to be extradited to Czech after he serves his term. [379]

Criminal gangs in Slovakia are comprised of criminal gangs from former Yugoslav Republics, Germany, Russia, Ukraine, Albania, Italy, and Poland. There are only two NGOs dealing with the issue of trafficking of women. They do focus on children. There is hardly any published information regarding trafficking in persons in Slovakia.[380]

TURKMENISTAN is a Country of Origin.

During the cotton harvest season, children as young as 10 years of age are used for labor in the rural areas. [381]

UKRAINE is a Country of Origin and Transit.

A 1992-1994 criminal investigation revealed the trafficking of newborn infants from maternity wards.

According to police data, about 12,000 children are abandoned by their parents annually. About one-half of these children are 3 to 7 years old. Ukrainian state boarding schools have about 50,000 orphaned children and children who are left without parental care. About 40,000 more children are placed under guardianship.

The police are currently searching for about 20,000 parents who have abandoned their children. This situation constitutes the foundation for trading and kidnapping children and teenagers in the Ukraine. They are for sale because the resources for their support are insufficient.

They can be sold not only for adoption, but also for working in brothels. One of the major examples of trafficking of children from Ukraine that made the legislators adopt a law against trafficking in people was that the Lviv Regional Prosecutor's Office found that newborn children from maternity hospitals were being trafficked abroad.

According to the data of the Ukrainian Parliamentary Commission in Human Rights, citizens of other countries (USA, Switzerland, Canada, Germany, France) illegally adopted and took over 800 babies abroad. About 130 of them were Ukrainian citizens. [382]

Under Ukrainian law, prostitution is not a criminal offense, rather a civil offense, like drinking alcohol in public places, which is considered a minor infraction. Keeping brothels or pimping carries a prison term of up to five years. Under the Ukrainian law, trafficking of women and children is incorporated in the term, "trafficking in people." Some experts believe that there should be a separate law for children. In Ukraine, the number of trafficked girls has not been fully documented, but trafficking of human beings in Ukraine is a huge business. This conclusion is based upon the number of trafficked children and teenagers. Approximately, 12,000 children are abandoned by their parents annually. Half of these children are between the ages of 3-7. State orphanages house approximately

50,000. Another 40,000 are placed under guardianship. Kids are sold for adoption and to work in brothels. In the Ternopil region, 124 orphans were taken abroad for operations, and 56 of them failed to return to the Ukraine. Women are exported to Türkiye, Cyprus, former Yugoslavia, Bosnia and Herzegovina, Croatia, United Arab Emirates, Syria, China, The Netherlands, Canada, Japan, Russia, Poland, Hungary, Czech Republic, Greece, Germany, Italy, Spain, Russia, United Arab Emirates, Israel, and the United States. Prostitution is not a modern phenomenon in the former Soviet States, but it was never as rampant as it is today because in years past, the ideology condemned prostitution, women were not as economically desperate, police were closely monitoring prostitution and pimping, and trafficking anyone across borders was virtually impossible. The ever-growing gap between the rich and the poor is a catalyst for the growth in prostitution. The proposals of employment abroad most commonly involve such kinds of jobs as waitresses, striptease dancers, singers or dancers in restaurants, masseuses, hotel maids, governesses, cleaners, tutors, manicurists, or seasonal workers.

Sometimes the women are explicitly recruited as prostitutes and know that they will work in the sex-sector, but do not know they will be held in forced labor or slavery. A trafficker gets US$200-$5,000 for recruiting a woman to work abroad.[383]

UZBEKISTAN is a Country of Origin.

In Greece, more than 40 percent of minors in prostitution are from neighboring or regional countries, including Uzbekistan, Kazakhstan, Armenia, Albania, and Iraq. Women and girls in Uzbekistan are trafficked particularly to the Persian Gulf and Türkiye.[384]

No one bothers to notify law enforcement when girls are abducted or lured away.[385]

MIDDLE EAST AND NORTHERN AFRICA

ALGERIA is a Country of Origin.

In 1997, UNICEF criticized Sudan, Uganda, and Algeria for brutalizing their children in political and military conflicts.

BAHRAIN is a Country of Destination.

Eastern European and Africa girls are trafficked to Bahrain.

EGYPT is a Country of Origin.

Child prostitution is rare.[386] But, child labor in Egypt has been labelled a "catastrophic phenomenon" by researchers and child rights advocates. The number of child laborers under the age of fifteen could exceed 4 million. Most of them worked in mechanical workshops. Others worked on farms, and in the chemical, steel, and construction industries. Girls working as housekeeper were physically and sexually abused. Children earned one-sixth of adult wages. [387]

IRAN is a Country of Origin and Transit.

Women had no rights under the law in Iran. An Iranian woman's divorce was not recognized in another country, unless it was first recognized in Iran. The custodianship of children did not belong to their mothers. A prostitute could be buried alive or stoned to death.

IRAQ is a Country of Origin.

Years of sanctions have led to an increase in prostitution. In Greece, more than 40 percent of the minors in prostitution are from neighboring countries, including Uzbekistan, Kazakhstan, Armenia, Albania, and Iraq. [388]

ISRAEL is a Country of Destination.

An academic filed a lawsuit against the Kibbutz Ruhama, resulting in the exposure of hundreds of cases of rape, sexual abuse, and incest in Israel. [389]

Thousands of women and girls have been trafficked to Israel for sex trade. It is not illegal to traffick women and girls *to* Israel for prostitution, but it is illegal to instigate or traffick women and girls *to leave* Israel for prostitution. [In order words, you can bring them in, but you cannot take them out.] Under Israel law, it is not illegal to engage in prostitution, although some laws criminalize activities associated with prostitution. The age of consent is 16. The methods by which the girls are procured, like rape, assault, abduction, and false imprisonment are criminal offenses.[390]

Children's rights activists estimate that there may be several hundred child prostitutes. There is a growing market for child pornography. It is not necessarily produced there but is imported and sold freely. [391]

Organized crime money from the former Soviet Union has been invested in Israeli real estate, businesses, and banks for the last seven years. In Israel, there is no law against laundering money or belonging to an illegal operation. This mob is profiting from prostitution. In the last few years, brothels and peepshows have arrived in Tel Aviv and Haifa. They traffick not only Russian prostitutes, but Eastern European victims and hold them in slavery-like conditions. The traffickers pay between $10,000-$15,000 for one of the victims.[392]

JORDAN is a Country of Destination.

In April 2001, Queen Rania of Jordan launched a conference on the use of children as soldiers in the Middle East and North Africa. It is the first-ever-regional conference calling on all governments worldwide to stop using children under 18-years of age as soldiers. [393]

KUWAIT is a Country of Destination.

See **Sri Lanka** note for references to **Kuwait**.

LEBANON is a Country of Transit and Destination.

According to Etienne Kashakedi, a Congolese politician, it is common to see Lebanese men buy street children for sex on the streets of Kinsasha, Congo.[394]

MOROCCO is a Country of Origin.

Teenage prostitution in urban centers has been estimated in the tens of thousands by NGO activists. [395]

OMAN is a Country of Origin.

Forced child labor has been forbidden since 1973 so it is not common to find children working. There is a market for forced child exploitation for camel jockeying. [396]

QATAR is a Country of Origin and Destination.

Mauritanian slaves are sometimes exported to Sheikhs in Qatar and the United Arab Emirates. There have been reports of children forced into camel jockeying.[397]

SAUDI ARABIA is a Country of Destination.

In mid-1997 hundreds of Indonesian women and girls, most under 20 years old, were found to be in prostitution. [398]

SYRIA is a Country of Origin.

Law does not prohibit forced child labor. There have been cases of child labor. Children were used as domestic slaves. [399]

UNITED ARAB EMIRATES (UAE) is a Country of Destination.

See **Qatar** note for reference to **UAE**.

In November 2000, Dubai Police rescued two Pakistani brothers, ages 4 and 6, who were kidnapped to work as camel jockeys. They were kidnapped from their homes in northwest Pakistan in August 2000, and flown to UAE through Iran with forged passports and false birth certificates. They were then sold to a Pakistani man in UAE for $5,445 each. In September 2000, a Pakistani boy escaped after being kidnapped to work as a camel jockey. In 1999, two boys — Pakistani and Bangladeshi — were rescued after being kidnapped to work as camel jockeys.[400]

Young Eastern European girls (Russian/Polish/Hungarian) were flown to Abu Dhabi for 30-day periods for about $30,000 under the guise of a modeling shoot. The girls were held as sex slaves. The modeling agency denies any knowledge. [401]

YEMEN is a Country of Origin and Destination.

Street children are in and around Sana. Child labour is common, especially in the commercial agricultural business. The International Labor Organization predicted that 431,000 children between the ages of 10-14 would be working in 2000. [402]

SOUTH ASIA

Most female victims are 10-15 years old. Even 4-year-old girls were abused. Some are forced to serve up to 10 customers per day. In 1990 in Southeast Asia, workers noticed that there were no 12—14-year-olds in villages. [403]

In March 2001, Radhika Coomaraswamy, an expert from Sri Lanka appointed to report to the United Nation's Human Rights Commission on violence against women released a report about women and children in Bangladesh, Nepal, and India. She interviewed young girls in brothels in Mumbai and Kolkata (Calcutta), India. Most of the girls were held against their wills, tortured, degraded, severely beaten, and repeatedly raped. They were deprived of food and water until they submitted sexually, and most were forced to service more than 10 clients a night. Not only were the boys and girls used for prostitution, but were trafficked for organ harvesting, forced into begging, forced into labor in sweatshops, forced into marriages or domestic service.

In 1992, there were about 8 million brothel workers in India and another 7.5 million call girls. The average age in the 1990s for recruitment was between 10-14, and the study goes on to say that up to half of this population may be infected with AIDs.

Although Coomaraswamy believes that laws should be strengthened to prevent, prosecute, and punish traffickers, she also contends that opportunities for financial independence are even more crucial. She also concludes that police corruption compounds the problem.

Victims claim that many police are brothel clients and on good terms with brothel owners, traffickers, and pimps. In all three countries — Bangladesh, Nepal, and India — police corruption is endemic and taken for granted. The research found that the trafficking routes were the same as the migration patterns. The governments seem serious about eradicating human trafficking, but the institutions needed to implement laws and policies were non-existent. [404]

AFGHANISTAN is a Country of Origin.

According to UNICEF, the children are traumatized by the 20-year war. Children as young as 8 and 9 have been reported in prostitution in Taliban-controlled Afghanistan. [405]

BANGLADESH is a Country of Origin.

Many children grow up on the street. Twenty-three percent of the population is between 10-19 years of age; many girls under fifteen are married off, although this is against the law. [406]

A total of 3,391 children were missing and 3,397 other children were trafficked out of the country in 2000. Of the 3,397 trafficked, 1,683 were boys. Most of the boys were under 10 and trafficked to be used as camel jockeys. In 1999, the number of kidnapped children was 987.

More girls are kidnapped than boys. The girls were kidnapped and sexually abused. Law enforces, politicians and border patrols are thought to be involved in the trade. [407]

INDIA is a Country of Origin and Destination.

A Swiss couple was arrested for luring children to perform pornographic acts for photography and film. There are links to Indian pornographic website in Canada. The Swiss couple visited Thailand and Sri Lanka.[408]

India accounts for the largest number of child prostitutes in the world (400,000 or 15 percent). They come from Bihar, West Bengal, Uttar Pradesh, Maharashtra, Karnataka, Rajasthan, Nepal, and Bangladesh. The HIV/AIDS epidemic is the main cause for the increase in demand for child prostitutes. Fifty percent are from Nepal and Bangladesh, and 50 percent are under 16 years of age. Virgins are in high demand. Child prostitutes who work for four years have had on average at least four-six abortions. Twenty percent of Mumbai brothel prostitutes are under 18 and 50 percent of them are infected with HIV.[409]

Hundreds of thousands of girls end up in brothels, or as cheap domestic labor in homes or sweatshops in India and Pakistan.

UNICEF warned India to be very wary of foreign agencies seeking to adopt orphaned children because of the earthquake. [410]

NEPAL is a Country of Origin.

A 45-year-old Nepalese man was arrested for selling over three hundred prostitutes to India over 10 years.[411]

An estimated 200,000 Nepalese girls — 30 percent are minors — work as prostitutes in Indian brothels. There is an average of 5,000-7,000 girls exported to India annually. The average age used to be 14-16 years of age; it has dropped to 10-14 years of age. Nepal is one of the most accessible areas for sex traffickers working in South and West Asia.[412]

Nepal appointed women as border patrol guards to prevent trafficking into India. Mahiti Nepal, a local NGO, has stopped more than 400 girls from crossing.[413]

Former trafficked victims stand guard on borders with India to prevent girls from being trafficked into the sex trade. These victims first took their posts in 1997. They have caught 70 smugglers and 240 girls. Some former prostitutes serviced 30 men daily. Most of the girls are 14 or 15. One victim hung herself. One victim was sold for $700 to a pimp.[414]

PAKISTAN is a Country of Destination.

There is an increase in the 10—15-year-olds as prostitute. The average age used to be fifteen. Today, there is a flourishing market of Bangladeshi girls between 8-18 years of age in Karachi Slums. Auctions are held to buy Bangladeshi, Burmese, and

Afghan girls. The younger and more beautiful girls can be bought for US$375-$500. Groups of 10-20 girls for brothels and pimps are bought for US$1,250-$5,000. The police are complicit in the prostitution market.

Seventy percent of girls in police custody experience physical and sexual abuse by police. Debt bondage is the primary tool of exploiters.[415]

SRI LANKA is a Country of Origin.

Sri Lankan girls are more literate and socially mobile than other girls in South Asia. There are 10,000 prostitutes in brothels who are 6—14-year-olds. There are another 10,000 prostitutes in tourist resorts who are 10-19 years of age. Girls are sent to Gulf Region countries, such as Saudi Arabia and Kuwait, to work as domestic workers. They live in sex slave conditions. They are also sent to India as well. [416]

Young Sri Lankan boys in fishing towns along the southern coast are the most vulnerable. Victims of foreign paedophiles range in age from 8-14. Children and their families, out of shame, are reluctant to report the crimes. In 1996, 18 school-boys were hired out to foreigners for sex. The heroin was used to lure the boys. In 2001, two Sri Lanka men were convicted and sentenced to 34 years in prison. One of the boys, 12 at the time, claimed to have been lured and hooked on heroin by a schoolteacher. He and his friends were asked to perform sex acts on three foreign men. A fourth filmed it. The boys were paid $3 each and told to go home. The group was abused three times. One music teacher showed the boys pornographic videos of boys having sex with men. The teacher gave the boys free drugs, and then offered drugs to the boys, who were then hooked, and demanded that they pay for the drugs. They could not pay so the teacher said that he would give them money if they did what they saw in the films. The boys obliged. None of the boys received professional counseling. Sri Lanka has only 35 psychiatrists and 8 psychologists.[417]

Child pornography is on the rise, even literature promoting incest and seduction of children is on the rise. In Sri Lanka, more than 100,000 children are vagrants, working in tea kiosks, restaurants, and as domestic servants. Some are used as transporters of drugs and other contraband. They are both male and female, and as young as 11. They are forced to work in the brothels. The rebel Liberation Tigers of Tamil Eelam use both boys and girls as child soldiers. Although the legislature has passed laws prohibiting child labor, it is basically unenforceable because of police corruption, bribery, and use of political influence. [418]

Paedophilia is soaring in Sri Lanka. Ninety percent of cases reported involve Sri Lankan citizens. One case reported was of a teacher impregnating a nine-year-old girl.[419]

WESTERN HEMISPHERE

CANADA is a Country of Transit and Destination.

Two convicted paedophiles, who were serving time in jail, were charged with operating a paedophile ring, from prison. It was called "The Family." It was comprised of about twenty-five paedophiles who live in Toronto. The child pornography was confiscated from the prison. The children were between 5-14 years of age. The distribution was done via mail, as opposed to the internet. In Canada, the maximum sentence for possessing and distributing child pornography is five years. The maximum sentence for manufacturing child pornography is 10 years. [420]

Approximately 1.3 million Canadian children live below the poverty line. That is up from 400,000 10 years ago. Ninety percent of child and teen prostitution is comprised of aboriginal children. [421]

UNITED STATES is a Country of Origin and Destination.

US Reports indicate that approximately 50,000 of women and girls are trafficked to the US annually in sex trade. Many are from Russia, Ukraine, Thailand, Mexico, the Czech Republic, and China. [422]

In October 2000, a US sergeant was arrested for possession and distributing child pornography. He served at the US military base at Camp Darby outside of Pisa, Italy. [423]

Three US citizens — two men and one woman — were charged with drugging, abducting, and forcing an 11-year-old girl from Oregon into prostitution in Vancouver, British Columbia. The girl was noticed "kiddie" stroll, which is one of the Red-Light Districts in the city. The girl met the three adults at a mall in Portland, Oregon weeks earlier. She was living with a foster family in Oregon and had been reported missing. The two men had attended an elite Jesuit prep school. Officers said that the younger girls usually are not put out on the streets in the unobstructed view. They are usually in "off-street" locations where they cannot be seen. The average age of entry into the prostitution in British Columbia is 14. The youngest prostitute who had been seen by the law enforcement officials up until that point was a 12-year-old.[424]

According to a US Central Intelligence Agency Report, victims trafficked to the United States usually end up in large cities, such as Los Angeles, Chicago, New York City, and Miami. Mobs in the United States that traffick women and children include syndicates from Türkiye, Pakistan, Iran, China, South America, Russia, India, North America, and Sri Lanka, which is Canada's number one source of refugee claimants. [425]

Five men, who were part of one of the largest trafficking syndicates in the United States, importing women from China, Thailand, Korea, Malaysia, and Vietnam, were convicted. The longest sentence was 33 months in jail. Part of the problem was that every one of the victims had been deported prior to trial. Had the US Attorney been able to prove that the women were coerced or forced into prostitution, the sentences may have been higher. [426]

MEXICO is a Country of Origin, Transit, and Destination.

There have not been many reports, which focus on children specifically in a country or region. This report shows six areas, and the focus was totally on the children.

Acapulco: About 1.4 percent of the girls aged 10-12 are married or living with a partner. Activities revolve around tourists. More than 500 Red-Light establishments and bars are registered, but there are plenty more that are unregistered. Girls as young as 13-17 work in bars and restaurants as waitresses. On Condesa Beach, groups of 40 or more boys from 14-17 prostitute themselves. They encounter gays from Mexico, Canada, and the US. Some of these boys are transvestites at night or work in gay bars. Some of the police extort the children.

Mexican clients pay the children less. Girls may charge 50 pesos, and the boys may charge 200 pesos. About 400 street children prostitute themselves in the city. Children leave home because they were raped, neglected, and sexual abused, use drugs, and need money. The street children who prostitute themselves are sometimes taken to hotels and locked up for weeks to make pornographic films. The children do not speak about their clients. Others, like waiters, taxi drivers, receptionists, security guards in nightclubs, valet parking attendants, street sellers, and the like offer and promote the services of the children. Their families, lovers, and pimps exploit the girls. There is a high rate of abortion. Girls 15-18 work as prostitutes for private parties.

Sometimes the children who make the films are given toys, food, a bed, occasional drugs, as well as money. Some girls go to school in the morning and work as prostitutes in the afternoon. Some children film their friends and sell the tapes commercially. Doctors claim that one-fifth of those prostituted are children.[427]

Cancun: Again, activities revolve around tourism. There are increasingly more children involved in prostitution. Adolescent boys work as transvestites in shows or as prostitutes for homosexuals. Most of the girls who prostitute themselves are 15-17. There are two groups: waitresses and dancers, and dancers are paid more. In the area around Parian, there are low-level bars and clubs. The internet promotes tourism with *escorts, both boys and girls.* There are clandestine brothels in most parts of town. Many taxi drivers are middlemen for the child prostitutes and clients. Girls who work in the hotels usually live in the hotel area. [428]

Ciudad Juarez: Violence is the second cause of death in this town. Most of the young girls who work in maquiladoras need to supplement their earnings, so they prostitute themselves. Most of the 200 murders here have occurred after rape and harassment. There is a high incidence of violence toward women here. About 4,000 girls and women work in the 350 licensed establishments. Eighty percent of these establishments are located in an area where they are 27 registered massage parlors. Boys, especially those between 12 and 17, prostitute themselves to support their drug addictions. Some older drug addicts will pimp younger children, especially girls 14-17. Cocaine is used to induce prostitution. There is a large drug community here. This area has the highest level of ill-treated children by their family members in Mexico. Many of the children go to the streets to escape familial abuse. It is common for girls as young as 13 to prostitute themselves. Their parents sell some of the children to middlemen who then sell them as adopted children to people in the United States.[429]

Guadalajara: There are approximately 2,000 street children. Eighty percent of them prostitute themselves to survive. Boys are more predominate on the street. The average age of the children is 12-17. Local gays and foreign tourists prostitute boys. There are boys as young as 7. The boys will go with foreigners in exchange for food, a bed, a roof, clothes, and higher payments if they allow themselves to be filmed. This phenomenon exists here as well as in **Puerto Vallarta.** Prosecutions are difficult because the children do not snitch on the predators. The girls prostitute themselves at the hotels. Most of them are 13-17, but there are girls as young as 8. Girls leave home because of neglect, alcoholic parents, and violence. Most of the girls take drugs and have been arrested for petty theft. Again, there are middlemen like taxi drivers and waiters, and the like. Children will prostitute themselves in the market and bus station. In 1998 there were 94 cases of rape against children aged 13-17. [430]

Tapachula: This is an area where there is a lot of illegals immigrated children who work in prostitution. Las Huacas is the Red-Light District, which is composed of 15-20 bars where prostitution is prolific. Owners pay the corrupt police. The children are sometimes locked up in the bars and prostitution establishments. Their pimps and clients make the girls drink alcohol.

Girls from Central America work in the parks and squares in the center of town. About 1,800 children work on the street. Very few local boys prostitute themselves here with homosexuals. Those who do are from Central America or neighboring regions. About 800 women prostitute themselves in brothels, and authorities suspect that of those, there are about 150 who are minor girls. Children are trafficked for illegal adoptions, sold by their families, or debt bondage. Many of the girls 15-17 work in bars and canteens and are from Guatemala, Honduras, and El Salvador. Girls as young as 13 worked in boarding houses. Many of the pimps make the girls work from 2pm-2am. [431]

Tijuana: About 70 percent of the children work on the street to survive. Some of them are 8-10 years old, although the majority are 12-17. Fifty percent of them work regularly; the others work occasionally. Most of the clients are gay people from the United States. Balboa Park is a meeting place for homosexuals, paedophiles, and children. There is a strong paedophile community in Tijuana, which defends their rights to have sex with children. Some young children take the paedophiles to other children for sex. In other words, some children are pimping. Some filmed the children. The children get paid $20 for a brief time to $200 for the full day to $300 if they are willing to be filmed. The girls working in the hotels are between the ages of 13-17. Some girls are controlled by pimps or are controlled by representatives and some work independently. There are incredibly young children in clandestine brothels. There is an extraordinarily strong link between drugs and prostitution. Young children have died of AIDS. Children are trafficked across the border. Sex tourism is a daily occurrence. The number of children prostituted is not firm, but experts believe it to be around 900.[432]

According to Caza Alliance, an NGO, thousands of children are victims of Mafias involved in child prostitution and child pornography. Children face the possibility of sterility at 12, abortion at 13, or AIDS at 14.

The Center for Research and Advanced Study in Social Anthropology counted 5,000 minors, 90 percent of them female, working in prostitution or child pornography. Sixteen and 17- year-old girls are trafficked to Chips, Mexico, for prostitution. The UN lists Mexico as the number one center for the supply of young children to North America. The majority are sent to international paedophile organizations. Most of the children over 12 ends up as prostitutes.

Mexico is one of the favored destinations of paedophile sex tourist from Europe and the United States. Well-organized networks in the Cuauhtemoc Zone, which has the highest concentration of sex trade in the country has an exploitation system where adolescents are married and then convinced to work to pay off some exceptionally incurred debts. [433]

CENTRAL AMERICA/LATIN AMERICA

There are two hundred million children under the age of 18 and 18-20 million children are under 15 years old and work full time. Almost 60 percent live in poverty. Six million aged eighteen and under are subject to physical abuse. Exploitation of children in the workplace perpetuates intergenerational poverty. [434] There is a growing child prostitution problem in Central America. Throughout Latin America, because of the substantial number of abandoned children, child sexual exploitation has increased.[435] Three years after the 1996 Brasilia Seminar, only two Latin American countries, Argentina, and Brazil, responded to the issue of child prostitution. Brazil focused on sex tourism. Argentina mobilized legislators, judges, educators, and doctors to offer support to sexually exploited children. [436]

Child rights advocate Bruce Harris, director of Caza Alliance, says that governments in Central America have paid little attention to the issue of child prostitution. [437]

ARGENTINA is a Country of Origin and Destination.

Many babies were kidnapped from their mothers while their mothers were held in military detention camps and sold to childless military couples. [438]

Child prostitution is growing at an alarming rate while the age is decreasing.[439] Sex tourism is thriving in Argentina, especially for paedophiles.[440]

BELIZE is a Country of Origin.

A human development department spokesperson claims there were rare reports of trafficking of children for prostitution. Rather, children are trafficked as migrant workers. [441]

BOLIVIA is a Country of Origin.

Child prostitution is in large numbers. [442]

Child labor is a problem in Bolivia. [443]

BRAZIL is a Country of Origin and Destination.

An estimated one million children are believed to enter the sex market. In Brazil alone, it is believed that between 500,000-2 million children are forced into prostitution. There are approximately 500,000 girls in prostitution. [444]

Portugal and Spain are the principal destinations for Brazilian women and children forced into prostitution. There are many Brazilian women in The Netherlands, Belgium, and France.

Brazil is considered the largest Latin American source of women engaged in the European sex trade. In 1998, Spanish authorities returned 461 women to Brazil. Trafficking of Brazilian women begins in neighboring Suriname.

There are reports of Brazilian prostitutes in Paraguay. [445] Some 23,000 refugees are in Brazil. Eighty percent are African. Some are from the former Yugoslavia.

A German man was arrested for allegedly trafficking three children: 2 girls, ages 2 and 10, and a 5-year-old boy. He is suspected of being involved in a pedophilia and organ trafficking syndicate. [446]

The Brazilian government pays poor families to send their children to school [as opposed to some African countries where impoverished families must pay school tuition]. [447]

In Port Murtinho, with a population of 11,000, there are 6 locations for prostitution. In Coruma, a population of 87,000, there are 16 prostitution locations.

In Campo Grande, with a population of 600,000, there are 12 prostitution locations where there are hundreds of girls in prostitution for sex tourism. They are from Sao Paulo, Goias, Parana, Minas Gerais, Paraguay, and Chile. [448]

In the northern Amazonian region, sexual exploitation of children is centered around brothels that cater to mining settlements. In the large urban centers, children, principally girls, who leave home because of abuse or sexual exploitation often prostitute themselves on the streets to survive. In the cities along the northeast coast, sexual tourism exploiting children is prevalent, and involves networks of travel agents, hotel workers, taxi drivers, and others who actively recruit children and even traffick them outside the country. Child prostitution also is developed in the areas served by the country's navigable rivers, particularly in ports and at the international borders. In port cities, crews from cargo vessels are a primary clientele. The report notes that although trafficking develops in part to meet the demands of foreigners, the local population sustains the business.[449]

CHILE is a Country of Origin.

The Chilean Ministry of Justice estimates that there are 10,000 children engaged in prostitution.

COLOMBIA is a Country of Origin.

An estimated 25,000 children — both boys and girls under the age of 18 — are prostitutes.[450]

Colombia is notorious for murdering street children. UNICEF claims that there are approximately 35,000 child prostitutes in Colombia. Sex tourism is on the rise. Middle-aged foreigners pay $10 to child prostitutes for sex. Many of these children are often addicted to drugs. [451]

Approximately 1.5 million Colombians have been turned into internal refugees due to the decades old civil war. Of those, nearly 1 million are children. Some rebels kill parents who refuse to enlist their children in the guerilla force. In Usume, a slum district on the outskirts of Bogota, a boy is killed every eight days. [452]

The Revolutionary Armed Forces of Colombia — FARC — recruits children under the age of 18 and has for years. Colombian officials claim that 50 percent of FARC fighters are underage. They send the children out first to the front line to test enemy locations and for landmines. FARC is not unique. Experts say that approximately 300,000 children have been recruited. Children are lured by promises of money, food, and social status.[453]

Six children, ages 8-10, who were on an elementary school hiking trip, were killed allegedly by rebels. [454]

COSTA RICO is a Country of Origin.

Costa Rico is emerging as sex tourism country. Consequently, the government is posting warnings on the internet. Foreigners, especially people from the United States, come to Costa Rico in search of sex with children. Adult prostitution is legal in Costa Rico. Up until 1999, sex with a child was legal. Today, if an adult has sex with a child, he may be facing up to 2-10 years in prison for child abuse.[455]

The Office of the President reports that approximately 2,500 children were being sexually exploited. In late 1999, two people from the United States in the tourist area of Quepos were charged with taking photographs of children to post on pornographic internet websites. [456]

According to Caza Alliance, an NGO, in 1999 a Costa Rican pimp was jailed for eight years after being convicted for entrapping impoverished girls into a prostitution ring.

CUBA is a Country of Origin.

Cuba has a thriving sex tourism trade and children, primarily girls as young as 13, are prostitutes. [457]

DOMINICAN REPUBLIC is a Country of Origin and Destination.

25,000 children, primarily between 12-17 years old, are prostitutes. Of that, 64 percent are girls and 36 percent are boys. [458]

There is a growing concern that individuals who are coming to adopt children may in fact be using the children for child pornography and sex trade. [459]

ECUADOR is a Country of Origin.

Children are trafficked from Ecuador to Venezuela. In 1998, the numbers were "alarming," says Vladimir Villegas, Venezuelan Parliamentarian.

There is a large sex trade, sex tourism, child prostitution, and especially with girls under 18 in urban areas. [460]

EL SALVADOR is a Country of Origin.

Network for Infants and Adolescents (RIA) found that child prostitution "is out of control, but the authorities do not recognize it." [461]

GUATEMALA is a Country of Origin.

Catholic Report states that the army — exclusively — carried out the hundreds of child abductions over the course of the 36-year civil war. [462]

It is difficult to combat child sexual exploitation because of poor legislation in Central American countries and the reluctance of children to speak out after being victimized.[463]

According to Caza Alliance, a Central American organization working with street children, the street children regularly sold themselves for sex, extensively used drugs, and almost all of them had contracted sexually transmitted diseases. Guatemala is notorious for murdering street children by authorities, as well as illegal methods of adoption.

GUYANA is a Country of Origin.

Many teenage girls are involved in prostitution. [464]

HONDURAS is a Country of Origin.

In the 1980s and 1990s, there were three hundred unsolved child killings. Police and security forces are implicated in thirty-six of the killings. Rodrigo Valladares Pineda, son of Honduras' Human Rights Commissioner, shot a 10-year-old street beggar in Teguciagalpa, Honduras' capital.[465]

Child prostitutes do not speak out because of fear of retaliation and because what they do supports their families.[466]

The largest amount of young female prostitutes is found in tourist areas of Antiqua, Tecun Umah, Panajachel.[467]

NICARAGUA is a Country of Origin.

In July 2000, the Nicaraguan Family Ministry found five hundred child prostitutes in Managua.

Approximately 150 of these children serviced at least 5 clients daily. [468]

PANAMA is a Country of Origin.

Dominican Republic girls are trafficked for prostitution to Panama. [469]

PERU is a Country of Origin.

A 14-year-old girl tells her story about working as a prostitute since 7-years of age.
[470]

It is estimated that 500,000 prostitutes are minors. [471]

SURINAME is a Country of Origin and Destination.

Young girls are trafficked and forced into prostitution. Girls are brought from the interior of the country to the city and to various mining locations in the interior. [472]

URUGUAY is a Country of Origin.

Child labor and children working as street vendors is a problem in Uruguay.[473]

VENEZUELA is a Country of Origin.

In December 1999, floods and mudslides ravaged Venezuela's central Caribbean coastline. Approximately 120 children were missing. Even though these children had been rescued and their faces were shown on television, these children were not reunited with families. It was feared that these children had been adopted mistakenly or illegally or ended up in the hands of traffickers. [474]

There is a thriving sex tourism trade, as well as child prostitution. There are estimates that 40,000 children are prostitutes, and that 22 percent are boys. [475]

Endnotes

[1] Koppel, Naomi, Associated Press, *WHO: 3M AIDS Deaths in 2000,* November 24, 2000. [2] World Health Organization 2000 Report, published by The World Health Organization. [3] Interpol Press Release, February 21, 2001.

[4] Australian Broadcasting Corporation, January 28, 2001.

[5] REPORT on the Communication from the Commission to the Council and the European Parliament, published by the European Commission, May 2, 2000.

[6] Interview with Interpol Agents, Lyon, France, July 11, 2000.

[7] www.taasa.org/currentissues/chldprostit.htm, *Social Implications of Child Prostitution,* February 26, 2001.

[8] Machel, Graca, *Impact on Armed Conflict on Children,* United Nation's 1995 Report, published by United Nations.

[9] United States Information Agency, Office of Research and Media Reaction, *Poverty in Russia: Just How Bad is It?* United States Information Agency Opinion Analysis, Washington, DC, January 12, 1999.

[10] Associated Press, *The Silent Crises,* European Children's Trust, October 12, 2000, as reported in Associated Press.

[11] Interview with International Organization of Migration Official, anonymous, Tirana, Albania, July 30, 2000.

[12] Interview with Paul Holmes, Inspector of Vice and Clubs, Metropolitan Police, London, England, June 13, 2000.

[13] Schengen Agreement of 1990; APPLYING THE SCHENGEN AGREEMENT OF 14 JUNE 1985 BETWEEN THE GOVERNMENTS OF THE STATES OF THE BENELUX ECONOMIC UNION, THE FEDERAL REPUBLIC OF GERMANY, AND THE FRENCH REPUBLIC, ON THE GRADUAL ABOLITION OF CHECKS AT THEIR COMMON BORDERS

The Kingdom of Belgium, the Federal Republic of Germany, the French Republic, the Grand Duchy of Luxembourg, and the Kingdom of The Netherlands, hereinafter called the Contracting Parties,

Taking as their basis the Schengen Agreement of 14 June 1985 on the gradual abolition of checks at their common borders,

Having decided to implement the intention expressed in that agreement of bringing about the abolition of checks at their common borders on the movement of persons and facilitating the transport and movement of goods,

Whereas the Treaty establishing the European Communities, supplemented by the Single European Act, provides that the internal market shall comprise an area without internal frontiers,

Whereas the aim pursued by the Contracting Parties coincides with that objective, without prejudice to the measures to be taken to implement the provisions of the Treaty,

Whereas the implementation of that intention requires a series of appropriate measures and close co- operation between the Contracting Parties... ."

[14] Interview with Paul Holmes, Inspector of Vice and Clubs, Metropolitan Police, London, England, June 13, 2000.

[15] Interview with John Rabun, Vice President and Chief Operating Officer, National Center for Missing & Exploited Children, Alexandria, Virginia, April 16, 2001.

[16] Interview with Dr. Louise Shelley, Professor, American University, Washington, DC, May 30, 2000. [17] Interview with Paul Holmes, Inspector of Vice and Clubs, Metropolitan Police, London, England, June 13, 2000.

[18] Interview with Paul Holmes, Inspector of Vice and Clubs, Metropolitan Police, London, England, June 13, 2000.

[19] Shelley, Dr. Louise, American University, Washington, DC, *The Exploitation and Export of Women from Russia: Scale and Scope,* March 11, 1999; *Paying the Price: Organized Crime has Exacted a Heavy Toll on Russian's Economy,* published in The Russian, April 1997, *Organized Crime in the Former Soviet Union,* published in Problems of Post- Communism, January/February 1995; Interview with Dr. Louise Shelley, Professor, American University, Washington, DC, May 30, 2000.

[20] Interview with former National Security Agency Analyst, anonymous, Washington, DC, October 2000.

[21] McLaughlin, Daniel, Reuters, *Russia's Top Prosecutor Blasts 'Corrupt' Officials,* January 12, 2001.

[22] Hitt, Jack, The New York Times, *Bandits in the Global Shipping Lanes,* August 20, 2000.

[23] Tyler, Patrick, International Tribune, *From Under a Couch, an Effort to Stop Corruption in Ukraine,* February 26, 2001.

[24] The New York Times, *German Report on Milosevic's Money Trail,* October 16, 2000.

[25] Smith, R. Jeffrey, The Washington Post, *Fall of Milosevic Sparks Hunt for Riches,* March 11, 2001.

[26] Interview with international security agent, anonymous, Washington, DC, May 26, 2000.

[27] Interview with Dr. Louise Shelley, Professor, American University, Washington, DC, May 30, 2000.

[28] Interview with Roberto, a hotel driver, Rome, Italy, July 17, 2000.

[29] E-mail to Author from anonymous former National Security Agency Agent, Spring 2001.

[30] Interview with Colonel Rizzo, Gaurdia di Finanza, Bari, Italy, July 25, 2000.

[31] Interview with Armando Ramirez, United States Customs Attaché, Rome, Italy, July 18, 2000.

[32] Interview with Alberto, a Kosovar trafficker, Brussels, Belgium, June 24, 2000.

[33] Interview with Paul Holmes, Inspector of Vice and Clubs, Metropolitan Police, London, England, June 13, 2000.

[34] Hill, Amelia, The OBSERVER, *Child Sex for Sale — Teenage Slaves Brought to Order,* January 14, 2001.

[35] Interview with Colonel Rizzo, Gaurdia di Finanza, Bari, Italy, July 25, 2000.

36 Interview with Customs Official, anonymous, London, England, August 4, 2000.

37 Interview with Alberto, a Kosovar trafficker, Brussels, Belgium, June 24, 2000.

38 ZENIT New Agency, December 19, 2000. Bishops 'Report claims that 20,000 prostitutes are in France, and 5,000-6,000 on the street. "At the European level, the Episcopal document calls on organizations to oppose the position of some states that are determined to "regulate" prostitution, to make it a job. There is no such thing as "good" or "bad" prostitution, judged differently because of the free consent of the person who prostitutes herself."

39 Interviews with David Gaylor, Detective Superintendent, Organisational Services, Sussex, England and Paul Holmes, Inspector of Vice and Clubs, Metropolitan Police, London, England, July 6, 2000.

40 Interview with anonymous expatriates working and living in Albania, Rogner Hotel, Tirana, Albania, July, August 2000.

41 Interview with United States Ambassador to Albania, The Honorable Joseph Limprecht, Tirana, Albania, August 1, 2000.

42 Interviews with anonymous expatriates, Tirana, Albania, July, August 2000.

43 Interview with Fabiola Laco-Ergo, Vice-President, Useful to Albanian Women, Tirana, Albania, July 26, 2000.

44 Interview with Francesco, a bartender, Sheraton Hotel, Bari, Italy, July 21, 2000.

45 Interview with John van Weeten, Task Force Albania, Tirana, Albania, July 30, 2000.

46 Interview with Fabiola Laco-Ergo, Vice-President, Useful to Albanian Women, Tirana, Albania, July 26, 2000.

47 Interview with Kenn Underwood, United Nations Weapons Expert, EOD Solutions, LTD, Explosive Ordnance Disposal, Essex, England, Tirana to Rome Flight, August 3, 2000.

48 Hedges, Christopher, The New York Times, July 11, 1998.

49 Hedges, Christopher, The New York Times, July 11, 1998; Flounders, Sara, International Action Center, *NATO Troops Seize Mining Complex,* August 24, 2000.

50 Flounders, Sara, International Action Center, *NATO Troops Seize Mining Complex,* August 24, 2000. 51 International Action Center, *"Why are NATO Troops Demanding to Leave Kosovo and Bosnia?"* February 10, 2001.

52 Schweid, Barry, Associated Press, *Albania PM: End Kosovo Violence,* August 23, 2000.

53 Moore, Patrick, The Balkan Report, *Companies Pledge to Build Burgas-Vlora Pipeline,* August 22, 2000.

54 Hayden, Robert, University of Pittsburgh, E-mail to author, August 4, 2000.

55 Hayden, Robert, University of Pittsburgh, E-mail to author, August 4, 2000.

56 Interview with Alberto, a Kosovar trafficker, Brussels, Belgium, June 24, 2000.

[57] Agence Europe, Brussels, EU/COUNCIL of EUROPE — Public Hearing on Trafficking of Women, April 3, 2001.

[58] Interview with Anna, a victim in a safe house, Tirana, Albania, August 2, 2000.

[59] Myers, Steven Lee, The New York Times, *Inquiry into Abuse by GIs in Kosovo Faults Training,* September 19, 2000.

[60] Bulman, Erica, Associated Press, *Abject Poverty Behind Sex Slavery Sales, says United Nations,* March 26, 2001.

[61] Interview with Nick, a Kosovar, Le Steak Restaurant, New York, June 6, 2000.

[62] Trouble & Strife, *Uncomfortable Truths,* Summer 2000. [63] Trouble & Strife, *Uncomfortable Truths,* Summer 2000. [64] Trouble & Strife, *Uncomfortable Truths,* Summer 2000.

[65] Pisik, Betsy, The Washington Times, *UN: AIDS Being Spread by its Peacekeepers,* July 8, 2000.

[66] Interview with Paul Kagame, President of Rwanda, Washington, DC, September 2000.

[67] Interview with Interpol Officials, Lyon, France, July 11, 2000.

[68] Interviews with Yrii, a driver, Tirana, Albania, July 26-August 3, 2000.

[69] Interview with Marcos, a self-proclaimed Nigerian pimp, Vienna, Austria, June 18, 2000.

[70] Simons, Marlise, The New York Times, *Balkan Gangs Stepping Up Violence, Dutch Say,* November 30, 2000.

[71] Interview with Paul Holmes, Inspector of Vice and Clubs, Metropolitan Police, London, England, June 13, 2000, July 6, 2000, and David Gaylor, Detective Superintendent, Organisational Services, Sussex, England, July 2000, conducted by Sheelagh Taylor, London, England.

[72] Interview with Massimo Sardi, Co-Director, ERASM, Etudes et Recherches Appliquees a la Sociologie et au Marketing, Geneva, Switzerland, July 12, 2000.

[73] Interview with David Gaylor, Detective Superintendent, Organisational Services, Sussex, England, London, England, July 6, 2000.

[74] Reuters, *Brussels are Albanians,* Brussels, Belgium, November 15, 1999.

[75] Interview with Marjan Huls, Amsterdam Vice Squad, Amsterdam, The Netherlands, July 27, 2000.

[76] Interview with a Madam, anonymous, Geneva, Switzerland, July 11, 2000.

[77] Agence France Presse, *Trafficking in Women and Children — Only Drugs or Illicit Arms More Profitable than Sex in Italy,* July 13, 2000.

[78] Interview with an anonymous trafficker, Vlora, Albania, July 30, 2000.

[79] Sestanovic, Muhamed, Crimes Against the Psychological Integrity of Children.

[80] Koja, G.J. HURINET, *8000 Albanian Girls Work as Prostitutes in Italy,* published by HURINET, July 25, 1998.

[81] United Press International, *British Note Albanian Refugee Smuggling,* London, England, April 7, 1998. [82] Koja, G.J., HURINET, *8000 Albanian Girls Work as Prostitutes in Italy,* published by HURINET, July 25, 1998;

International Organization for Migration, May 7, 1996; International Organization for Migration, *Trafficking in Women for Sexual Exploitation to Italy,* June 1996; Specter, Michael, The New York Times, *Traffickers 'New Cargo: Naïve Slavic Women,* January 11, 1998; Caritas, The Institute of Race Relations, London, United Kingdom, *European Race Audit Bulletin,* November 25, 1997; USA TODAY, *Pedophilia Ring Uncovered in Italy,* November 1997.

[83] Organization for Security and Cooperation in Europe, ODIHR Proposed Action Plan of Activities to Combat Trafficking in Human Beings, June 1, 2000.

[84] Fleishman, Jeffrey, The Philadelphia Inquirer, *Illegal Routes Thrive on Hopes of Millions,* published by The Philadelphia Inquirer, February 4, 2000.

[85] Interior Ministry of the Federation of Bosnia-Herzegovina, June 2000.

[86] Reuters, *Bosnian Club Raids Set 177 Women Free,* March 4, 2001.

[87] Interview with Chuck de Caro, former CNN Investigative Reporter, March 9, 2001.

[88] Interview with Philippe Boudin, Directeur, Comite Contre l'Esclavage Moderne, child migrant worker expert, Paris, France, July 3, 2000.

[89] British Broadcasting Company, April 11, 2000.

[90] Agence France Presse, May 25, 1998.

[91] Zenica, Medica — Infoteka Special edition, *"Rape — A Specific Trauma, A Specific Type of Violence: Our Work Experience with Rape Survivors in the War in Bosnia-Herzegovina,* May 1997.

[92] Potts, Carla, Youth Mine Action Ambassador, *Lest We Forget: Bosnia & Landmines,* June 6, 2000.

[93] Filipova, Rossitza Pencheva, Animus Association Foundation, *Legal Study on the Combat of Trafficking in Women for the Purpose of Forced Prostitution in Bulgaria,* March 20, 2000.

[94] United Nations Human Rights Country Profile, Bulgaria, March 1999.

[95] Simeonov, Simeon, Sofia Police Directorate, EDT, *Bulgaria Sex Club Urges Lawmakers to Legalize Prostitution,* September 12, 1997.

[96] M2 Presswire, Karajkovic, Assistant Minister of Justice, United Nations, *Women's Anti-Discrimination Committee Concludes Consideration of Croatia's Initial Report,* January 28, 1998.

[97] Reuters, *Croatia Becomes Centre for Human Smuggling,* July 6, 2000.

[98] Gall, Carlotta, The New York Times, *A Feeble Croatia Seeks to Recoup Billions Lost to Corruption,* September 3, 2000.

[99] Swardson, Anne, The Washington Post, *Croatian General Is Given 45 Years for War Crimes,* March 3, 2000.

[100] Reuters, *Croat Police Break Human Smuggling Chain,* April 7, 2001.

[101] Security Intelligence News Service, *Sex Slave Trade Serious Problem in Kosovo,* June 9, 2000.

[102] Philips, John, The TIMES, *Migrants Take the Minefield 'Package Tour,* London, England, December 6, 2000.

[103] Interview with anonymous trafficker, Paris, France, July 1, 2000.

[104] Myers, Steven Lee, The New York Times, *Inquiry into Abuse by GIs in Kosovo Faults Training,* September 19, 2000.

[105] Myers, Steven Lee, The New York Times, *Inquiry into Abuse by GIs in Kosovo Faults Training,* September 19, 2000.

[106] Agence France Presse, Trafficking in Women and Children — Internationals in Kosovo Push Up Demand for Prostitutes, June 20, 2000.

[107] Erlanger, Steven, The New York Times, *Aide Takes Stock of UN in Kosovo,* July 17, 2000.

[108] Hanson, Ivor, The New York Times, *Kosovo's Young Get by With a Little Help from the West,* February 11, 2001.

[109] McKenzie, Steve, SUNDAY MAIL, *Scots-based Commandos are Helping to Wage War Against Mafia- run Sex Slavery,* February 4, 2001.

[110] Taki's Column, New York Press, July 13, 2000.

[111] Montenegrin Women Lobby Report, *Current Situation on Sex Trafficking in Montenegro,* June 19, 2000.

[112] United Nation Report on Trafficking in Women, Montenegro, Podgorica, October 2000.

[113] A November 1999 letter written by Alexis S. Troubetzkoy, a Humanitarian, to Paul-Louis de Gendt, a Brussels restaurant owner, given to author, Brussels, Belgium, June 23, 2000.

[114] Reuters, *Romania Court Jails British Priest on Sex Charges,* July 9, 1998.

[115] McNeil, Jr., Donald G., The New York Times, *Romania, Under Pressures, Improves,* January 13, 2001.

[116] Popa, Madalina, Sanse Egale Pentru Femei, *Legal Study on the Combat of Trafficking in Women for the Purpose of Forced Prostitution in Romania,* March 2000.

[117] Popa, Madalina, *Sanse Egale Pentru Femei, Legal Study on the Combat of Trafficking in Women for the Purpose of Forced Prostitution in Romania,* March 2000.

[118] McGrory, Daniel, TIMES, *Chinese Migrants Wait for Serbs to Decide Their Fate,* October 14, 2000. [119] TIMES, *Leading Article: Enemy of the People, The Political Case for Trying Milosevic in Belgrade,* April 5, 2001.

[120] Sage, Adam, The TIMES, *Witness Recalls Day UN Troops Permitted Massacre,* April 4, 2001.

[121] United States Department of State Human Rights Report, Slovenia Report, February 2000.

[122] Interview with Tom Erents, Crime Investigator Adviser, National Police Agency, The Hague, The Netherlands, June 27, 2000.

[123] Interview with Jim Nagle and Jim Gibbons, US Customs Service Agents, Fairfax, Virginia, May 2000; Interview with Tom Erents, Crime Investigator Adviser, National Police Agency, The Hague, The Netherlands, June 27, 2000.

[124] Interview with Jim Reynolds, International Paedophilia Consultant, London, England, June 11, 2000.

[125] Interview with Tom Erents, Crime Investigation Adviser, National Police Agency, The Hague, The Netherlands, June 27, 2000; Interview with Jim Nagle and Jim Gibbons, US Customs Service Agents, Fairfax, Virginia, May 2000; Interview with Jola Vollebregt, National Police Agency, The Hague, The Netherlands, Amsterdam,

The Netherlands, June 25, 27, 2000; Interview with Carlos Schippers, National Police Agency, Amsterdam, The Netherlands, June 25, 2000.

126 Interview with Jim Reynolds, International Paedophilia Consultant, London, England, June 11, 2000.

127 Interview with John Rabun, Vice President and Chief Operating Officer, The National Center for Missing & Exploited Children, Alexandria, Virginia, April 13, 2001.

128 Interview with Jim Reynolds, International Paedophilia Consultant, London, England, June 11, 2000; Interview with Tom Erents, Crime Investigation Adviser, National Police Agency, The Hague, The Netherlands, June 27, 2000; Interview with Jola Vollebregt, National Police Agency, The Hague, The Netherlands, June 27, 2000.

129 Interview with Jim Nagle and Jim Gibbons, US Customs Service Agents, Fairfax, Virginia, May 2000.

130 Interview with Madam Colleen, Paris, France, July 2, 2000.

131 Interview with Madam Colleen, Paris, France, July 2, 2000.

132 Interview with Joseph Wolf, Senior Special Agent, US Customs Service, London, July 5, 2000.

133 Interview with Jim Reynolds, International Paedophilia Consultant, London, England, June 11, 2000; Interview with Carlos Schippers, National Police Agency, Amsterdam, The Netherlands, June 25, 2000; Interview with Marjan Huls, Amsterdam Vice Squad, Amsterdam, The Netherlands, June 28, 2000; Interview with Jola Vollebregt, National Police Agency, The Hague, The Netherlands, June 27, 2000; Interview with Tom Erents, Crime Investigation Adviser, National Police Agency, The Hague, The Netherlands, June 27, 2000.

134 Interview with Marcos, a Nigerian self-proclaimed trafficker, Vienna, Austria, June 18, 2000.

135 Interview with President Arap Moi of Kenya, Washington, DC, February 2000; Interview with The Honorable Richard Seziberra, Rwandan Ambassador to the United States, Washington, DC, October 2000. 136 Interview with Paul Holmes, Inspector of Vice and Clubs, Metropolitan Police, London, England, June 13, 2000; Interview with Maria Delaney, University College, Cork, Ireland, London, July 2000, conducted by Sheelagh Taylor; Interview with David Gaylor, Detective Superintendent, Organisational Services, Sussex, England, London, July 2000, conducted by Sheelagh Taylor; Interview with Jola Vollebregt, National Police Agency, The Hague, The Netherlands, June 27, 2000; Interview with Carlos Schippers, National Police Agency, Amsterdam, The Netherlands, June 25, 2000; Interview with Marjan Huls, Amsterdam Vice Squad , Amsterdam, The Netherlands, June 27, 2000; Interview with Merel Hoogendoorn, Campagne-coordinator, Terres des Hommes, Amsterdam, The Netherlands, June 26, 2000; Interview with Michael Looney, US Customs Service Agent, Paris, France, June 30, 2000; Interview with Vera Lesko, President, Vlora Women Hearth, London, England, July 6, 2000; Interview with Fabiola Laco- Ergo, Vice President, Useful to Albanian Women, Tirana, Albania, July 27, 2000.

137 Interview with Paul Holmes, Inspector of Vice and Clubs, Metropolitan Police, London, England, June 13, 2000; Interview with Maria Delaney, University College, Cork, Ireland, London, July 2000, conducted by Sheelagh Taylor; Interview with David Gaylor, Detective Superintendent, Organisational Services, England, London, July 2000, conducted by Sheelagh Taylor; Interview with Jola Vollebregt, National Police Agency, The Hague, The Netherlands, June 27, 2000; Interview with Carlos Schippers, National Police Agency, Amsterdam, The Netherlands, June 25, 2000; Interview with Marjan Huls, Amsterdam Vice Squad, Amsterdam, The Netherlands, June 27, 2000; Interview with Merel Hoogendoorn, Campagne-coordinator, Terres des Hommes, Amsterdam, The Netherlands, June 26, 2000; Interview with Michael Looney, US Customs Service Agent, Paris, France, June 30, 2000; Interview with Vera Lesko, President, Vlora Women Hearth, London, England, July 6,

2000; Interview with Fabiola Laco-Ergo, Vice President, Useful to Albanian Women, Tirana, Albania, July 27, 2000.

[138] Interview with Paul Holmes, Inspector of Vice and Clubs, Metropolitan Police, London, England, June 13, 2000; Interview with Maria Delaney, University College, Cork, Ireland, London, July 2000, conducted by Sheelagh Taylor; Interview with David Gaylor, Detective Superintendent, Organisational Services, Sussex, England, London, July 2000, conducted by Sheelagh Taylor; Interview with Jola Vollebregt, National Police Agency, The Hague, The Netherlands, June 27, 2000; Interview with Carlos Schippers, National Police Agency, Amsterdam, The Netherlands, June 25, 2000; Interview with Marjan Huls, Amsterdam Vice Squad, Amsterdam, The Netherlands, June 27, 2000; Interview with Merel Hoogendoorn, Campagne-coordinator Terres des Hommes, Amsterdam, The Netherlands, June 26, 2000; Interview with Michael Looney, US Customs Service Agent, Paris, France, June 30, 2000; Interview with Vera Lesko, President, Vlora Women Hearth, London, England, July 6, 2000; Interview with Fabiola Laco-Ergo, Vice President, Useful to Albanian Women, Tirana, Albania, July 27, 2000.

[139] Interview with Paul Holmes, Inspector of Vice and Clubs, Metropolitan Police, London, England, June 13, 2000; Interview with Maria Delaney, University College, Cork, Ireland, London, July 2000, conducted by Sheelagh Taylor; Interview with David Gaylor, Detective Superintendent, Organisational Services, Sussex, England, London, July 2000, conducted by Sheelagh Taylor; Interview with Jola Vollebregt, National Police Agency, The Hague, The Netherlands, June 27, 2000; Interview with Carlos Schippers, National Police Agency, Amsterdam, The Netherlands, June 25, 2000; Interview with Marjan Huls, Amsterdam Vice Squad, Amsterdam, The Netherlands, June 27, 2000; Interview with Merel Hoogendoorn, Campagne-coordinator, Terres des Hommes, Amsterdam, The Netherlands, June 26, 2000; Interview with Michael Looney, US Customs Service Agent, Paris, France, June 30, 2000; Interview with Vera Lesko, President, Vlora Women Hearth, London, England, July 6, 2000; Interview with Fabiola Laco-Ergo, Vice President, Useful to Albanian Women, Tirana, Albania, July 27, 2000.

[140] Interview with Paul Holmes, Inspector of Vice and Clubs, Metropolitan Police, London, England, June 13, 2000; Interview with Maria Delaney, University College, Cork, Ireland, London, July 2000, conducted by Sheelagh Taylor; Interview with David Gaylor, Detective Superintendent, Organisational Services, Sussex, England, London, July 2000, conducted by Sheelagh Taylor; Interview with Jola Vollebregt, National Police Agency, The Hague, The Netherlands, June 27, 2000; Interview with Carlos Schippers, National Police Agency, Amsterdam, The Netherlands, June 25, 2000; Interview with Marjan Huls, Amsterdam Vice Squad, Amsterdam, The Netherlands, June 27, 2000; Interview with Merel Hoogendoorn, Campagne-coordinator, Terres des Hommes, Amsterdam, The Netherlands, June 26, 2000; Interview with Michael Looney, US Customs Service Agent, Paris, France, June 30, 2000; Interview with Vera Lesko, President, Vlora Women Hearth, London, England, July 6, 2000; Interview with Fabiola Laco-Ergo, Vice President, Useful to Albanian Women, Tirana, Albania, July 27, 2000.

[141] Interview with Max Guido, the Secretary General of Caritas Diocesana, Rome, Italy, July 20, 2000.

[142] Interview with Roberto, a hotel driver in Rome, Italy, July 18, 2000.

[143] Documentary shown to author and translated by Jola Vollebregt, National Police Agency, The Hague, The Netherlands, June 27, 2000, produced and released by Dutch Television, 2000.

[144] Interviews with victims in Albanian safe house, Tirana, Albania, August 2, 2000. [145] Interviews with victims in Albanian safe house, Tirana, Albania, August 2, 2000. [146] Interviews with victims in Albanian safe house, Tirana, Albania, August 2, 2000.

[147] Interview with Antoinette Looney, wife of Michael Looney, US Customs Service Agent, Paris, France, July 4, 2000.

[148] Interview with Paul Holmes, Inspector of Vice and Clubs, Metropolitan Police, London, England, June 13, 2000.

[149] Interviews with victims and prostitutes throughout the summer of 2000 in London, England, Vienna, Austria, Brussels, Belgium, Amsterdam, The Netherlands, Paris, France, Milano, Roma, Naples, Bari, Lecce, Brindisi, and Tuscany, Italy, Geneva, Switzerland, Tirana, Durres, Vlora, and Berat, Albania; Interviews with boys at the Il Faro Foundation, Rome, Italy, July 18, 2000.

[150] Osava, Mario, Inter Press Service, *Trafficking in Humans — A 7.0 Billion-Dollar Business,* November 29, 2000.

[151] *Knaus/Kartusch/Reiter,* Combat of Trafficking in Women for the Purposes of Forced Prostitution, Boltzmann Institute of Human Rights, Vienna 2000.

[152] The International Criminal Tribunal for Rwanda, Indictment and Sentencing documents for Jean Paul Adayesu, 1996 and 1998.

[153] Reuters, *UN Court Convicts Bosnian Serbs in Rape,* February 22, 2001.

[154] Interview with Mark Talisman, Vice Chairman of the Holocaust Museum, Washington, DC, March 9, 2001.

[155] Levchenko, Kateryna, *La Strada Ukraine, Legal Study on the Combat of Trafficking in Women for the Purpose of Forced Prostitution in Ukraine*, December 1999, page 22, footnote 28.

[156] REPORT on the communication from the Commission to the Council and the European Parliament "For further actions in the fight against trafficking in women," Committee on Women's Rights and Equal Opportunities, published by European Commission, May 2, 2000.

[157] Interview with Dr. Louise Shelley, Professor, American University, Washington, DC, May 30, 2000; Interview with Paul Holmes, Inspector of Vice and Clubs, Metropolitan Police, London, England, June 13, 2000.

[158] The Report of the Secretary-General, General Assembly of the United Nations, 50th Session, published by the United Nations, 1995.

[159] Interview with David Ould, Anti-Slavery Organization, London, England, June 13, 2000.

[160] As defined by Human Rights Standards for The Treatment of Trafficked Person, prepared by the Foundation Against Trafficking in Women, the International Human Rights Law Group, and the Global Alliance Against Traffick in Women, published by the Foundation Against Trafficking in Women.

[161] Machel, Graca, *Impact of Armed Conflict on Children,* United Nations Report, 1995, published by the United Nations.

[162] Agence France Presse, August 31, 2000.

[163] Interview with Paul Holmes, Inspector of Vice and Clubs, Metropolitan Police, London, England, June 13, 2000.

[164] Interview with Jola Vollebregt, National Policy Agency, The Hague, The Netherlands, June 27, 2000.

[165] Interview with Paul Holmes, Inspector of Vice and Clubs, Metropolitan Police, London, England, June 13, 2000; Interview with Carlos Schippers, National Police Agency, Amsterdam, The Netherlands, June 25, 2000; Interview with Jola Vollebregt, National Police Agency, Amsterdam, The Netherlands and The Hague, The Netherlands, June 25 and 27, 2000; Interview with David Gaylor, Detective Superintendent, Organisational Services, Sussex, England, London, July 9, 2000; Interview with anonymous Belgium law enforcement officials, June 19, 2000; Interview with Colonel Rizzo, Gaurdia di Finanza, Bari, Italy, July 25, 2000; Interview with Interpol Officials, Lyon, France, July 11, 2000; Interview with John Rabun, Vice President and Chief Operating Officer, The National Center for Missing & Exploited Children, Alexandria, Virginia, April 16, 2001; Interview with Jim Nagle and Jim Gibbons, US Customs Service Agents, Fairfax, Virginia, June 8, 2000; Interview with Tom Erents, Crime Investigation Adviser, National Police Agency, The Hague, The Netherlands, June 27, 2000; Interview with Marjan Huls, Amsterdam Vice Squad, Amsterdam, The Netherlands, June 28, 2000.

[166] Austad, Jan, Interpol, E-mail to author, August 25, 2000.

[167] Tarm, Michael, The New York Times, June 13, 2000.

[168] Interview with Armando Ramirez, US Customs Service Attaché, Rome, Italy, July 18, 2000.

[169] Cushman, John J., The New York Times, *Reputed Head of Drug Ring Taken to U.S. After Arrest,* August 27, 2000.

[170] Doland, Angela, Associated Press, *Interpol Looks for New Direction in Fighting Cybercrime,* October 14, 2000.

[171] Interpol website, www.interpol.com, June 2000 and February 2001.

[172] Interview with Interpol officials, July 11, 2000.

[173] Interview with Jola Vollebregt, National Police Agency, The Hague, The Netherlands, June 27, 2000.

[174] Interview with Armando Ramirez, US Customs Service Attaché, Rome, Italy, July 18, 2000.

[175] Shelley, Dr. Louise, American University Professor, Washington, DC, Problems of Post-Communism, *Organized Crime in the Former Soviet Union,* January/February 1995.

[176] Interview with Jola Vollebregt, National Police Agency, Amsterdam and The Hague, The Netherlands, June 25 and 27, 2000.

[177] Interview with John Rabun, Vice President and Chief Operating Officer, The National Center for Missing & Exploited Children, Alexandria, Virginia, April 16, 2001.

[178] Interview with Jim Nagle and Jim Gibbons, US Customs Service Agents, Fairfax, Virginia, June 8, 2000.

[179] Interview with US Customs Service Agents in Paris, Rome, London, summer of 2000 and O'Neill, Sean, Daily Telegraph, *Girl, 8, Raped to Order on the Internet Sex Show Attack Led to Downfall of Paedophile Club.* February 14, 2001.

[180] Graff, Peter, Reuters News Service, December 21, 2000, *Russian Police Crack U.S., Europe Child Porn Ring.*

[181] Interview with Interpol officials, Lyon, France, July 11, 2000.

[182] Interview with Interpol officials, Lyon, France, July 11, 2000.

[183] Simonsson, Lennart, Associated Press, *Swedish Police Uncover Paedophile Ring,* January 17, 2001. [184] Rabun, John, Vice President and Chief Operating Officer of National Center for Missing & Exploited Children, Internal National Center for Missing & Exploited Children Memo, January 11, 2001.

[185] Ananova, *Mother Jailed Over Internet Chat Room Under-Age Sex,* April 10, 2001.

[186] Veysey, Wayne, PA News, *Taskforce Launched to Combat Internet Paedophiles,* March 28, 2001. [187] Interview with Paul Holmes, Inspector of Vice and Clubs, Metropolitan Police, London, England, August 4, 2000.

[188] Interview with Doris Stoisser, Austrian journalist, Vienna, Austria, June 18, 2000.

[189] Interview with John Rabun, Vice President and Chief Operating Officer, National Center for Missing & Exploited Children, Alexandria, Virginia, April 16, 2001.

[190] Interview with John Rabun, Vice President and Chief Operating Officer, National Center for Missing & Exploited Children, Alexandria, Virginia, April 16, 2001

[191] Presentation of Henk J. Hagen to the Eleventh Meeting of the Interpol Standing Working Party Offences Against Minors, Lyon, France, May 1998; Letter from Henk J. Hagen at Interpol to Sabrina Deligia, a journalist, August 26, 1999.

[192] Presentation of Henk J. Hagen to the Eleventh Meeting of the Interpol Standing Working Party Offences Against Minors, Lyon, France, May 1998; Letter from Henk J. Hagen at Interpol to Sabrina Deligia, a journalist, August 26, 1999.

[193] Presentation of Henk J. Hagen to the Eleventh Meeting of the Interpol Standing Working Party Offences Against Minors, Lyon, France, May 1998; Letter from Henk J. Hagen at Interpol to Sabrina Deligia, a journalist, August 26, 1999.

[194] Presentation of Henk J. Hagen to the Eleventh Meeting of the Interpol Standing Working Party Offences Against Minors, Lyon, France, May 1998; Letter from Henk J. Hagen at Interpol to Sabrina Deligia, a journalist, August 26, 1999.

[195] Presentation of Henk J. Hagen to the Eleventh Meeting of the Interpol Standing Working Party Offences Against Minors, Lyon, France, May 1998; Letter from Henk J. Hagen at Interpol to Sabrina Deligia, a journalist, August 26, 1999.

[196] Nationwide New Proprietary Ltd., 2001, The Australian, *India: Indian Children Fall Easy Prey to Paedophiles,* April 12, 2001.

[197] Hinchey-Bancroft, Timothy, Pravda Ru, *UN Organization: Statistics Quote 300,000 Child Prostitutes in USA,* December 12, 2000.

[198] Zenit.org, *Salesian Assails Sexual Tourism in Third World,* October 9, 2000.

[199] Interviews with United States Customs Service Agents, Fairfax, Virginia, June 8, 2000, and Paul Holmes, Inspector of Vice and Clubs, Metropolitan Police, London, England, June 13, 2000.

[200] Interview with Nigerian traffickers, Vienna, Austria, June 18, 2000.

[201] United Nation Human Rights Country Profile, Belgium, September 1999.

[202] Reuters, *Belgian Paedophile Dutroux Sentenced for Escape,* June 19, 2000.

203 Associated Press, *Dutroux Case on Child Sex Murders to go on Trial in 2002,* January 30, 2001.

204 Casert, Raf, Associated Press, *Senate Uncovers Exploitation of Brazilian, African,* March 19, 2001.

205 Asian Daily News, February 17, 2001.

206 Ford, Richard, The Times, *French to Reduce Police at Ports,* January 29, 2001.

207 Thiessen, Tamara, Singapore Press Holding, Ltd., *France — Land of Lost Children,* October 20, 2000.

208 Xinhua News Agency, November 8, 2000.

209 International Tribune, January 8, 2001.

210 Rodriguex, Zoriada Ramirez, Report from Latin America, *Making the Harm Visible, Global Sexual Exploitation of Women and Girls, Speaking Out and Providing Services,* Published by The Coalition Against Trafficking in Women, February 1999.

211 Cohen, Roger, The New York Times, *The Oldest Profession Seeks New Market in West Europe,* September 19, 2000.

212 Ceska Tiskova Kancelar, June 28, 2000.

213 Ceska Tiskova Kancelar, December 1, 2000.

214 Cohen, Roger, The New York Times, *Most Recent Killing May Push Germans to Act on Hate Crime,* August 21, 2000.

215 Cohen, Roger, The New York Times, *Germans Faults 'Silence 'About Attacks on Immigrants,* July 31, 2000.

216 Ceska Tiskova Kancelar, *Schily Complains about Poor Cooperation Against Child Sex,* July 15, 2000.

217 Paterson, Tony, The Guardian, *For Germans 'Using Under-Age Prostitutes,* December 19, 2000.

218 Radio Prague/Central Europe Online, *Child Prostitution: Czech, German Ministers Unite Efforts,* April 9, 2001.

219 Interview with Eva Eberhardt, Principal Associate, ACE Associates, London, England, October 4, and 7, 2000.

220 United Nation Human Rights Country Profile, Ireland, 2000.

221 Interview with Grace Cerutti, US Customs Service Agent, Rome, Italy, July 18, 2000. 222 British Broadcasting Company, *Italy Prepares for Refugee Onslaught,* March 27, 1999. 223 British Broadcasting Company, *Boats Collide off Italian Coast,* May 27, 1999.

224 Johnson, Richard with Paul Froelich and Chris Wilson, The New York Post, *3 Busted in Milan Rape of Model, 15,* March 2, 2001.

225 Hancock, Julia, Reuters, *Italy Charges 1,491 in Internet Pedophilia Case,* October 28, 2000.

226 Olson, Elizabeth, The New York Times, *Liechtenstein Found to Be Lax in Monitoring of Bank Deals,* September 1, 2000.

227 Interview with private driver in London, August 3, 2000.

[228] Factbook on Global Sexual Exploitation — The Netherlands, 2000.

[229] Reuters, *Dutch Police Arrest Three in Large Child Porn Raid,* November 1, 2000.

[230] Foreign Information Division, Ministry of Foreign Affairs, *Dutch Policy on Prostitution Questions and Answers,* 2000.

[231] Agence France Presse, July 16, 1998.

[232] Associated Press, *Death-Prostitution,* March 25, 2000.

[233] Interview with self-proclaimed Nigerian pimps and traffickers in Vienna, Austria, June 18, 2000.

[234] Olson, Elizabeth, The New York Times, *Switzerland Freezes Shady $1 Billion in a Year,* June 27, 2000.

[235] Interview with Eva Eberhardt, Principal Associate, ACE Associates, London, England, October 4 and 7, 2000.

[236] Deutsch, Anthony, Associated Press, *Dutch Open Proceedings Against Nine Suspects in Dover Human Trafficking Case,* March 5, 2001.

[237] Hoge, Warren, The New York Times, *Dutch Truck Driver Sentenced in Chinese Immigrant Deaths,* April 6, 2001.

[238] Reuters, *Foreign Prostitutes Become Sex Slaves in Britain,* June 2, 2000.

[239] Interview with David Gaylor, Detective Superintendent, Organisational Services, Sussex, England, London, England, July 6, 2000; Child Labor Law News Service, posted to web at allAfrica.com, *Checks Tightened on Voodoo Girls Caught in Sex,* April 3, 2001.

[240] Associated Press, *Danish Detain 37 for Child Porn,* September 14, 2000.

[241] The Washington Times, July 2000.

[242] Interview with Derrick Patagen, tourist who visited Finland and Estonia in August 2000, Washington, DC, September 17, 2000.

[243] Coalition Against Trafficking in Women Fact Book, citing Norwegian consulate in Murmansk, "statement by the Network North Against Prostitution and Violence."

[244] Latvia News Agency, *Ruthless Sexual Abuse of Children All Around the Baltic Sea,* January 18, 2001. [245] Interview with Eva Eberhardt, Principal Associate, ACE Associates, London, England, October 4 and 7, 2000.

[246] Sybnerova, Stanislave and Sheu, Harald, Charles University Prague, *Legal Study on the Combat of Trafficking in Women for the Purpose of Forced Prostitution in the Czech Republic,* September 1999. [247] Ceska Tiskova Kancelar, December 1, 2000.

[248] Ceska Tiskova Kancelar, October 10, 2000.

[249] Ceska Tiskova Kancelar, *Police Cooperate with NGOS in Fighting Pimping,* November 29, 2000. [250] Cohen, Roger, The New York Times, *The Oldest Profession Seeks New Market in West Europe,* September 19, 2000.

[251] Feher, Lenke, Institute for Legal Sciences of the Hungarian Academy of Sciences, National Institute Criminology, University of Miskolv, *Legal Study on the Combat of Trafficking in Women for the Purpose of Forced Prostitution in Hungary,* 2000.

[252] Kirk, Karl Peter, South China Morning Post, *Hungary: Trade in Women Spurs Action by UN,* September 7, 2000.

[253] Polish News Agency, *Polish Police Detain More Than 20 Foreigners Involved in the Trafficking of Women for Sex Exploitation,* September 6, 2000.

[254] Erlanger, Steven, The New York Times, *Poland finds Itself the Border Copy of West Europe,* August 28, 2000.

[255] Deutsche Presse Agentur, *Alien Smuggling Via Poland on Decline,* June 19, 2000.

[256] Finkel, Andrew, The Times, *Fifty Migrants Missing off Turkish Coast,* January 2, 2001.

[257] Associated Press, *Death-Prostitution,* March 25, 2000.

[258] Frantz, Douglas, Istanbul Journal, *Flotsam Adrift on Anceitn Streets: A City 's Young,* August 29, 2000.

[259] United Press International, December 1997, citing by Coalition Against Trafficking in Women, Greece — Facts on Trafficking and Prostitution.

[260] Papasotiriou, Alexis, Radio Free Europe, *Greece: Private Business Invest in Balkan Economies,* October 25, 1999.

[261] Associated Press, *Greek Police Detain Kurdish Illegals,* November 19, 2000.

[262] British Broadcasting Company, World, August 1, 1999.

[263] Liste Afrique, August 5, 1999.

[264] International Herald Tribune, *West Africa Awaits Sign from Child Slave 's Ship,* April 16, 2001; Reuters, *No Child Slaves Are Found as Ship Reaches Benin,* April 17, 2001.

[265] Interview with The Honorable Ambassador Richard Seziberra, Rwandan Ambassador to the United States, March 18, 2001.

[266] United States Human Rights Reports for 1999: Botswana, United States Department of State, February 25, 2000.

[267] United States Department of Labor, *Prostitution of Children,* 1996; WAO- Afrique, *Child Trafficking in West and Central Africa,* submission to the United Nations Working Group on Contemporary Forms of Slavery, published by the United Nations, June 1999.

[268] Promotion de l'Enfant et de l'Environement and L'Action Sociale et Developpement.

[269] Panafrican News Agency, *International Labour Organization Report Points to Evils of Child Trafficking,* April 11, 2001.

[270] Central African Republic's Report to the United Nations Committee on the Rights of the Child, published by the United Nations, October 2000.

[271] United States Department of State, Human Rights Report, Central African Republic, 1999.

272 United States Human Rights Report for 1999: Chad, United States Department of State, February 25, 2000.

273 Interview with Nigerian pimps and traffickers in Vienna, Austria, June 18, 2000.

274 Panafrican News Agency, *Child Laboour, a Blight in Cote D 'Ivoire,* December 26, 2000.

275 Lederer, Edith M., Associated Press, *UN: Congo Crisis Affecting Millions,* November 29, 2000.

276 Allio, Emmy, New Vision, *Uganda to Hand Over Congo Kids Tomorrow,* February 21, 2001.

277 Panafrican News Agency, *Des Enfants "Transparents" dans les Rues de Kinshasa,* March 6, 2001.

278 Committee on Rights of the Children Report for Djibouti, published by United Nations, May 30, 2000.

279 United States Department of State Country Profile, Equatorial Guinea, February 25, 2000.

280 Matloff, Judith, Christian Science Monitor, *In Africa, Money Is not Only Reason Young Girls are Sexually Exploited,* September 12, 1996.

281 Gebriel, Alem W., The Daily Monitor, Opinion, *Exploitation of Child Labour Needs Due Attention,* February 20, 2001.

282 Badjan, Isatour, The Independent, *Discourse with a Sociologist,* Banjul, The Gambia, April 12, 2001. 283 Coalition against Trafficking of Women Fact Book, citing Samuel Saprong, *Women Take Initiative to Better Their Lot: Human Rights,* Africa News, June 1998).

284 United Nations Integrated Regional Information Network, Distributed by All African Global Media, *Child Traffickers Arrested,* April 12, 2001.

285 Afrifa, Dr. A., Department of Psychology, University of Ghana, Ghanaian Chronicle (Accra), *Child Rape: A National Disgrace,* April 4, 2001.

286 Farah, Douglas, The Washington Post, *Refugee Tide Swells in West Africa,* February 13, 2001.

287 Okoko, Tervil, Panafrican News Agency, *Man Kills Wife to Sell Their Baby,* September 21, 2000.

288 Reuters, *United Nations Appeal for Food Aid for Four Million Kenyans,* February 15, 2001.

289 Interview with David Ould, Anti-Slavery Organization in London, England, June 13, 2000.

290 Group Interview at the Center for Population Development Assistance, organized by Maria Nagorski, May 26, 2000.

291 www.globalmarch.org/worstformsreport/world/lesotho, April 13, 2001

292 Onishi, Norimitsu, New York Times, *Guinea in Crises as Area 's Refugees Pour In,* February 20, 2001. 293 United States Department of State, Human Rights Reports, 1999; United Nations, Concluding Observations on Madagascar.

294 Interview with Bob Griffin, retired businessman, Londolozi Game Reserve, South Africa, April 2, 2001.

295 www.globalmarch.org/worstformsreport/world/Mali, April 13, 2001.

296 United States Department of Labor, *Prostitution of Children,* 1996.

[297] Ackbarally, Nassseem, Panafrican News Agency, *Report Says Child Prostitution Rampant in Mauritius,* October 9, 2000.

[298] Davidson, Howard, Board Member, International Centre for Missing & Exploited Children, *Memo to International Centre for Missing & Exploited Children,* September 14, 2000, presented in London, England, October 5, 2000.

[299] www.globalmarch.org/worstformsreport/world/Niger, April 13, 2001.

[300] Bassey, Okon, African News Service, *Human Trafficking,* August 7, 2000.

[301] The NEWS (Lagos), *Obasanjo Had Goose Pimples; Interview with Mrs. Titi, M*arch 28, 2001.

[302] Reuters, *Nigerian Flog Muslim Girl,* January 27, 2001.

[303] United States Department of State, *Human Rights Report,* 1999.

[304] Interview with The Honorable Richard Seziberra, Rwandan Ambassador to the United States, Washington, DC, October 30, 2000.

[305] United Nations Integrated Regional Information Network, *Adopted Orphans Exploited and Tormented,* April 2, 2001.

[306] Panafrican News Agency, *African NGOs Meet on Child Abuse,* February 5, 2001.

[307] Interview with Paul Holmes, Inspector of Vice and Clubs, Metropolitan Police, London, England, June 13, 2000.

[308] Fofana, Lansana, Inter Press Service, *Militia Admits Recruiting Child Soldiers,* June 29, 2000.

[309] Ghanaian Times, August 11, 1999.

[310] Wren, Christopher, The New York Times, *UN Weighs Return to Somalia to Aid Leaders,* January 12, 2001.

[311] Nation Multimedia Group Public Co., Ltd, THE NATION (Bangkok) *Thai Women Rescued from Abroad,* November 30, 2000.

[312] Davidson, Howard, Board Member, International Centre for Missing & Exploited Children, *Memo to International Centre for Missing & Exploited Children,* September 14, 2000.

[313] Swindells, Steven, Reuters, *Child Sex Trafficking on Rise in South Africa,* December 5, 2000.

[314] Dynes, Michael, The Times, *Mbeki Agrees Drug Plan for HIV Babies,* January 27, 2001.

[315] World Entertainment News Network, December 21, 2000.

[316] Brummer, Stefaans, Mail and Guardian, *Sports Bodies Kept on Paedophile,* October 20, 2000.

[317] British Broadcasting Company, News, *Cape Town Mayor Resigns Over Pornography,* September 13, 2000.

[318] Swindells, Steve, Reuters, *Child Sex Trafficking on Rise in South Africa,* November 23, 2000.

[319] SAPA Domestic News Wire, *South Africa: Child Sex Lucrative Market — Report,* November 22, 2000.

[320] Cauvin, Henri, The New York Times, *South Africa Veils Crime Date, Faulting System,* August 3, 2000. [321] Molo Songololo Report to the 13th International Congress on Child Abuse and Neglect, *Trafficking of Children for Sexual Exploitation,* September 2000.

322 United Nations Integrated Regional Information Network, Distributed by All Africa Global Media, *Harassment and Rape Hampering Girls' Education,* March 28, 2001.

323 Samayende, Sizwe, African Eye News Service, *Mandela Children's Fund Supports Anti-Rape Group,* April 11, 2001.

324 Panafrican News Agency, *Child Porno TV Show Causes Anguish in South Africa,* March 29, 2001.

325 Interview with Swaziland Ambassador to the United States, Spring 2000.

326 Molo Songololo Report to the 13th International Congress on Child Abuse and Neglect, *Trafficking of Children for Sexual Exploitation,* September 2000.

327 Miller, Steve, The Washington Times, *NAACP to Call for Sanctions on Sudan,* February 7, 2001.

328 The New York Times, Editorial, January 13, 2001.

329 Inter Press Service, July 25, 1997.

330 Bangkok Post, *Thai Girls Lured to Sex Trade in Africa,* August 24, 1998; Vandeberg, St. Petersburg Times, *Invisible Women Shown in Russia's Demographics,* October 13, 1997.

331 African News Agency, *Child Peddling Serious Problem in Togo and Benin,* March 23, 1998.

332 Amnesty International, *Uganda: Stolen Children, Stolen Lives,* September 18, 1997.

333 Child Rights Information Network, *Exploited Children in Uganda,* March 6, 2001.

334 Nalumansi, Lillian, New Vision, *Uganda: Street Children Rise,* March 3, 2001.

335 Matloff, Judith, Christian Science Monitor, *In Africa, Money Is not Only Reason Young Girls Are Sexually Exploited,* September 12, 1996.

336 d'Arcy, Susan, Sunday Times, *Sex Curb on the Way,* December 17, 1995.

337 Nationwide General News; Federal Parliament, *Stiff Jail Terms Set for Sex Slavery,* June 29, 1999.

338 Australian Associated Press, *Man in Court Over Thai Child-Sex Tourism,* January 25, 2001.

339 Handshin, Mia, Advertiser, *Our Shame of Sexually Exploited Children,* May 23, 2000.

340 Darragh, David, West Australian, *Teacher Filmed Girl Rape,* December 8, 2000.

341 Harden, Blaine, The New York Times, *Burmese, Repression, AIDS and Denial,* November 14, 2000.

342 Gray, Laurence, Commentary, The Los Angeles Times, *The Dark Side of Tourism Preys on the Children of Cambodia,* December 12, 2000.

343 Reuters, *Cambodia Vows to Crack Down on Sex Tourism,* September 26, 2000.

344 Johnson, Kay, South China Morning Post, *Paedophile's Light Sentence Weakens Crackdown,* November 22, 2000.

345 Reuters, *United States Man Charged with Raping Underage Cambodian Girl,* December 17, 2000. 350 Associated Press, *Briton Tried Behind Closed Doors in Pedophilia Case,* November 20, 2000.

347 Reuters, *China Gang Leaders Get Death for Women Trafficking,* October 21, 2000.

348 Harder, James, INSIGHT Magazine, October 2000.

349 Gall, Carlotta, The New York Times, *China's Migrants Find Europe's Open Back Door,* August 22, 2000.

350 Rosenthal, Elisabeth, The New York Times, *Despite High Risk, Chinese Go West,* 2000.

351 Mydans, Seth, The New York Times, *Sexual Violence as Tool of War: East Timor's Women Pay a Toll,* March 21, 2001.

352 Antara, Asia Pulse Pte, Ltd., *Child Prostitution Attracting Foreign Businessmen,* April 10, 2001.

353 Associated Press, *Japanese Ringleader of Nude-Model Internet,* November 30, 2000.

354 Inter Press Service, *Japanese — Tougher Laws Sought on Child Pornography,* June 16, 2000.

355 Reuters, *Singapore Arrests All-Woman Porn Syndicate Suspects,* January 10, 2001.

356 International Labour Organization — Country Paper: Mongolia, September 1999; United States Department of State, Human Rights Report, Mongolia, 1999.

357 New Zealand Herald, *Natural Born Killer at 15,* February 17, 2000; New Zealand Herald, *Police Raid Parlor Using Thai Prostitutes,* April 6, 1999; Coalition Against Trafficking in Women-Asia Pacific, Trafficking in Women and Prostitution in the Asia Pacific, 1996.

358 Mulrooney, Paul, New Zealand Watchdog Group, Interactive Association of New Zealand, *Foreign Help to Fight Pornography,* January 6, 2001.

359 Agnote, Dario, Kyodo News, Sex *Trade Key Part of S.E. Asian Economies,* August 18, 1998; Gabriela, Diana Mendoza, TODAY, *RP Has 400,000 Prostitutes,* February 25, 1998; Kane, June, *Sold for Sex,* 1998; Coalition Against Trafficking in Women Fact Book, citing Sol. F. Juvida, *Philippines — Children: Scourge of Child Prostitution,* Inter Press Service, October 12, 1997, citing UNICEF and NGO sources; Dallon, David, *Sex in Manila; Just One More Growth Industry,* Ending Child Prostitution, Pornography and Trafficking Bulletin, March 1997; Coalition Against Trafficking in Women Fact Book, citing *375,000 Filipino Women and Kids Are into Prostitution,* Philippine Daily Inquirer, July 26, 1997; Ending Child Prostitution, Pornography, and Trafficking Bulletin, *Manila Imposes Heavy Term on Aust Paedophile,* March-April, 1996; Coalition Against Trafficking in Women Fact Book, citing Lira S. Dalagin, *150 Pinays Sold as Sex Slaves in Africa,* Manila Chronicle, May 31, 1995, citing Bureau of Immigration; NGO Coalition for Monitoring the CRC, Supplementary Report on the Implementation of CRC, submission to the United Nations, published by the United Nations, January 1995; Manila News Bulleting, November 22, 1990.

360 Kyodo News, September 23, 1998.

361 Nation Multimedia Group Public Co., Ltd. THE NATION (Bangkok) *Thai Women Rescued from Abroad,* November 30, 2000.

362 Bai-Ngern, Pongsak, Nation Multimedia Group Public Co., Ltd, THE NATION (Bangkok), *Child-Sex Scandal Rocks the Senate,* January 20, 2001; Associated Press, *Senator Surrenders to Police on Child Sex,* January 23, 2001.

363 Morley, Mary, The Daily Universe, Brigham Young University, *BYU Professor says Sexual Slavery a Growing Problem,* March 8, 2001.

364 International Tribune, January 8, 2001.

365 Ending Child Prostitution, Pornography and Trafficking International, 1999, *A Step Forward;* United States Department of State, Human Rights Report, Armenia, 1999.

366 Carpenter, Dave, Associated Press, *Baku Looks to Prosper from Oil,* October 12, 1997.

367 Ending Child Prostitution, Pornography and Trafficking Newsletter, May 1999; United Nations CRC, Comments on Belarus, 1994.

368 World Congress Against the Commercial Exploitation, August 1996; Karlen, Helena and Christene Hagnen, Ending Child Prostitution, Pornography and Trafficking International, *Commercial Sexual Exploitation of Children in Some Eastern European Countries,* March 1996.

369 McNeil, Jr., Donald G., The New York Times, *Estonia's President: Un-Soviet and Unconventional,* April 7, 2001.

370 Kazakh Commercial, TV, British Broadcasting Company, Mercyhurst, September 3, 2000.

371 Associated Press, *Thousands of Women left Kyrgystan to Work,* December 21, 2000.

372 Ending Child Prostitution, Pornography and Trafficking Bulletin, citing the GUARDIAN, August 1996.

373 Associated Press, WORLD STREAM, August 31, 2000.

374 Associated Press, *Human Rights Group says Trafficking in Women Remain,* June 15, 2000.

375 United States Department of State, Human Rights Report, 1999.

376 Allenova, Oga and Marina Oborina, World Press Service, *Russia: Slaves of Shari'ah,* March 30, 2000.

377 Warnecke, Grace, Winrock Foundation, Kyiv, Russia, E-mail to Author, August 14, 2000.

378 Graff, Peter, Independent Newspapers (UK) Limited, *UK: Child Porno Videos Sold from Russia in 'National Geographic 'Boxes,* March 27, 2001.

379 Ceska Tiskova Kancelar, *Czech Photographer Sentenced for Child Pornography in Slovakia,* December 9, 2000.

380 Burcikova, Petra, Koollarova, Henrieta, and Kruzlizkova, Tatiana, *Legal Study on the Combat of Trafficking in Women for the Purpose of Forced Prostitution in Slovakia,* September 1999.

381 United States Department of State Human Rights Report, Turkmenistan, February 25, 2000.

382 Estes, Richard J., University of Pennsylvania, *Combat of Trafficking in Women for the Purpose of Forced Prostitution: Ukraine Country Report,* October 2000.

383 Levchenko, Kateryna, La Strada Ukraine, *Legal Study on the Combat of Trafficking in Women for the Purpose of Forced Prostitution in Ukraine,* December 1999.

384 ECPAT International, *A Step Forward,* 1999; US Department of State, Human Rights Report, 1999.

385 Associated Press, *Human Rights Group Says Trafficking in Women Remain,* June 15, 2000.

386 International Save the Children Alliance, *Children's Rights: Reality or Rhetoric?,* 1999.

387 Nasraw, Salah, Associate Press/Boston Globe, *Egypt: Child Labor Activists Urge Government Action,* April 14, 2001.

388 Dallas Morning News, *Effectiveness of Iraq Sanctions Not Clear,* September 29, 1997; ECPAT International. *A Step Forward,* 1999.

389 Kiley, Sam, The Times, *Perfect Kibbutz Lifestyle Hid Rape and Child Abuse,* January 21, 2001. 390 Amnesty International, *Israel — Human Rights Abuses of Women Trafficked from Countries of the former Soviet Union into Israel's Sex Industry,* May 2000.

391 United States Department of State Human Rights Report, 1999; Coalition Against Trafficking in Women Fact Book, citing CEDAW Report, April 8, 1997.

392 Connolly, Kevin, British Broadcasting Company, *Investigates Russian's Mafia Covert Invasion of Israeli Society,* November 21, 1998

393 Press Release by The Coalition to Stop the Use of Child Soldiers, posted to the web allAfrica.com, April 5, 2001.

394 Interview with Etienne Tshisekedi, declared Congolese Presidential candidate, Washington, DC, March 15, 2001.

395 United States Department of State Human Rights Report, 1999.

396 www.globalmarch.org/worstformsreport/world/oman, April 13, 2001

397 www.globalmarch.org/worstformsreport/world/qatar, April 13, 2001.

398 Coalition Against Trafficking in Women Fact Book, citing *Hundreds of RI's Women Believed to Work as Prostitutes in Saudi Arabia,* Kompas, February 7, 1997, citing Indonesia's Minister for Women's Affairs.

399 www.globalmarch.org/worstformsreport/world/syria, April 13, 2001.

400 Reuters, *Unite Arab Emirates Police Rescue Two Kidnapped Pakistani Boys,* November 5, 2000.

401 Stern, Jared Paul, The New York Post, *Sheik Looks to East for Sex Slaves,* March 2001.

402 **www.globalmarch.org/worstformsreport/world/yemen,** April 13, 2001.

403 Interview with David Ould, Anti-Slavery Organization, London, England, June 13, 2000.

404 Bulman, Erica, Associated Press, *Abject Poverty Behind Sex Slavery Sales, says United Nations,* March 26, 2001.

405 Coalition Against Trafficking in Women Fact Book, citing *Taliban's Law Drives Women to Suicide,* May 27, 1998.

406 Shamim, Ishrat, *Girl Child, Trafficking and HIV/AIDS: South Asian Perspective, 2000.*

407 Xinhua News Agency, *Children Trafficking a Serious Problem in Bangladesh,* March 26, 2001.

408 India Express, *Swiss Couple Held for Soliciting Kids in Mumbai,* December 18, 2000. 409 Shamim, Ishrat, *Girl Child, Trafficking and HIV/AIDS: South Asian Perspective,* 2000. 410 Reuters, February 9, 2001.

411 Kathmandu Post via Nepal News (November 8, 2000).

412 Shamim, Ishrat, *Girl Child, Trafficking and HIV/AIDS: South Asian Perspective, 2000.*

413 United Press International, *Women Guards Stem Teen Trade,* June 20, 2000.

414 Los Angeles Times, June 26, 2000.

415 Shamim, Ishrat, *Girl Child, Trafficking and HIV/AIDS: South Asian Perspective,* 2000. 416 Shamim, Ishrat, *Girl Child, Trafficking and HIV/AIDS: South Asian Perspective,* 2000. May 30, 2000.

417 Wijedasa, Namini, Associated Press, *Fighting Paedophiles,* January 1, 2001.

418 Kyodo News, *Sri Lanka Urged to Tackle Child Trafficking,* January 6, 2001.

419 Jayasinghe, Christine, *Paedophilia Surge Strains Inadequate Legal System,* February 26, 2001.

420 Zitrin, Richard, APB News, *Cops Bust Prison-Based Child Porn Ring,* September 20, 2000.

421 Inter Press Service, *Rights-Canada: Pimps, Paedophiles Prey On... ,* December 7, 2000.

422 Pleming, Sue, Reuters, *New Data Base Documents Trafficking of Women,* March 7, 2001.

423 Associated Press, *US Sergeant Jailed in Italy on Child Pornography Charges,* January 17, 2001.

424 Joyce, Greg, Calgary Herald News, Americans Face Slew of Charges Resulting from 11-year-old Who Worked Street, February 27, 2001.

425 RCMP Intelligence Report, Mary 24, 2000.

426 Davis, Joyce M. and Nomi Morris, Knight Ridder News Service, *Fighting the Slave Trade,* January 22, 2001.

427 Azaola, Elena, UNICEF-DIF, *Boy and Girl Victims of Sexual Exploitation in Mexico,* June 2000. 428 Azaola, Elena, UNICEF-DIF, *Boy and Girl Victims of Sexual Exploitation in Mexico,* June 2000. 429 Azaola, Elena, UNICEF-DIF, *Boy and Girl Victims of Sexual Exploitation in Mexico,* June 2000. 430 Azaola, Elena, UNICEF-DIF, *Boy and Girl Victims of Sexual Exploitation in Mexico,* June 2000. 431 Azaola, Elena, UNICEF-DIF, *Boy and Girl Victims of Sexual Exploitation in Mexico,* June 2000. 432 Azaola, Elena, UNICEF-DIF, *Boy and Girl Victims of Sexual Exploitation in Mexico,* June 2000.

433 SIPAX Report, *Women and Low Intensity Warfare,* January 1998; Hall, Allan, The Scotsman, August 25, 1998; The Indian Express, *Global Law to Punish Sex Tourists Sought by Britain and EU,* November 21, 1997.

434 Financial Times, *Street Children: Latin America and Caribbean,* November 17, 2000.

435 Reuters, *Child Prostitution, growing Central America,* September 6, 2000.

436 Rodriguex, Zoriada Ramirez, Report from Latin America, *Making the Harm Visible, Global Sexual Exploitation of Women and Girls, Speaking Out and Providing Services,* Published by The Coalition Against Trafficking in Women, February 1999.

437 United Nations Wire, San Pedro Sula La Prensa, *Activist Criticizes Central American Governments on Child Prostitution Problem,* April 9, 2001.

438 Krauss, Clifford, The New York Times, *Argentine Court Ruling Could Open the Military to Prosecution,* March 8, 2001.

439 Ending Child Prostitution, Pornography and Trafficking International, *A Step Forward,* 1999.

[440] Kane, June, *Sold for Sex*, 1998.

[441] United States Department of State Human Rights Report, Belize, Washington, DC, 1999.

[442] United States Department of Labor, *Prostitution of Children*, Washington, DC, 1996.

[443] www.globalmarch.org/worstformsreport/bolivia, April 13, 2001.

[444] Ending Child Prostitution Pornography and Trafficking Bulletin, *Child Prostitution, Volume, 4/1, 1996-97*; Bangkok Post, *Experts Meet in Brazil to Fight Child Sex Slavery*, April 18, 1996.

[445] The Inter Press Service, *Trafficking in Humans — A 7.0 Billion Dollar Business*, November 29, 2000.

[446] Agencia South America, *Brazilian Authorities Accuse German of Trafficking*, March 2001.

[447] Financial Times, *Street Children: Latin America and Caribbean*, November 17, 2000.

[448] SEJUP, *Child Prostitutes Used in Sex Tourism in Pantannal*, September 17, 1997.

[449] United States Department of State Human Rights Report, Columbia 1999. [450] United States Department of State Human Rights Report, Columbia, 1999. [451] Australian Broadcasting Corporation, January 28, 2001.

[452] Dudley, Steven, The Washington Post, *Children of War Fill Colombia's Slums*, August 8, 2000.

[453] Forero, Juan, The New York Times, *A Child's Vision of War: Boy Guerrillas in Colombia*, December 17, 2000.

[454] Krauss, Clifford, The New York Times, Colombia Pledges to Investigate Killing of 6 Children by Troops, August 20, 2000.

[455] Associated Press, *Costa Rica Fights Child Prostitution on the Internet*, June 10, 2000.

[456] Reuters, *Child Prostitution Growing in Central America*, September 6, 2000.

[457] United States Department of State Human Rights Report, Cuba, Washington, DC, 1999; Kane, June, *Sold for Sex*, 1998.

[458] International Save the Children Alliance, *Children's Rights: Reality or Rhetoric?* 1999, citing UNICEF survey, 1999.

[459] United States Department of State Human Rights Report, Dominican Republic, Washington, DC, 1999. [460] United States Department of State Human Rights Report, Ecuador, Washington, DC, 1999; Kane, June, *Sold for Sex*, 1998.

[461] Reuters, *Child Prostitution, Growing Central America*, September 6, 2000.

[462] The Washington Post, *The Americas, 2000*.

[463] Reuters, *Child Prostitution, Growing Central America*, September 6, 2000.

[464] United States Department of State Human Rights Report, Guyana, Washington, DC, 1999.

[465] Financial Times, *Street Children: Latin America and Caribbean*, November 17, 2000.

[466] Reuters, Child Prostitution, Growing Central America, September 6, 2000.

[467] Reuters, Child Prostitution, Growing Central America, September 6, 2000.

[468] Reuters, Child Prostitution, Growing Central America, September 6, 2000

[469] International Organization for Migration, Trafficking in Women from the Dominican Republic for Sexual Exploitation, June 1996.

[470] Street Children, *Lydia Puma, A Fourteen-Year-Old Girl from Cusco, Peru, Her Voice,* April 19, 1997.

[471] United States Department of Labor, *Prostitution of Children,* Washington, DC, 1996.

[472] United States Department of State Human Rights Report, Suriname, Washington, DC, 1999.

[473] www.globalmarch.org/worstformsreport/uruguay, April 13, 2001.

[474] COMTEX Newswire, *Report: Rescued Children Missing in Venezuela,* July 16, 2000.

[475] Ending Child Prostitution Pornography and Trafficking Bulletin, *Venezuela Losing War against Sexual Exploitation of Children,* October 1996.

Bibliography

Ackbarally, Nassseem, Panafrican News Agency, Report Says Child Prostitution Rampant in Mauritius, October 9, 2000.

African News Agency, Child Peddling Serious Problem in Togo and Benin, March 23, 1998.

Afrifa, Dr. A., Department of Psychology, University of Ghana, Ghanaian Chronicle (Accra), Child Rape: A National Disgrace, Accra, Ghana, April 4, 2001.

Agence Europe, Brussels, EU/COUNCIL of EUROPE — Public Hearing on Trafficking of Women, Brussels, April 3, 2001.

Agence France Presse, August 31, 2000.

Agence France Presse, July 16, 1998.

Agence France Presse, May 25, 1998.

Agence France Presse, Trafficking in Women and Children — Internationals in Kosovo Push Up Demand for Prostitutes, June 20, 2000.

Agence France Presse, Trafficking in Women and Children — Only Drugs or Illicit Arms More Profitable than Sex in Italy, July 13, 2000.

Agencia South America, Brazilian Authorities Accuse German of Trafficking.

Agnote, Dario, Kyodo News, Sex Trade Key part of Southeast Asian Economies, August 18, 1998. Allenova, Oga and Marina Oborina, World Press Service, Russia: Slaves of Shari'ah, March 30, 2000. Allio, Emmy, New Vision, Uganda to Hand Over Congo Kids Tomorrow, February 21, 2001.

Amnesty International, Israel — Human Rights Abuses of Women Trafficked from Countries of the Former Soviet Union into Israel's Sex Industry, May 2000.

Amnesty International, Uganda: Stolen Children, Stolen Lives, September 18, 1997.

Ananova, Mother Jailed Over Internet Chat Room Under-Age Sex, London, England, April 10, 2001. Antara, Asia Pulse Pte, Ltd., Child Prostitution Attracting Foreign Businessmen, April 10, 2001.

Asian Daily News, February 17, 2001.

Associated Press, Briton Tried Behind Closed Doors in Pedophilia Case, November 20, 2000. Associated Press, Costa Rica Fights Child Prostitution on the Internet, June 10, 2000.

Associated Press, Danish Detain 37 for Child Porn, September 14, 2000. Associated Press, Death-Prostitution, March 25, 2000.

Associated Press, Dutroux Case on Child Sex Murders to go on Trial in, January 30, 2001. Associated Press, Greek Police Detain Kurdish Illegals, November 19, 2000.

Associated Press, Human Rights Group says Trafficking in Women Remain, June 15, 2000. Associated Press, Japanese Ringleader of Nude-Model Internet, November 30, 2000.

Associated Press, Senator Surrenders to Police on Child Sex, January 23, 2001. Associated Press, The Silent Crises, European Children's Trust, October 12, 2000. Associated Press, Thousands of Women Left Kyrgystan to Work, December 21, 2000.

Associated Press, US Sergeant Jailed in Italy on Child Pornography Charges, January 17, 2001. Associated Press, World Stream, August 31, 2000.

Austad, Jan, Interpol, Lyon, France, Email to Author, August 25, 2000.

Australian Associated Press, Man in Court Over Thai Child-Sex Tourism, January 25, 2001.

Australian Broadcasting Corporation, January 28, 2001.

Azaola, Elena, UNICEF-DIF, Boy and Girl Victims of Sexual Exploitation in Mexico, June 2000. Badjan, Isatour, The Independent, Discourse with a Sociologist, Banjul, The Gambia, April 12, 2001. Bai-Ngern, Pongsak, Nation Multimedia Group Public Co., Ltd, THE NATION (Bangkok), Child-Sex Scandal Rocks the Senate, January 20, 2001.

Bangkok Post, Experts Meet in Brazil to Fight Child Sex Slavery, Bangkok, Thailand, April 18, 1996. Bangkok Post, Thai Girls Lured to Sex Trade in Africa, Bangkok, Thailand, August 24, 1998.

Bassey, Okon, African News Service, Human Trafficking, August 7, 2000.

British Broadcasting Company, Boats Collide off Italian Coast, London, England, May 27, 1999.

British Broadcasting Company, Italy Prepares for Refugee Onslaught, London, England, March 27, 1999. British Broadcasting Company, London, England, April 11, 2000.

British Broadcasting Company, News, Cape Town Mayor Resigns Over Pornography, London, England, September 13, 2000.

British Broadcasting Company, World, August 1, 1999.

Brummer, Stefaans, Mail and Guardian, Sports Bodies Kept on Paedophile, London, England, October 20, 2000.

Brussa, Licia, Editor, Health Migration Sex Work, The experience of TAMPEP, Transnational AIDS/STD prevention among migrant prostitutes in Europe, published by TAMPEP International Foundation, The Netherlands, Amsterdam, December 1999.

Bulman, Erica, Associated Press, Abject Poverty Behind Sex Slavery Sales, says United Nations, March 26, 2001.

Burcikova, Petra, Koollarova, Henrieta, and Kruzlizkova, Tatiana, Legal Study on the Combat of Trafficking in Women for the Purpose of Forced Prostitution in Slovakia, published by the Ludwig Boltzmann Institute of Human Rights, Vienna, Austria, September 1999.

Caritas, The Institute of Race Relations, European Race Audit Bulletin, London, UK, November 25, 1997. Carpenter, Dave, Associated Press, Baku Looks to Prosper from Oil, October 12, 1997.

Casert, Raf, Associated Press, Senate Uncovers Exploitation of Brazilian, African, March 19, 2001. Cauvin, Henri, The New York Times, South Africa Veils Crime Date, Faulting System, New York, New York, USA, August 3, 2000.

Central African Republic's Report to the United Nations Committee on the Rights of the Child, New York, New York, USA, October 2000.

Ceska Tiskova Kancelar, Czech Photographer Sentenced for Child Pornography in Slovakia, December 9, 2000.

Ceska Tiskova Kancelar, December 1, 2000.

Ceska Tiskova Kancelar, June 28, 2000.

Ceska Tiskova Kancelar, October 10, 2000.

Ceska Tiskova Kancelar, Police Cooperate with NGOS in Fighting Pimping, November 29, 2000. Ceska Tiskova Kancelar, Schily Complains about Poor Cooperation against Child Sex, July 15, 2000. Child Labor Law News Service, posted to web at allAfrica.com, Checks Tightened on Voodoo Girls Caught in Sex, April 3, 2001.

Child Rights Information Network, Exploited Children in Uganda, March 6, 2001.

Coalition Against Trafficking in Women — Asia Pacific, Trafficking in Women and Prostitution in the Asia Pacific, 1996.

Coalition Against Trafficking in Women Fact Book, April 8, 1997.

Coalition Against Trafficking in Women Fact Book, citing 375,000 Filipino Women and Kids Are into Prostitution, Philippine Daily Inquirer, July 26, 1997.

Coalition Against Trafficking in Women Fact Book, citing Hundreds of RI's Women Believed to Work as Prostitutes in Saudi Arabia, Kompas, February 7, 1997, citing Indonesia's Minister for Women's Affairs. Coalition Against Trafficking in Women Fact Book, citing Lira S. Dalagin, 150 Pinays Sold as Sex Slaves in Africa, Manila Chronicle, May 31, 1995.

Coalition Against Trafficking in Women Fact Book, citing Norwegian Consulate in Murmansk, "Statement by the Network North Against Prostitution and Violence."

Coalition Against Trafficking in Women Fact Book, citing Sol. F. Juvida, Philippines — Children: Scourge of Child Prostitution, Inter Press Service, October 12, 1997.

Coalition Against Trafficking in Women Fact Book, citing Taliban's Law Drives Women to Suicide, May 27, 1998.

Coalition Against Trafficking of Women Fact Book, citing Samuel Saprong, Women Take Initiative to Better Their Lot: Human Rights, Africa News, June 1998.

Cohen, Roger, The New York Times, Germans Faults 'Silence 'About Attacks on Immigrants, New York, New York, USA, July 31, 2000.

Cohen, Roger, The New York Times, Most Recent Killing May Push Germans to Act on Hate Crime, New York, New York, USA, August 21, 2000.

Cohen, Roger, The New York Times, The Oldest Profession Seeks New Market in West Europe, New York, New York, USA, September 19, 2000.

Committee on Rights of the Children Report for Djibouti, published by United Nations, New York, New York, USA, May 30, 2000.

COMTEX Newswire, Report: Rescued Children Missing in Venezuela, July 16, 2000.

Connolly, Kevin, British Broadcasting Company, Investigates Russian's Mafia Covert Invasion of Israeli Society, London, England, November 21, 1998.

Cushman, John J., The New York Times, Reputed Head of Drug Ring Taken to U.S. After Arrest, New York, New York, USA, August 27, 2000.

d'Arcy, Susan, Sunday Times, Sex Curb on the Way, London, England, December 17, 1995.

Dallas Morning News, Effectiveness of Iraq Sanctions Not Clear, Dallas, Texas, USA, September 29, 1997.

Dallon, David, Sex in Manila; Just One More Growth Industry, ECPAT Bulletin, March 1997. Darragh, David, West Australian, Teacher Filmed Girl Rape, December 8, 2000.

Davidson, Howard, Board Member, International Centre for Missing & Exploited Children, Memo to ICMEC, September 14, 2000, presented in London, England, October 5, 2000.

Davis, Joyce M. and Nomi Morris, Knight Ridder News Service, Fighting the Slave Trade, January 22, 2001.

Deutsch, Anthony, Associated Press, Dutch Open Proceedings Against Nine Suspects in Dover Human Trafficking Case, March 5, 2001.

Deutsche Presse Agentur, Alien Smuggling Via Poland on Decline, June 19, 2000.

Documentary, How 10,000 Bulgaria are being "Screwed" by Western European shown to author and translated by Jola Vollebregt, The Hague, The Netherlands, produced by Dutch Television, June 27, 2000.

Doland, Angela, Associated Press, Interpol Looks for New Direction in Fighting Cybercrime, October 14, 2000.

Dragnich, Alex, N., **Serbs and Croats, The Struggle in Yugoslavia**, published by Harcourt Brace & Company, New York, New York, 1992.

Dudley, Steven, The Washington Post, Children of War Fill Colombia's Slums, Washington, DC, August 8, 2000.

Dynes, Michael, The TIMES, Mbeki Agrees Drug Plan for HIV Babies, London, England, January 27, 2001.

E-mail to Author, Anonymous former National Security Analyst, National Security Agency, Washington, DC, Spring 2001.

E-mail to Author, Anonymous United States Custom Official, United States Customs Agency, Washington, DC, Summer 2000.

Ending Child Prostitution, Pornography, and Trafficking Bulletin, Child Prostitution, Volume, 4/1, 1996- 97,

Ending Child Prostitution, Pornography, and Trafficking International, A Step Forward, 1999.

Ending Child Prostitution, Pornography, and Trafficking Bulletin, Manila Imposes Heavy Term on Aust Paedophile, March- April 1996.

Erlanger, Steven, The New York Times, Aide Takes Stock of UN in Kosovo, New York, New York, USA, July 17, 2000.

Erlanger, Steven, The New York Times, Poland finds Itself the Border Copy of West Europe, New York, New York, USA, August 28, 2000.

Estes, Richard J., University of Pennsylvania, Combat of Trafficking in Women for the Purpose of Forced Prostitution: Ukraine Country Report, Philadelphia, Pennsylvania, October 2000.

Farah, Douglas, The Washington Post, Refugee Tide Swells in West Africa, Washington, DC, February 13, 2001.

Feher, Lenke, Institute for Legal Sciences of the Hungarian Academy of Sciences, National Institute Criminology, University of Miskolv, Legal Study on the Combat of Trafficking in Women for the Purpose of Forced Prostitution in Hungary, published by Ludwig Boltzmann Institute of Human Rights, Vienna, Austria, 2000.

Filipova, Rossitza Pencheva, Animus Association Foundation, Legal Study on the Combat of Trafficking in Women for the Purpose of Forced Prostitution in Bulgaria, published by Ludwig Boltzmann Institute of Human Rights, Vienna, Austria, March 20, 2000.

Financial Times, Street Children: Latin America and Caribbean, London, England, November 17, 2000. Finkel, Andrew, The Times, Fifty Migrants Missing off Turkish Coast, London, England, January 2, 2001. Fleishman, Jeffrey, The Philadelphia Inquirer, Illegal Routes Thrive on Hopes of Millions, Philadelphia, Pennsylvania, USA, February 2000.

Flounders, Sara, International Action Center, NATO Troops Seize Mining Complex, August 24, 2000. Fofana, Lansana, Inter Press Service, Militia Admits Recruiting Child Soldiers, June 29, 2000.

Ford, Richard, The Times, French to Reduce Police at Ports, London, England, January 29, 2001. Foreign Information Division, Ministry of Foreign Affairs, Dutch Policy on Prostitution Questions and Answers, The Hague, The Netherlands, 2000.

Forero, Juan, The New York Times, A Child's Vision of War: Boy Guerrillas in Colombia, New York, New York, USA, December 17, 2000.

Frantz, Douglas, Istanbul Journal, Flotsam Adrift on Ancient Streets: A City's Young, Istanbul, Türkiye, August 29, 2000.

Gabriela, Diana Mendoza, TODAY, RP Has 400,000 Prostitutes, published by TODAY, Arlington, Virginia, USA, February 25, 1998.

Gall, Carlotta, The New York Times, A Feeble Croatia Seeks to Recoup Billions Lost to Corruption, New York, New York, USA, September 3, 2000.

Gall, Carlotta, The New York Times, China's Migrants Find Europe's Open back Door, New York, New York, USA, August 22, 2000.

Gebriel, Alem W., The Daily Monitor, Opinion, Exploitation of Child Labour Needs Due Attention,

February 20, 2001.

Ghanaian Times, Accra, Ghana, August 11, 1999.

Glenny, Misha, The Fall of Yugoslavia, The Third Balkan War, published by Penguin Group, New York, New York, 1992.

Graff, Peter, Independent Newspapers (UK) Limited, UK: Child Porno Videos Sold from Russia in National Geographic 'Boxes, London, England, March 27, 2001.

Graff, Peter, Reuters News Service, Russian Police Crack U.S., Europe Child Porn Ring, December 21, 2000.

Gray, Laurence, Commentary, Los Angeles Times, The Dark Side of Tourism Preys on the Children of Cambodia, Los Angeles, California, USA, December 12, 2000.

Hagen, Henk J., Interpol, Letter to Sabrina Deligia, Lyon, France, August 26, 1999.

Hagen, Henk J., Interpol, Presentation to the Eleventh Meeting of the Interpol Standing Working Party Offences Against Minors, Lyon, France, May 1998.

Hall, Allan, The Scotsman, August 25, 1998.

Hancock, Julia, Reuters, Italy Charges 1,491 in Internet Pedophilia Case, October 28, 2000.

Handshin, Mia, Advertiser, Our Shame of Sexually Exploited Children, published by the Advertiser, May 23, 2000.

Hanson, Ivor, The New York Times, Kosovo's Young Get by With a Little Help from the West, New York, New York, USA, February 11, 2001.

Harden, Blaine, The New York Times, Burmese, Repression, AIDS and Denial, New York, New York, USA, November 14, 2000.

Harder, James, INSIGHT Magazine, Washington, DC, USA, 2000.

Hayden, Robert, University of Pittsburgh, Email to Author, Pittsburgh, Pennsylvania, USA, August 4, 2000.

Hedges, Christopher, The New York Times, New York, New York, USA, July 11, 1998.

Hill, Amelia, The OBSERVER, Child Sex for Sale — Teenage Slaves Brought to Order, London, England, January 14, 2001.

Hinchey-Bancroft, Timothy, Pravda. Ru, UN Organization: Statistics Quote 300,000 Child Prostitutes in USA, December 12, 2000.

Hitt, Jack, The New York Times, Bandits in the Global Shipping Lanes, New York, New York, USA, August 20, 2000.

Hoge, Warren, The New York Times, Dutch Truck Driver Sentenced in Chinese Immigrant Deaths, New York, New York, USA, April 6, 2001.

Houston Chronicle, Houston, Texas, November 30, 1999.

Hroni, Sotiraq, Politics Differently, published by Fatmir Toci, Tirana, Albania, 1996.

Hupchick, Dennis P. and Harold E. Cox, The Historical Atlas of Eastern Europe, St. Martin's Press, New York, New York, 1996.

India Express, Swiss Couple Held for Soliciting Kids in Mumbai, Mumbai (Bombay), India, December 18, 2000. Inter Press Service, Japanese — Tougher Laws Sought on Child Pornography, June 16, 2000.

Inter Press Service, July 25, 1997.

Inter Press Service, Rights-Canada: Pimps, Paedophiles Prey On, December 7, 2000.

Inter Press Service, Trafficking in Humans — A 7.0 Billion Dollar Business, November 29, 2000. Interior Ministry of the Federation of Bosnia-Herzegovina, Sarajevo, Bosnia-Herzegovina, June 2000.

International Action Center, Why are NATO Troops Demanding to Leave Kosovo and Bosnia? February 10, 2001.

International Herald Tribune, West Africa Awaits Sign from Child Slave's Ship, Paris, France, April 16, 2001.

International Labour Organization — IPEC, Country Paper: Mongolia, September 1999. International Organization for Migration, Geneva, Switzerland, May 7, 1996.

International Organization for Migration, Trafficking in Women for Sexual Exploitation to Italy, Geneva, Switzerland, June 1996.

International Organization for Migration, Trafficking in Women from the Dominican Republic for Sexual Exploitation, Geneva, Switzerland, June 1996.

International Save the Children Alliance, Children's Rights: Reality or Rhetoric? citing UNICEF survey, New York, New York, USA, 1999.

International Tribune, Paris, France, January 8, 2001. Interpol Press Release, Lyon, France, February 21, 2001. Interpol website, www.interpol.com.

Interview with Agnes Fournier de Saint Maur, head of Branch, Trafficking in Human Beings Branch, Interpol, Lyon, France, July 11, 2000.

Interview with Alberto, a Kosovar trafficker, Brussels, Belgium, June 24, 2000.

Interview with Angela Walker, London, England, Summer 2000.

Interview with anonymous Belgium law enforcement officials, June 19, 2000. Interview with an anonymous Customs official, London, England, August 4, 2000.

Interview with anonymous expatriates working and living in Albania, Tirana, Albania, July, August 2000. Interview with anonymous former National Security Analyst, National Security Agency, Washington, DC, October 2000.

Interview with anonymous International Organization of Migration Official, Tirana, Albania, July 30, 2000. Interview with anonymous International Security Expert, Washington, DC, May 26, 2000.

Interview with anonymous Madam, Geneva, Switzerland, July 11, 2000. Interview with an anonymous private driver in London, England, August 3, 2000.

Interview with anonymous Sacra Corona Unita Mafia Lieutenant, Naples, Italy, July 2000. Interview with anonymous trafficker, Paris, France, July 1, 2000.

Interview with anonymous trafficker, Vlora, Albania, July 30, 2000.

Interview with Antoinette Looney, wife of Michael Looney, US Customs Service Attaché, Paris, France, July 4, 2000.

Interview with Armando Ramirez, US Custom Service Attaché, Rome, Italy, July 18, 2000.

Interview with Asian and African women at the Center for Population Development Assistance, organized by Maria Nagorski, May 26, 2000.

Interview with Bill, a driver, Geneva, Switzerland, July 10, 2000

Interview with Bob Griffin, retired businessman, Londolozi Game Reserve, South Africa, April 2, 2001. Interview with Carlos Schippers, National Police Agency, Amsterdam, The Netherlands, June 25, 2000. Interview with Charlie II, a driver, Naples, Italy, July 21, 2000.

Interview with Charlie, a hotel driver, Milan, Italy, July 14, 15, 2000. Interview with Children at IL Faro Foundation, Rome, Italy, July 18, 2000.

Interview with Chuck de Caro, former CNN Investigative Reporter, Washington, DC, March 9, 2001. Interview with Colonel Rizzo, Gaurdia di Finanza, Bari, Italy, July 25, 2000

Interview with David Gaylor, Detective Superintendent, Organisational Services, Sussex, England, London, England, July 6, 2000.

Interview with David Gaylor, Detective Superintendent, Organisational Services, Sussex, England, London, England, July 2000, conducted by Sheelagh Taylor.

Interview with David Ould, Anti-Slavery Organization in London, England, June 13, 2000. Interview with Derrick Pitkanen, Washington, DC, USA, September 17, 2000.

Interview with Doris Stoisser, an Austrian journalist, Vienna, Austria, June 18, 2000.

Interview with Dr. Louise Shelley, Professor, American University, Washington, DC, May 30, 2000. Interview with Etienne Tshisekedi, declared Congolese Presidential candidate, Washington, DC, March 15, 2001.

Interview with Eva Eberhardt, Principal Associate, ACE Associates, London, England, October 4, and 7, 2000.

Interview with Fabiola Laco-Ergo, Vice President, Useful to Albanian Women, Tirana, Albania, July 26, 2000.

Interview with Fabiola Laco-Ergo, Vice President, Useful to Albanian Women, Tirana, Albania, July 28, 2000.

Interview with Francesco, bartender, who used to live in Tirana, Albania, Sheraton Hotel, Bari, Italy, July 21, 2000.

Interview with Grace Cerutti, United States Customs Service Agent, Rome, Italy, July 18, 2000. Interview with Interpol Officials, Lyon, France, July 11, 2000.

Interview with Irene Ivison, Coalition for Removal of Pimping, London, England, June 12, 2000. Interview with Irene, Ivison, a mother, whose daughter was lured into prostitution and later murdered by a client, June 2000.

Interview with James Gibbons, Senior Special Agent, United States Customs Service, Fairfax, Virginia, June 8, 2000.

Interview with James Nagle, United States Customs Agent, Fairfax, Virginia, June 8, 2000. Interview with Jan Austad, Interpol, Lyon, France, July 11, 2000.

Interview with Jim Reynolds, International Paedophilia Consultant, London, England, June 11, 2000. Interview with John Rabun, Vice President and Chief Operating Officer, National Center for Missing & Exploited Children, Alexandria, Virginia, April 16, 2001.

Interview with John van Weeten, President, Task Force Albania, Tirana, Albania, July 30, 2000. Interview with Joseph Limprecht, United States Ambassador to Albania, Tirana, Albania, August 1, 2000. Interview with Joseph Wolf, Senior Special Agent, United States Customs Service, London, July 5, 2000. Interview with Juliet Singer, National Missing Helpline, London, England, June 2000.

Interview with Kenn Underwood, Director, EOD Solutions, LTD, Tirana to Rome Flight, August 3, 2000. Interview with Lady Lisa, London, England, Summer 2000.

Interview with Linda Regan, Senior Research Officer, Child and Woman Abuse Studies Unit, University of North London, London, England, July 6, 2000.

Interview with Liz Kelly, Director, Child and Woman Abuse Studies Unit, University of North London, London, England, July 6, 2000.

Interview with Louie, Herman, and Mark, Brussels Police Officers, Brussels, Belgium, June 20, 2000. Interview with Luigi Colombetti, Paris, France, June 28- July 5, 2000.

Interview with Madam Colleen, Paris, France, July 2, 2000.

Interview with Marcos, a self-proclaimed Nigerian pimp and trafficker, Vienna, Austria, June 18, 2000. Interview with Maria Delaney, University College, Cork, Ireland, London, England, July 2000, conducted by Sheelagh Taylor.

Interview with Marjan Huls, Amsterdam Vice Squad, Amsterdam, The Netherlands, June 28, 2000. Interview with Mark Talisman, Vice-Chairman of the Holocaust Museum, Washington, DC, March 9, 2001.

Interview with Mary Banotti, European Member of Parliament, Brussels, Belgium, June 20, 2000. Interview with Massimo Sardi, Co-Directeur, Etudes et Recherches Appliquees a la Sociologie et au Marketing, Geneva, Switzerland, July 12, 2000.

Interview with Max Guido, Secretary General of Caritas Diocesana, Rome, Italy, July 20, 2000. Interview with Melvin, a hotel driver, London, England, June 16, 17, 2000.

Interview with Merl Hoogendoorn, Campagne-Coordinator, Terre des Hommes, Amsterdam, The Netherlands, June 26, 2000.

Interview with Michael Looney, United States Customs Attaché, Paris, France, June 30, 2000. Interview with Nick, a Kosovar, Le Steak Restaurant, New York, June 6, 2000.

Interview with Nigerian traffickers and pimps in Vienna, Austria, June 18, 2000. Interview with Oliver Limet, Brussels, Belgium, June 22, 2000.

Interview with Patsy Sorensen, Lid van het Europees Parlement, Europees Parlement, Vienna, Austria, June 19, 2000.

Interview with Paul Holmes, Inspector of Vice and Clubs, Metropolitan Police, London, England, June 13, 2000.

Interview with Paul Holmes, Inspector of Vice and Clubs, Metropolitan Police, London, England, August 4, 2000.

Interview with Paul Holmes, Inspector of Vice and Clubs, Metropolitan Police, London, England, July 6, 2000.

Interview with Paul Ikponwosa Oviawe, Terre des Hommes, Amsterdam, The Netherlands, June 26, 2000. Interview with Paul Kagame, President of Rwanda, Washington, DC, September 2000.

Interview with Paul-Louis de Gendt, La Brouette, Brussels, Belgium, June 21-24, 2000.

Interview with Philippe Boudin, Directeur, Comite Contre l'Esclavage Moderne, Paris, France, July 3, 2000.

Interview with Richard Seziberra, Rwandan Ambassador to the United States, Washington, DC, October 30, 2000.

Interview with Richard Seziberra, Rwandan Ambassador to the United States, Washington, DC, March 18, 2001.

Interview with Roberto, a hotel drive, Rome, Italy, July 17, and 18, 2000. Interview with Ruby, Parisian Club owner, Paris, France, June 30, July 1, 2000. Interview with Swaziland Ambassador to the United States, Spring 2000.

Interview with Tom Erents, Crime Investigation Adviser, National Police Agency, The Hague, The Netherlands, June 27, 2000.

Interview with Vera Lesko, President, Vlora Women Hearth, London, England, July 6, 2000. Interview with Victims in Albanian safe houses, Tirana, Albania, August 2, 2000.

Interview with Victims, London, England, Vienna, Austria, Brussels, Belgium, Amsterdam, The Netherlands, Paris, France, Geneva, Switzerland, Milan, Italy, Rome, Italy, Naples, Italy, Bari, Italy, Brindisi, Italy, Lecce, Italy, Tuscany, Italy, Berat, Albania, Durres, Albania, Vlora, Albania, Tirana, Albania, Summer 2000.

Interview with Jola Vollebregt, National Police Agency, Amsterdam, The Netherlands, June 25, 2000. Interview with Jola Vollebregt, National Police Agency, The Hague, The Netherlands, June 27, 2000. Interview with Yrii, a driver, Albania, Tirana, July 26-August 3, 2000.

Ivison, Irene, *Fiona's Story, A Tragedy of Our Times*, published by Virago Press, a division of Little Brown and Company, London, England, 1997.

Jayasinghe, Christine, Paedophilia Surge Strains Inadequate Legal System, February 26, 2001.

Johnson, Kay, South China Morning Post, Paedophile's Light Sentence Weakens Crackdown, November 22, 2000.

Johnson, Richard with Paul Froelich and Chris Wilson, The New York Post, 3 Busted in Milan Rape of Model, 15, New York, New York, USA, March 2, 2001.

Joyce, Greg, Calgary Herald News, Americans Face Slew of Charges Resulting from 11-year-old Who Worked Street, Calgary, Canada, February 27, 2001.

Judah, Tim, **Kosovo, War and Revenge**, published by Yale University Press, New Haven Connecticut, London, England, 2000.

Kane, June, Sold for Sex, 1998.

Karlen, Helena and Christene Hagnen, ECPAT International, Commercial Sexual Exploitation of Children in Some Eastern European Countries, March 1996.

Kathmandu Post via Nepal News, Kathmandu, Nepal, November 8, 2000.

Kazakh Commercial, TV, British Broadcasting Company, London, England, September
3, 2000.

Kiley, Sam, The Times, Perfect Kibbutz Lifestyle Hid Rape and Child Abuse, London,
England, January 21, 2001.

Kirk, Karl Peter, South China Morning Post, Hungary: Trade in Women Spurs Action by
UN, September 7, 2000.

Knaus/Kartusch/Reiter, Combat of Trafficking in Women for the Purposes of Forced
Prostitution, published by Boltzmann Institute of Human Rights, Vienna, Austria,
2000.

Koja, G.J. HURINET, 8000 Albanian Girls Work as Prostitutes in Italy, July 25, 1998.
Koppel, Naomi, Associated Press, WHO: 3M AIDS Deaths in 2000, November 24,
2000.

Krauss, Clifford, The New York Times, Argentine Court Ruling Could Open the Military
to Prosecution,

New York, New York, USA, March 8, 2001.

Krauss, Clifford, The New York Times, Colombia Pledges to Investigate Killing of 6 Children by Troops,

New York, New York, USA, August 20, 2000. Kyodo News, September 23, 1998.

Kyodo News, Sri Lanka Urged to Tackle Child Trafficking, January 6, 2001.

Latvia News Agency, Ruthless Sexual Abuse of Children All Around the Baltic Sea, January
18, 2001. Lederer, Edith M., Associated Press, UN: Congo Crisis Affecting Millions,
November 29, 2000.

Letter given to author by Louis-Paul de Gendt, Brussels, Belgium, June 23, 2000.

Levchenko, Kateryna, La Strada Ukraine, Legal Study on the Combat of Trafficking in
Women for the Purpose of Forced Prostitution in Ukraine, page 22, footnote 28, published by Ludwig Boltzmann Institute of Human Rights, Vienna, Austria, December
1999.

Liste Afrique, August 5, 1999.

Los Angeles Times, Los Angeles, California, USA, June 26, 2000.

M2 Presswire, Karajkovic, Assistant Minister of Justice, United Nations, Women's Anti-Discrimination Committee Concludes Consideration of Croatia's Initial Report, New York, New York, USA, January 28, 1998.

Machel, Graca, Impact on Armed Conflict on Children, United Nation's 1995 Report, New York, New York, USA, 1995.

Malcolm, Noel, **Bosnia, A Short History**, published by Macmillan Publishers, Ltd., London, England, 1994. Malcolm, Noel, **Kosovo, A Short History**, published by Macmillan Publishers, Ltd., London, England, 1998.

Manila News Bulleting, Manila, The Philippines, November 22, 1990.

Martin, Stoddard, **The Sayings of Lord Byron**, published by Gerald Duckworth & Co. Ltd., London, England, 1990.

Matloff, Judith, Christian Science Monitor, In Africa, Money Is not Only Reason Young Girls are Sexually Exploited, Boston, Massachusetts, USA, September 12, 1996.

Mazower, Mark, **The Balkans, A Short History**, published in the United States by Random House, Inc, New York, New York and simultaneously in Canada by Random House of Canada Limited, Toronto, Canada published in Great Britain by Weidenfeld & Nicolson, a division of The Orion Publishing Group, London, England, 2000.

McGrory, Daniel, Times, Chinese Migrants Wait for Serbs to Decide Their Fate, London, England, October 14, 2000.

McKenzie, Steve, SUNDAY MAIL, Scots-based Commandos are Helping to Wage War Against Mafia-run Sex Slavery, London, England, February 4, 2001.

McLaughlin, Daniel, Reuters, Russia's Top Prosecutor Blasts 'Corrupt' Officials, London, England, January 12, 2001.

McNeil, Jr., Donald G., The New York Times, Estonia's President: Un-Soviet and Un-conventional, New York, New York, USA, April 7, 2001.

McNeil, Jr., Donald G., The New York Times, Romania, Under Pressures, Improves, New York, New York, USA, January 13, 2001.

Miller, Steve, The Washington Times, NAACP to Call for Sanctions on Sudan, Washington, DC, USA, February 7, 2001.

Molo Songololo Report to the 13th International Congress on Child Abuse and Neglect, Trafficking of Children for Sexual Exploitation, South Africa, September 2000.

Montenegrin Women Lobby Report, Current Situation on Sex Trafficking in Montenegro, Podgorica, Montenegro, June 19, 2000.

Moore, Patrick, The Balkan Report, Companies Pledge to Build Burgas-Vlora Pipeline, August 22, 2000. Morley, Mary, The Daily Universe, Brigham Young University, BYU Professor says Sexual Slavery a Growing Problem, Brigham Young University, Salt Lake City, Utah, USA, March 8, 2001.

Mulrooney, Paul, New Zealand Watchdog Group, Interactive Association of New Zealand, Foreign Help to Fight Pornography, Auckland, New Zealand, January 6, 2001.

Mydans, Seth, The New York Times, Sexual Violence as Tool of War: East Timor's Women Pay a Toll,

New York, New York, USA, March 21, 2001.

Myers, Steven Lee, The New York Times, Inquiry into Abuse by GIs in Kosovo Faults Training, New York, New York, USA, September 19, 2000.

Nalumansi, Lillian, New Vision, Uganda: Street Children Rise, March 3, 2001.

Nasraw, Salah, Associated Press/Boston Globe, Egypt: Child Labor Activists Urge Government Action, Boston, Massachusetts, USA, April 14, 2001.

Nation Multimedia Group Public Co., Ltd, THE NATION (Bangkok) Thai Women Rescued from Abroad, Bangkok, Thailand, November 30, 2000.

Nationwide General News: Federal Parliament, Stiff Jail Terms Set for Sex Slavery, June 29, 1999. Nationwide News Proprietary Ltd., 2001, The Australian, India: Indian Children Fall Easy Prey to Paedophiles, Sydney, Australia, April 12, 2001.

New Zealand Herald, Natural Born Killer at 15, Auckland, New Zealand, February 17, 2000.

New Zealand Herald, Police raid Parlor Using Thai Prostitutes, Auckland, New Zealand, April 6, 1999. Non-Governmental Organization Coalition for Monitoring the CRC, Supplementary Report on the Implementation of CRC, submission to the United Nations, New York, New York, USA, January 1995. O'Neill, Sean, Daily Telegraph, Girl, 8, Raped to Order on the Internet Sex Show Attack Led to Downfall of Paedophile Club, London, England, February 14, 2001.

Okoko, Tervil, Panafrican News Agency, Man Kills Wife to Sell Their Baby, September 21, 2000.

Olson, Elizabeth, The New York Times, Liechtenstein Found to Be Lax in Monitoring of Bank Deals, New York, New York, USA, September 1, 2000.

Olson, Elizabeth, The New York Times, Switzerland Freezes Shady $1 Billion in a Year, New York, New York, USA, June 27, 2000.

Onishi, Norimitsu, The New York Times, Guinea in Crises as Area's Refugees Pour In, New York, New York, USA, February 20, 2001.

Organization for Security and Cooperation in Europe, ODIHR Proposed Action Plan of Activities to Combat Trafficking in Human Beings, published by Organization for Security and Cooperation in Europe, June 1, 2000.

Osava, Mario, Inter Press Service, Trafficking in Humans — A 7.0 Billion-Dollar Business, November 29, 2000.

Panafrican News Agency, African NGOs Meet on Child Abuse, February 5, 2001. Panafrican News Agency, Child Laboour, a Blight in Cote D'Ivoire, December 26, 2000.

Panafrican News Agency, Child Porno TV Show Causes Anguish in South Africa, March 29, 2001. Panafrican News Agency, Des Enfants "Transparents" dans les Rues de Kinshasa, March 6, 2001. Panafrican News Agency, International Labour Organization Report Points to Evils of Child Trafficking, April 11, 2001.

Papasotiriou, Alexis, Radio Free Europe, Greece: Private Business Invest in Balkan Economies, October 25, 1999.

Paterson, Tony, The Guardian, For Germans 'Using Under-Age Prostitutes, London, England, December 19, 2000.

Philips, John, The Times, Migrants Take the Minefield 'Package Tour, London, England, December 6, 2000.

Pisik, Betsy, The Washington Times, UN: AIDS Being Spread by its Peacekeepers, Washington, DC, July 8, 2000.

Pleming, Sue, Reuters, New Data Base Documents Trafficking of Women, London, England, March 7, 2001.

Polish News Agency, Polish Police Detain More Than 20 Foreigners Involved in the Trafficking of Women for Sex Exploitation, Warsaw, Poland, September 6, 2000.

Popa, Madalina, Sanse Egale Pentru Femei, Legal Study on the Combat of Trafficking in Women for the Purpose of Forced Prostitution in Romania, published by the Ludwig Boltzmann Institute of Human Rights, Vienna, Austria, March 2000.

Potts, Carla, Youth Mine Action Ambassador, Lest We Forget: Bosnia & Landmines, Canada, June 6, 2000.

Promotion de l'Enfant et de l'Environement and L'Action Sociale et Developpement.

Rabun, John, Vice President and Chief Operating Officer, The National Center for Missing & Exploited Children, Internal NCMEC Memo, January 11, 2001.

Radio Prague/Central Europe Online, Child Prostitution: Czech, German Ministers Unite Efforts, Prague, The Czech Republic, April 9, 2001.

RCMP Intelligence Report, published by RCMP, Mary 24, 2000.

REPORT on the Communication from the Commission to the Council and the European Parliament, published by the European Commission, May 2, 2000.

REPORT on the Communication from the Commission to the Council and the European Parliament 'For further actions in the fight against trafficking in women.' Committee on Women's Rights and Equal Opportunities, published by European Commission, May 2, 2000.

Reuters, Belgian Paedophile Dutroux Sentenced for Escape, London, England, June 19, 2000. Reuters, Bosnian Club Raids Set 177 Women Free, London, England, March 4, 2001.

Reuters, Brussels are Albanians, London, England, November 15, 1999.

Reuters, Cambodia Vows to Crack Down on Sex Tourism, London, England, September 26, 2000. Reuters, Child Prostitution Growing in Central America, London, England, September 6, 2000. Reuters, China Gang Leaders Get Death for Women Trafficking, London, England, October 21, 2000. Reuters, Croat Police Break Human Smuggling Chain, London, England, April 7, 2001.

Reuters, Croatia Becomes Centre for Human Smuggling, London, England, July 6, 2000.

Reuters, Dutch Police Arrest Three in Large Child Porn Raid, London, England, November 1, 2000. Reuters, Foreign Prostitutes Become Sex Slaves in Britain, London, England, June 2, 2000.

Reuters, London, England, February 9, 2001.

Reuters, Nigerian Flog Muslim Girl, London, England, January 27, 2001.

Reuters, No Child Slaves Are Found as Ship Reaches Benin, London, England, April 17, 2001. Reuters, Romania Court Jails British Priest on Sex Charges, London, England, July 9, 1998.

Reuters, Singapore Arrests All-Woman Porn Syndicate Suspects, London, England, January 10, 2001. Reuters, UN Appeals for Food Aid for Four Million Kenyans, London, England, February 15, 2001. Reuters, UN Court Convicts Bosnian Serbs in Rape, London, England, February 22, 2001.

Reuters, Unite Arab Emirates Police Rescue Two Kidnapped Pakistani Boys, London, England, November 5, 2000.

Reuters, US Man Charged with Raping Underage Cambodian Girl, London, England, December 17, 2000. Rodriguex, Zoriada Ramirez, Report from Latin America, Making the Harm Visible, Global Sexual Exploitation of Women and Girls, Speaking Out and Providing Services, published by The Coalition Against Trafficking in Women, February 1999.

Rosenthal, Elisabeth, The New York Times, Despite High Risk, Chinese Go West, New York, New York, USA, 2000.

Sage, Adam, The Times, Witness Recalls Day UN Troops Permitted Massacre, London, England, April 4, 2001.

Samayende, Sizwe, African Eye News Service, Mandela Children's Fund Supports Anti-Rape Group, April 11, 2001.

SAPA Domestic News Wire, South Africa: Child Sex Lucrative Market — Report, South Africa, November 22, 2000.

Schengen Agreement of 1990; APPLYING THE SCHENGEN AGREEMENT OF 14 JUNE 1985 BETWEEN THE GOVERNMENTS OF THE STATES OF THE BENELUX ECONOMIC UNION, THE FEDERAL REPUBLIC OF GERMANY AND THE FRENCH REPUBLIC, ON THE GRADUAL ABOLITION OF CHECKS AT THEIR COMMON BORDERS...

Schweid, Barry, Associated Press, Albania PM: End Kosovo Violence, New York, New York, USA, August 23, 2000.

Security Intelligence News Service, Sex Slave Trade Serious Problem in Kosovo, June 9, 2000. SEJUP, Child Prostitutes Used in Sex Tourism in Pantannal, September 17, 1997.

Sestanovic, Muhamed, Crimes against the Psychological Integrity of Children.

Shamim, Ishrat, Girl Child, Trafficking and HIV/AIDS: South Asian Perspective, 2000.

Shelley, Dr. Louise, American University, Washington, DC, USA, Problems of Post-Communism, Organized Crime in the Former Soviet Union, published by Problems of Post-Communism, January/February 1995.

Shelley, Dr. Louise, American University, Washington, DC, USA, The Exploitation and Export of Women from Russia: Scale and Scope, published by Dr. Louise Shelley, March 11, 1999.

Shelley, Dr. Louise, American University, Washington, DC, USA, The Russian, Paying the Price: Organized Crime has Exacted a Heavy Toll on Russian's Economy, published in The Russian, April 1997. Simeonov, Simeon, Sofia Police Directorate, EDT, Bulgaria Sex Club Urges Lawmakers to Legalize Prostitution, September 12, 1997.

Simons, Marlise, The New York Times, Balkan Gangs Stepping Up Violence, Dutch Say, New York, New York, USA, November 30, 2000.

Simonsson, Lennart, Associated Press, Swedish Police Uncover Paedophile Ring, New York, New York, USA, January 17, 2001.

SIPAX Report, Women and Low Intensity Warfare, January 1998.

Smith, R. Jeffrey, The Washington Post, Fall of Milosevic Sparks Hunt for Riches, Washington, DC, USA, March 11, 2001.

Specter, Michael, The New York Times, Traffickers 'New Cargo: Naïve Slavic Women, New York, New York, USA, January 11, 1998.

Stern, Jared Paul, The New York Post, Sheik Looks to East for Sex Slaves, New York, New York, USA, March 2001.

Street Children, Lydia Puma, A Fourteen-Year-Old Girl from Cusco, Peru, Her Voice, Quito, Peru, April 19, 1997.

Swardson, Anne, The Washington Post, Croatian General Is Given 45 Years for War Crimes, Washington, DC, USA, March 3, 2000.

Swindells, Steve, Reuters, Child Sex Trafficking on Rise in South Africa, London, England, November 23, 2000.

Sybnerova, Stanislave and Sheu, Harald, Charles University Prague, Legal Study on the Combat of Trafficking in Women for the Purpose of Forced Prostitution in the Czech Republic, published by the Ludwig Boltzmann Institute of Human Rights, Vienna, Austria, September 1999.

Taki's Column, New York Press, New York, New York, USA, July 13, 2000. Tarm, Michael, The New York Times, New York, New York, USA, June 13, 2000.

The Coalition to Stop the Use of Child Soldiers, press release, posted to the web allAfrica.com, April 5, 2001.

The Indian Express, Global Law to Punish Sex Tourists Sought by Britain and EU, Mumbai (Bombay), India, November 21, 1997.

The International Criminal Tribunal for Rwanda, Indictment and Sentencing documents for Jean Paul Adayesu, 1996 and 1998, posted on the Internet at www.ictr.com, March 18, 2001.

The New York Times Editorial, New York, New York, USA, January 13, 2001.

The New York Times, German Report on Milosevic's Money Trail, New York, New York, USA, October 16, 2000.

The NEWS (Lagos), Obasanjo Had Goose Pimples; Interview with Mrs. Titi, Lagos, Nigeria, March 28, 2001.

The Report of the Secretary-General, General Assembly of the United Nations, 50th Session, New York, New York, USA, 1995.

The TIMES, Leading Article: Enemy of the People, The Political Case for Trying Milosevic in Belgrade, London, England, April 5, 2001.

Thiessen, Tamara, Singapore Press Holding, Ltd., France — Land of Lost Children, October 20, 2000. Troubetzkoy, Alexis S., Letter written to Paul-Louis de Gendt, November 1999, given to Author, Brussels, Belgium, June 23, 2000.

Trouble & Strife, *Uncomfortable Truths*, Summer 2000.

Tyler, Patrick, International Tribune, From Under a Couch, an Effort to Stop Corruption in Ukraine, Paris, France, February 26, 2001.

United Nation Human Rights Country Profile, Belgium, New York, New York, USA, September 1999. United Nation Human Rights Country Profile, Ireland, New York, New York, USA, September 1999. United Nation Report on Trafficking in Women, Podgorica, Montenegro, New York, New York, USA, October 2000.

United Nations CRC, Comments on Belarus, New York, New York, USA, 1994.

United Nations Human Rights Country Profile, Bulgaria, New York, New York, USA, March 1999. United Nations Integrated Regional Information Network, Adopted Orphans "Exploited and Tormented," New York, New York, USA, April 2, 2001.

United Nations Integrated Regional Information Network, Distributed by All African Global Media, Child Traffickers Arrested, New York, New York, USA, April 12, 2001.

United Nations Integrated Regional Information Network, Distributed by AllAfrica Global Media, Harassment and Rape Hampering Girls 'Education, New York, New York, USA, March 28, 2001. United Nations Wire, San Pedro Sula La Prensa, Activist Criticizes Central American Governments on Child Prostitution Problem, New York, New York, USA, April 9, 2001.

United Press International, British Note Albanian Refugee Smuggling, April 7, 1998.

United Press International, citing by Coalition Against Trafficking in Women, Greece — Facts on Trafficking and Prostitution, December 1997.

United Press International, Women Guards Stem Teen Trade, June 20, 2000.

United States Department of Labor, Prostitution of Children, 1996, Washington, DC, USA, 1996. United States Department of State Country Profile, Equatorial Guinea, Washington, DC, USA, February 25, 2000.

United States Department of State Human Rights Report, 1999, Washington, DC, USA, February 25, 2000. United States Department of State Human Rights Report, Armenia, 1999, Washington, DC, USA, February 25, 2000.

United States Department of State Human Rights Report, Belize, 1999, Washington, DC, USA, February 25, 2000.

United States Department of State Human Rights Report, Botswana, 1999, Washington, DC, USA, February 25, 2000.

United States Department of State Human Rights Report, Central African Republic, 1999, Washington, DC, USA, February 25, 2000.

United States Department of State Human Rights Report, Chad, 1999, Washington, DC, USA, February 25, 2000.

United States Department of State Human Rights Report, Columbia, 1999, Washington, DC, USA, February 25, 2000.

United States Department of State Human Rights Report, Cuba, 1999, Washington, DC, USA, February 25, 2000.

United States Department of State Human Rights Report, Dominican Republic, 1999, Washington, DC, USA, February 25, 2000.

United States Department of State Human Rights Report, Ecuador, 1999, Washington, DC, USA, February 25, 2000.

United States Department of State Human Rights Report, Guyana, 1999, Washington, DC, USA, February 25, 2000.

United States Department of State Human Rights Report, Mongolia, 1999, Washington, DC, USA, February 25, 2000.

United States Department of State Human Rights Report, Slovenia 1999, Washington, DC, USA, February 25, 2000.

United States Department of State Human Rights Report, Suriname, 1999, Washington, DC, USA, February 25, 2000.

United States Department of State Human Rights Report, Turkmenistan, 1999, Washington, DC, USA, February 25, 2000.

United States Department of State Human Rights Reports, Madagascar, 1999, Washington, DC, USA, February 25, 2000.

United States Information Agency, Office of Research and Media Reaction, Poverty in Russian: Just How Bad is It? United States Information Agency Opinion Analysis, Washington, DC, January 12, 1999.

USA TODAY, Pedophilia Ring Uncovered in Italy, published by USA TODAY, Arlington, Virginia, November 1997.

van Weeten, John, Task Force Albania, An Odyssey, published by John van Weenen, The Priory, Wollaston, Northamptonshire, England, 1998.

Vandeberg, St. Petersburg Times, Invisible Women Shown in Russia's Demographics, St. Petersburg, Russia, October 13, 1997.

Veysey, Wayne, PA News, Taskforce Launched to Combat Internet Paedophiles, March 28, 2001.

WAO- Afrique, Child Trafficking in West and Central Africa, submission to the United Nations Working Group on Contemporary Forms of Slavery, New York, New York, USA, June 1999.

Warnecke, Grace, Winrock Foundation, Kyiv, Russia, E-mail to Author, August 14, 2000. Washington Post, The Americas, 2000, Washington, DC, USA, 2000.

Washington Times, Washington, DC, USA, July 2000.

Wijedasa, Namini, Associated Press, Fighting Paedophiles, January 1, 2001.

World Congress Against Commercial Exploitation, New York, New York, USA, August 1996. World Entertainment News Network, December 21, 2000.

World Health Organization 2000 Report, published by The World Health Organization.

Wren, Christopher, The New York Times, UN Weighs Return to Somalia to Aid Leaders, New York, New York, USA, January 12, 2001.

www.globalmarch.org/worstformsreport/bolivia, April 13, 2001.

www.globalmarch.org/worstformsreport/uruguay, April 13, 2001.

www.globalmarch.org/worstformsreport/world/lesotho, April 13, 2001

www.globalmarch.org/worstformsreport/world/mali, April 13, 2001.

www.globalmarch.org/worstformsreport/world/niger, April 13, 2001.

www.globalmarch.org/worstformsreport/world/oman, April 13, 2001

www.globalmarch.org/worstformsreport/world/qatar, April 13, 2001.

www.globalmarch.org/worstformsreport/world/syria, April 13, 2001.

www.globalmarch.org/worstformsreport/world/yemen, April 13, 2001.

www.taasa.org/currentissues/chldprostit.htm,_Social Implications of Child Prostitution, February 26, 2001. Xinhua News Agency, Children Trafficking a Serious Problem in Bangladesh, Bangladesh, November 8, 2000.

Zenica, Medica — Infoteka Special Edition, Rape — A Specific Trauma, A Specific Type of Violence: Our Work Experience with Rape Survivors in the War in Bosnia-Herzegovina, published by Infoteka Special Edition, May 1997.

ZENIT News Agency, published by ZENIT News Agency, December 19, 2000.

Zenit.org, Salesian Assails Sexual Tourism in Third World, published by Zenit. Org, October 9, 2000. Zitrin, Richard, APB News, Cops Bust Prison-Based Child Porn Ring, published by APB News, September 20, 2000.

Acknowledgements

There are numerous individuals who opened the doors for me and agreed to be interviewed during this investigation. For security reasons, I cannot name you all. You know who you are — My warmest heartfelt thanks!

I owe the deepest gratitude to Ernie Allen and Nancy Dube of the International Centre for Missing & Exploited Children (ICMEC) for giving me this opportunity.

To the ICMEC Board, special thanks to Arnold Burns, Mary Banotti, Dan Broughton, John Libonati, Howard Davidson, Baron Daniel Cardon, and especially the late Eve Branson and the late Susanna Agnelli for "convincing me to go into Albania." Sincere thanks to Susanna's staff and the children at the Il Faro Foundation! And Charlie Morrison, too perfect, too professional, just too much fun!

To ICMEC's and the National Center for Missing & Exploited Children's (NCMEC) staff, especially, Jennifer Penta, John Rabun, Bria George, Linda Aquilino, Ruben Rodriquez, Michael Lynch, Sherry Bailey, Cheryl McLaughlin, Johnny Campbell, Terry Rauch, and Sheelagh Taylor, I could not have done this without you all. Thank you for your solid support and "patience" with me. I know it was not easy.

To Bob Bowlin of SONY and *his boys*, Bob Creighton, Don, and Christopher. Words cannot express thanks for those who protect. I know I am not an easy client!

To Noel Brown and the late Zyg Nagorski, you kicked this madness into *high gear!*

To Paul Holmes, Jola Vollebregt, Thomas Erents, Marjan Huls, Klaus Wilting, Jim Reynolds, David Gaylor, Agnes Fournier de Saint Maur, Jan Austad, Philippe Boudin, Carlos Schippers, and Colonel Rizzo, — you have my utmost respect. I still do not know how you do your jobs without going mad!

To Eva Eberhardt, Maria Delaney, Fabiola Laco-Ergo, Vera Lesko, Evis Berisha, Luigi Colombetti, Massimo Sardi, Kenn Underwood, Paul Lind, Merl Hoogendoorn, Paul-Louis de Gendt, Oliver Limet, Diane Grammer, Stana Buchowska , Vincent Di Maio, Linda Regan, Liz Kelly, Jim Strand, Karin Roncari, Angela Walker, Lady Lisa, Mrs. Josephine Anenih, Marianne Schertenleiz, Patty Sorensen, Dr. Louise Shelley, Ruby, Madam Colleen, Maria Nagorski, and the folks at CEDPA, and my drivers, Melvin, Charlie, Roberto, Charlie II, Wild Bill, and Yrii — an unbelievable indoctrination!

To the late Ed Turner — *true news hound* in his own right, who kept me sane with the trumpets calls of *"Copious Notes, Copious Notes!"*

To Ray Kelly, Richard Stroebel, and their colleagues at the US Customs Service — you opened my eyes, made me speechless, and connected the dots! Thank you for your trust!

To John van Weenen at Task Force Albania — what an education about the *Rock Age!*

To the Mums of the House and the girls in Albania especially, and the girls and boys I met in London, Vienna, Brussels, Amsterdam, Paris, Geneva, Milan, Rome, Naples, Bari, Lecce, Brindisi, and at the stations, hotels, clubs, discos, trains, and on the streets, bless you for sharing!

To Teresa and Hap Storer, who kept reminding me what this journey was all about — the children.

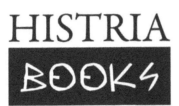 
 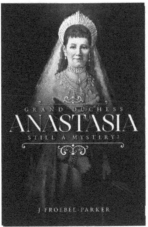